CW01237132

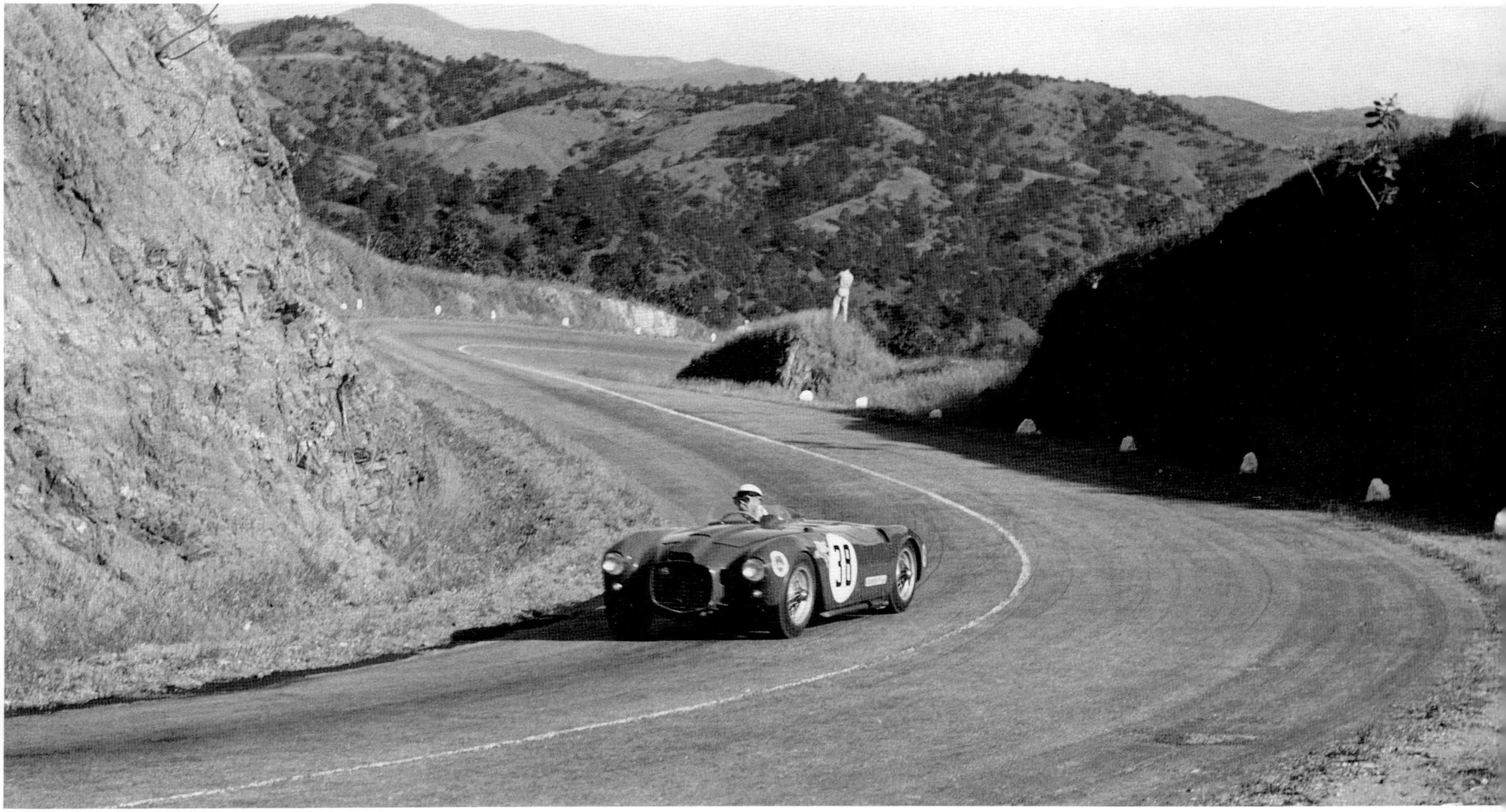
38

CARRERA PANAMERICANA

History of the Mexican Road Race 1950-1954

Daryl E. Murphy

Motorbooks International
Publishers & Wholesalers

*To Terry Lincoln (1942-1992), adventurer
and good friend*

First published in 1993 by Motorbooks International Publishers & Wholesalers, PO Box 2, 729 Prospect Avenue, Osceola, WI 54020 USA

© Daryl E. Murphy, 1993

All rights reserved. With the exception of quoting brief passages for the purposes of review no part of this publication may be reproduced without prior written permission from the Publisher

Motorbooks International is a certified trademark, registered with the United States Patent Office

The information in this book is true and complete to the best of our knowledge. All recommendations are made without any guarantee on the part of the author or Publisher, who also disclaim any liability incurred in connection with the use of this data or specific details

We recognize that some words, model names and designations, for example, mentioned herein are the property of the trademark holder. We use them for identification purposes only. This is not an official publication

Motorbooks International books are also available at discounts in bulk quantity for industrial or sales-promotional use. For details write to Special Sales Manager at the Publisher's address

Library of Congress Cataloging-in-Publication Data
Murphy, Daryl E.
   Carrera Panamericana : the Mexican road race, 1950-1954 / Daryl E. Murphy.
     p. cm.
   Includes index.
   ISBN 0-87938-734-3
   1. Carrera Panamericana, Mexico—History.
I. Title.
GV1034.C37M87   1993
796.7'2—dc20   92-33694
                                  CIP

Printed and bound in Hong Kong

On the front cover: Richie Ginther stands alongside the 1952 Ferrari 340 Mexico, chassis number 222 AT, that he co-piloted with Phil Hill in the 1953 Carrera Panamericana. *Phil Hill*

On the frontispiece: Newcomer Eugenio Castellotti rounds a curve near Oaxaca in his Lancia D23. *Lee Render photo, Dean Batchelor collection*

On the title page: Spectators fill the hillside and crowd the road for a view as Fernando Razo Maciel, a Mexican Buick driver, passes. Soldiers guarded the entire 1,930-mile course, with orders to shoot anything that strayed onto the road—which may explain the seeming orderliness of the crowd. *Don Downie*

Contents

	Preface	6
	Acknowledgments	7
Introduction	Run For The River	8
Chapter 1	Creating The Carrera Panamericana "Mexico"	11
Chapter 2	1950 Carrera Panamericana I	21
Chapter 3	1951 Carrera Panamericana II	39
Chapter 4	1952 Carrera Panamericana III: Sports Class	52
Chapter 5	1952 Carrera Panamericana III: Stock Class	64
Chapter 6	1953 Carrera Panamericana IV: Large Sports Class	73
Chapter 7	1953 Carrera Panamericana IV: Small Sports Class	93
Chapter 8	1953 Carrera Panamericana IV: Large & Small Stock Classes	101
Chapter 9	1954 Carrera Panamericana V: Large Sports Class	122
Chapter 10	1954 Carrera Panamericana V: Small Sports Class	144
Chapter 11	1954 Carrera Panamericana V: Small Stock Class	153
Chapter 12	1954 Carrera Panamericana V: Large Stock Class	161
Epilogue	Postmortem	177
Appendices	Carrera Panamericana Entries 1950-1954	179
	Carrera Panamericana Results 1950-1954	186
	Bibliography	190
	Index	191

Preface

When Carrera Panamericana began, it received scant notices in the media—even among the fledgling automotive periodicals of the time. Hence, sparse accurate information tends to be available, and practically no second or third sources exist for crosschecking and verification. To the nonautomotive press, it was an annual one-shot display of death-defying feats, and reporting of the event leaned toward the sensational.

Compounding the confusion, the official records kept by the Asociacion Nacional Automovilistica (ANA), the Mexican sanctioning body, which were originated in Spanish, were destroyed many years ago, and about the only surviving documents are some third-generation facsimiles of ANA magazines—in Spanish—and a few daily press reports.

Even the official records, however, are suspect owing to the vagaries of the language, the abilities of its translator, the officials who originated the records, and sundry clerical and typographic errors.

Added to all that is the Mexican custom of using the father's family name for what Anglo-Americans term a middle name, with the mother's family name being placed last. Also, oftentimes, the last name is indicated only by an initial. For instance, the name of Mexican driver Fernando Razo Maciel might appear as Fernando Razo M., or in a one-name listing, as Razo. By the same logic, American driver Troy Lynn Ruttman is variously listed as Troy Lynn R., or just plain Lynn.

The most obvious discrepancies have been eliminated with the help of a great number of interested people. Some judgment calls have been made, but by and large, this text should be the most complete and accurate history possible of the epic Carrera adventure. Enjoy!

Daryl E. Murphy
Irving, Texas
August 1992

Acknowledgments

Special thanks to those who contributed to research:
Harry Atkinson, Queensland, Australia
Robert Barkhimer, Los Gatos, California
Dean Batchelor, Woodland Hills, California
Tom Burniston, Long Beach, California
Antonio Perez Cosio, Mexico, DF
Bill Crawford, San Dimas, California
Tom Deal, El Paso, Texas
Don Downie, Kingman, Arizona
Max Ellis, Montebello, California
C. D. Evans, El Paso, Texas
Mark Gillett, Dallas, Texas
Bruce Gross, El Paso, Texas
Mary Keane, Mobil Corporation
Irv Kerbel, Lincolnwood, Illinois
Mitch Leland, Flintridge, California
Herschel McGriff, Green Valley, Arizona
Ak Miller, Pico Rivera, California
Larry Nicklin, Leo, Indiana
Tom Rudy, Lexington, Kentucky
Bob Russo, Riverside, California
Troy Ruttman, Venice, Florida
Jim Sitz, Los Angeles, California
Jean Ashley Stone, El Paso, Texas
Scott Yantis, El Paso, Texas

Introduction

Run For The River

The Carrera Panamericana became the meeting place for three worlds: the elite European race car manufacturers, their elaborate teams, and world champion drivers; the down-home American stock car fraternity and Indianapolis Brickyard contenders; and the third world, Mexico. Here, young Mexican boys crowd around the Siata Sport 8V of Californian Ernie McAfee seeking autographs before the start of the 1953 Carrera Panamericana "Mexico."
Dave Friedman

Carrera Panamericana: the Mexican Road Race. In its day, it was the longest, the fastest, and probably the wildest automobile race ever staged on an international scale. It became a World Championship event along with Le Mans, the Mille Miglia, Nürburgring, and the Tourist Trophy, and most drivers considered it the best—and the worst—of them all.

From 1950 to 1954, it was witnessed by over 10 million spectators along its nearly 2,000-mile course. Its route featured sea-level deserts where the fastest cars could reach 180mph and 10,000ft fogbound mountain passes that required first-gear operation.

Carrera Panamericana affected engineering and marketing philosophies from Modena to Michigan. Ferrari designed a model specifically for the race: the 340 Mexico. Lincoln was repositioned as a high-performance luxury sedan because of its successes in Mexico. And several other manufacturers adopted a south-of-the-border image in model names and advertising themes, such as Porsche with its Carrera model, named in honor of its race wins.

The Pan-Am was so unconventional and fascinating that it held the world's attention for a full week each year. It was one of the last of the great open road affairs in the classic point-A-to-point-B fashion. It was the only major event in which sports and stock cars could be compared on the same course at the same time. American and European drivers got their first look at each other, and the competition marked the return of US factory support to racing in America.

When the Carrera began in 1950, the world was less than five years past World War II, and only three past the Nürnberg War Crimes Trials. In retrospect, Americans lived what seemed to be a simple and uncomplicated world existence centered around hometown and region, but with a new wisdom from wartime experiences. If they were in the military, they likely traveled to places they'd never heard of, with cultures that existed formerly only on the pages of *National Geographic*. If they stayed home and worked in defense, they probably learned skills, met people, and handled equipment that was new to them. If they were a child, they were exposed to strange and romantic new facts and prejudices. And child and adult alike developed unswerving patriotism.

When the fighting ended, the rejoicing began, releasing pent-up spending orgies after four years of consumer deprivation. Everything had been rationed during wartime—

automobiles, paper, cosmetics, gasoline, food —and it took American industry nearly four years to fill the pipeline of demand.

Before the war, for instance, if you wanted to buy a new car, it cost you about $850, and you saved the money for its purchase. After the war—if you could even get the car—it cost twice as much, you might have to wait six months for delivery, and you probably financed it for $50 down and $50 a month out of your $2,500 annual salary.

When the first race started on May 5, 1950, Harry Truman was president, *All About Eve* had won that year's Academy Award, Sam Snead was making a record $35,758 for the year in professional golf, Henry Banks was American Automobile Association driving champion, and Johnny Parsons would win the Indianapolis 500 on Memorial Day at 124.2mph. The United States was a month away from entering a small Asian country named Korea for purposes of a "police action."

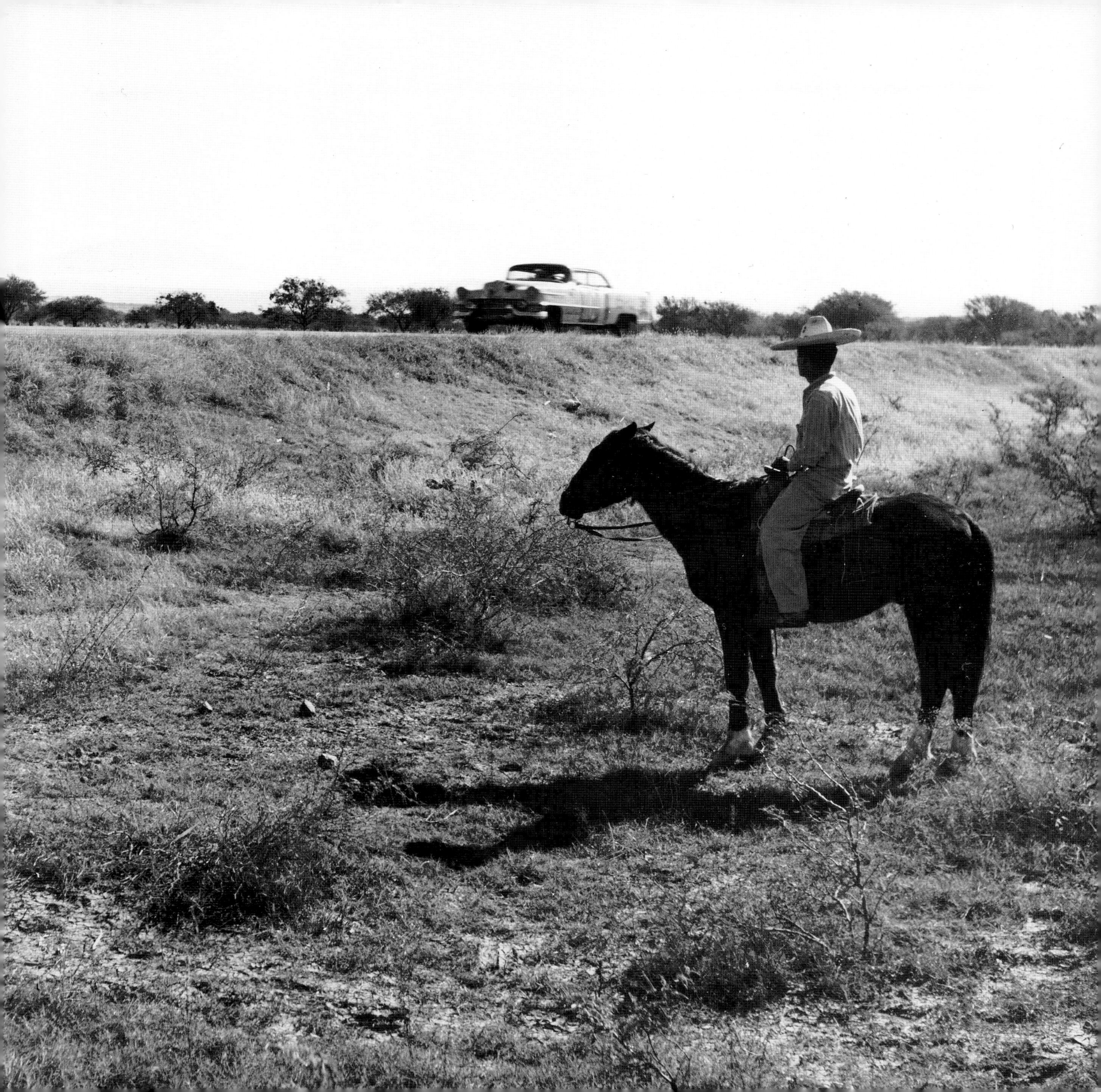

Chapter 1

Creating The Carrera Panamericana "Mexico"

The Adventurers Make Ready

It was summer 1945. Herschel McGriff sat in his father's prewar Hudson on the damp clay track that was Portland Speedway, hoping that no one would recognize him; he had told his father he was taking the car on a Sunday date.

World War II had been over just one month, and everyone seemed a little crazy. Things that had been put off for the duration were available again—although gas, tires, and particularly cars were still scarce. But the local race promoter was celebrating Japan's surrender by staging a "race-what-you-bring" event for all comers.

Even though he was just seventeen, McGriff had been driving heavy trucks for a logging company since 1942 in the mountains near Portland, Oregon, and had developed a feel for speed and handling on the tricky winding dirt pathways. A race against other drivers would help him decide if he was as good as he thought he was.

Starting on the outside of the sixth row, the slowest racer in the field, McGriff avoided a crashed Ford at the gun and flung the Hudson around the track. By the tenth of a scheduled twenty-five laps, he was in sixth place, but a wheel came off, and he was lapped by everyone—twice—while he refitted it. Then, on the last lap, the battery fell out of the car, and he had to coast over the finish line in eleventh place.

Not an auspicious beginning, but it was fun.

McGriff's father, however, was not amused and demanded $180 from McGriff for repairs to the family car.

By the next spring, McGriff had saved enough money to buy a 1940 Ford, and Portland Speedway had paved its track for a scheduled 100-lap opening race. Preparing his car with the help of friend Ray Elliott, McGriff entered knowing he could go the distance. He watched the veteran drivers and local hotshots battle for the lead for the first forty laps only to retire against a wall or smoking in the pits. Pacing himself to his best speed, by lap eighty, McGriff was in second place by a straightaway, and at the checkered flag, he had passed the leader to win the second race he had ever driven.

A Race of Heroic Proportions

In 1950, Mexico was to some an ancient and backward country stuck in the wrong century. Although it had given the United States tremendous economic support during World War II with its resources and products,

CARRERA PANAMERICANA "MEXICO"

Mexico seemed to some an ancient and backward land stuck in the wrong century, but postwar prosperity had allowed resumption of the grand plan of an international roadway to make the country accessible to trade and tourist. Don Downie

PAN-AMERICAN HIGHWAY SYSTEM IN MEXICO

- ▬▬▬ RACE ROUTE, MAY 5-9
- ─── OTHER PAVED ROUTES
- ▪▪▪▪▪ ALL-WEATHER SURFACE
- ═══ UNDER CONSTRUCTION

(FEEDER ROADS NOT SHOWN)

The first Carrera Panamericana stretched 2,135 miles across the entire length of Mexico and was run in eight separate legs, varying from 84 to 339 miles in length. Road & Track

the average American's view of the land south of the border was of an unstable and uneducated country with a population that filled its days lazing in the shade under sombreros or robbing tourists at gunpoint.

Texans thought even worse. Their prejudice had historic roots: Once a part of Mexico, the republic of Texas and later the state had been created in bloody battles just over a century earlier—and Texans had not forgotten the Alamo. By the middle of the twentieth century, the economically superior Texans looked upon Mexicans as a useful underclass, equating them unconsciously with blacks, as stated in a contemporary Texas politcal history by T. R. Fehrenbach.

But postwar prosperity had, among other things, allowed America to resume its grand plan of an international roadway, known as the Pan-American Highway. As Americans laid asphalt and concrete across Middle America, Mexicans were rushing to make more of their country accessible to both trade and tourist, hopefully bringing a new economic and social awareness to the country.

Two of the roads in Mexico—the Central Highway from the Texas border to México City and the Cristobal Colon (or Christopher Columbus) from the capital to the Guatemalan border—had been under construction since 1935 and were nearly complete. By the time they were done, they would represent about one-fourth of all the paved roads in the entire country and cost 500 million pesos, about $58 million.

With the anticipation of a link across Mexico connecting North America with Central America, the Asociacion Mexicana Automovilistica (AMA) and the Asociacion Nacional Automovilistica (ANA) began to talk about an event that would prove and publicize the nation's new artery.

The perfect answer was a race. No race of any significance had been held in the country since 1939, the course was almost done, and the enthusiasm was high. And it couldn't be just a little race, either; it had to be an event that would make the world sit up and take notice, a contest of heroic proportions and vast distances—a race that would bear witness to what Mexico had accomplished and what it was capable of doing.

Committees were organized, inquiries were made, and in March 1949, the ANA magazine began publishing a series of articles about the new highway and European road races—without making a connection between the two. Mexican President Miguel Aleman and Secretary of Communications Agustin Garcia Lopez offered their support—should such a race ever be scheduled.

By August, the complete list of committees was published and work began, still without a formal date set for the race because of the uncertainty of actual completion of the road.

A successful México City Pontiac dealer, Antonio Cornejo, was appointed general manager for the race. Stanford educated, the upper-class Cornejo was fluent in English and Spanish; he was a man who was used to getting things accomplished.

One of his first tasks was financing. The government provided a 250,000 peso ($28,900) seed fund, and Cornejo raised twice that amount from the states through which the race would pass and from contractors and assemblers of cars, accessories, and tires. Of the 750,000 peso fund, half would be designated as prize money.

Needing help from outside, Cornejo contacted the American Automobile Association (AAA)—then the biggest and most powerful race sanctioning body in the United States—to loan technical assistance in organization. Press releases were sent to hundreds of North American newspapers. Copies of the rules and entry blanks were sent to 600 registered AAA race car owners, drivers, and mechanics.

By mid-December, engineers of the Mexican Public Works were able to forecast that by February, not only would the highways be open, but all river crossings would have either permanent bridges or fords proper enough to permit a high-speed race.

The date of the start was set for May 5—*Cinco de Mayo*, the national holiday commemorating the Mexican victory over the invading French at Puebla in 1862—and the place would be Ciudad Juárez, across the Rio Grande from El Paso, Texas.

Even in Texas, El Paso was relatively remote from the rest of the state. In 1950, it was a hard day's drive from any other large city in Texas—560 miles from San Antonio, over 600 miles from Dallas, and 750 miles from Houston (when El Pasoans talked about going to the beach, they most probably meant the one in San Diego, California—it was closer than the one in Corpus Christi, Texas).

What this meant to the racers and crews going to Mexico was that they would be virtually inaccessible. They better have everything they needed before they left home.

For You a Rose in Portland Grows

Since 1945, Herschel McGriff had done well in Northwest stock car racing. By the spring of 1950, he had entered twelve races and won eight, capping the 1949 season by being crowned Northwest champion. At twenty-two,

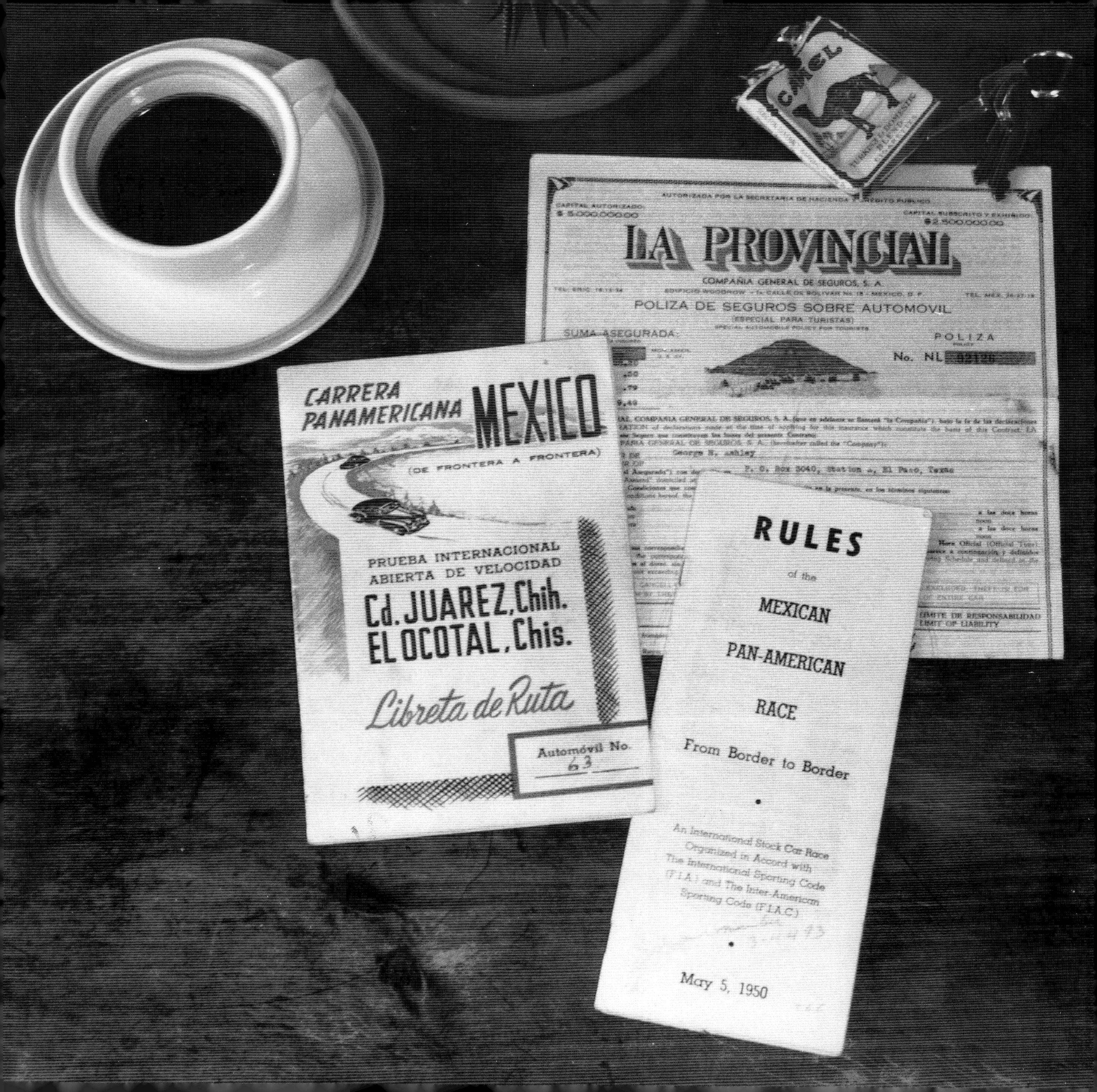
AUTORIZADA POR LA SECRETARIA DE HACIENDA Y CREDITO PUBLICO
CAPITAL AUTORIZADO $5.000.000.00
CAPITAL SUBSCRITO Y EXHIBIDO $2.500.000.00
LA PROVINCIAL
COMPAÑIA GENERAL DE SEGUROS, S. A.
POLIZA DE SEGUROS SOBRE AUTOMOVIL
(ESPECIAL PARA TURISTAS)
SUMA ASEGURADA
POLIZA
LIMITE DE RESPONSABILIDAD
LIMIT OF LIABILITY
CARRERA PANAMERICANA MEXICO
(DE FRONTERA A FRONTERA)
PRUEBA INTERNACIONAL ABIERTA DE VELOCIDAD
Cd. JUAREZ, Chih.
EL OCOTAL, Chis.
Libreta de Ruta
Automóvil No. 63
RULES
of the
MEXICAN
PAN-AMERICAN
RACE
From Border to Border
An International Stock Car Race Organized in Accord with The International Sporting Code (F.I.A.) and The Inter-American Sporting Code (F.I.A.C.)
May 5, 1950

he was a talented and already experienced oval track driver. He had married his high school sweetheart in 1948, and between races, still drove a truck in the lumber industry.

One of his biggest fans was Roy Sundstrom, a neighbor in Portland who helped McGriff and Ray Elliott maintain the succession of Fords that McGriff campaigned, and who reveled in the pit life at the racetrack.

Elliott was the one who brought the news of the Mexican Road Race to McGriff's and Sundstrom's attention. He belonged to the AAA and showed the two the letter he had received promoting the race. Sundstrom and McGriff discussed the contest often over the next several weeks, but they realized that running in the race would require a great deal of money—which neither had. The planning was fun, but without a lot of backing, they could not possibly swing it.

Then one Saturday in March, McGriff heard the honking of a horn in his driveway. He went to the door, and there were Sundstrom and Elliott in a brand-new Oldsmobile 88 two-door coupe, smiling and motioning him to the car.

"Whad'ya think, Hersh?" Sundstrom asked, beaming. "Think this'll get you to Mexico?"

An elated McGriff slid into the driver's seat and started the V-8 engine. "Sounds like a stuck lifter," he said solemnly as he listened to the engine. "You know, we're gonna need lots of tires, and a bigger fuel tank. . . . Good, it's got a stick shift; that Hydra-matic could be trouble in the mountains."

The three partners—for that's what Sundstrom wanted the group to be called—spent the rest of the weekend planning their great adventure. They all agreed that McGriff and Sundstrom would split the first 80 percent of any winnings, and Elliot would get the rest. Sundstrom posted their entry fee, and the trio went to work preparing the Olds.

Sundstrom hired a sign painter to decorate the car with roses on its doors and the slogan "For You a Rose in Portland Grows," and with a rush of civic pride named the vehicle *The Spirit of Portland*.

On Tuesday, Elliott found a 50-gallon saddle tank off a wrecked International truck, and by Friday, he had modified and mounted it in the Oldsmobile's trunk.

The trio found that a local General Tire dealer had General Squeegees on sale for $12 each and bought eight. They all tinkered with the car, and although none knew much about serious mechanicing, they did learn to mount the tires, a skill that would undoubtedly come in handy in Mexico.

On April 15, McGriff paid all of his bills, bought groceries for his young family, and left Portland with Elliott in the right seat and car owner Sundstrom perched unceremoniously on top of a pile of tires in the rear. The first night out, they stopped at Reno, Nevada, primarily because motel rates there were among the lowest in the country.

McGriff, who had left home virtually broke, put a dime in a slot machine and hit a jackpot.

"Damn! With luck like that, we're bound to win the race," he said as he struggled to carry the 1,500 coins to the cashier.

When the Oregon Oldsmobile arrived in El Paso, the men found the race headquarters and checked in.

Getting the Race Organized: Help from California

The 2,178-mile race would be run in nine legs varying in distances from 84 to 334 miles each over a period of five days. It would cover the entire length of Mexico from Ciudad Juárez on the Rio Grande to the village of El Ocotal on the Guatemalan border. Cars would start the race in numerical order at one-minute intervals, with five minutes between each group of twenty. On subsequent legs, they would start in the order in which they finished the previous leg. Each team would be furnished a route book, in which leg and accumulated race times would be recorded.

Cash prizes offered for each leg were 2,000 pesos ($232) for the win, 1,000 pesos ($116) for second, and 500 pesos ($58) for third. The first three places at the end of the race would receive 150,000 pesos ($17,442), 100,000 pesos ($11,630), and 50,000 pesos ($5,815.00) in

Each contestant was provided with a rulebook, and a route book for identification and recording of the official times at the end of each leg. This paperwork from the number 63 Cadillac of George Ashley also includes an auto insurance policy—necessary to enter Mexico in the car, but useless in the event of a racing accident.

15

Drivers and cars gathered in Ciudad Juárez on May 2, 1950, for inspection and the drawing of numbers and issuance of logbooks and race paraphernalia. Jean Ashley Stone collection

prize money. To put that money in the perspective of the time, the average price of a new 1950 Oldsmobile 88 was about 16,800 pesos ($2,100). The narrow prize money structure put competition on a pretty much all-or-nothing basis, and many US drivers hesitated at posting the $290.75 entry fee after assessing their chances.

Bob Estes, a California-based Lincoln-Mercury dealer and race car owner, was interested in sponsoring the personal Lincoln of AAA driver Johnny Mantz in the race. The two of them appointed themselves ambassadors of the southern California racing fraternity and went to Mexico. They drove nearly the entire course in a 1949 Lincoln borrowed from Estes' lot, inspecting—and practicing. They used the Pemex race gasoline; talked to Antonio Cornejo; and even checked out the race committee's books. Satisfied that everything was on

The collection of huts at El Ocotal on the Guatemalan border, which would be the finish of the 1950 Pan-Am. Jack Cansler photo, Jean Ashley Stone collection

the up and up, they returned to Los Angeles and took out an ad in the *Los Angeles Times* sanctioning California entrants.

Rules for car preparation were simple: keep it strictly stock. Allowable modifications included a 0.030in overbore for 1949–1950 models, 0.060in overbore for older models; replacement of shocks with stronger units; removal of hubcaps and fender skirts; and removal of the rear seat to install extra gas tanks and to carry spares and tools. An open exhaust was specifically forbidden, and seatbelts and helmets were encouraged but not required.

To the dismay of some racing veterans, the organizing committee was even going to provide room and board for all participants during the race—and free gasoline and oil. At the start of every leg, each crew would be provided a sack lunch and three warm Coca-Colas, plus the racers could look forward to a banquet each night at the stopover city.

A Potpourri of Cars and Drivers

The American concept of fast cars had always been the 2-ton luxury behemoths popularized in the twenties by Duesenberg, Packard, and the like, so the mindset, even among the racers, was that the bigger a car was, the faster and more stable it must be—and that was partly true. The most expensive—ergo the biggest—American automobiles of 1950 coincidentally had the most horsepower.

Packard and Lincoln were producing plenty of power from their old L-head engines, and in fact, the former had the most efficient of the group, with a better horsepower-per-cubic inch figure than the rest, but the flathead engine was nearing the end of its usefulness.

Cadillac and Oldsmobile had independently introduced two new, modern overhead-valve V-8s in 1949. These V-8s had shorter, more rigid crankshafts than their competitors and were also lighter, higher-revving, and yet more stressed for elevated compression ratios. The 331ci, 160hp Cadillac unit was 220lb lighter and 10hp stronger than the 346ci L-head V-8 it replaced and had five main bearings instead of the previous three. When the smaller Olds Rocket—303ci and 135hp—was dropped into the light sedan body of the 76/88 series, its nimbleness and favorable

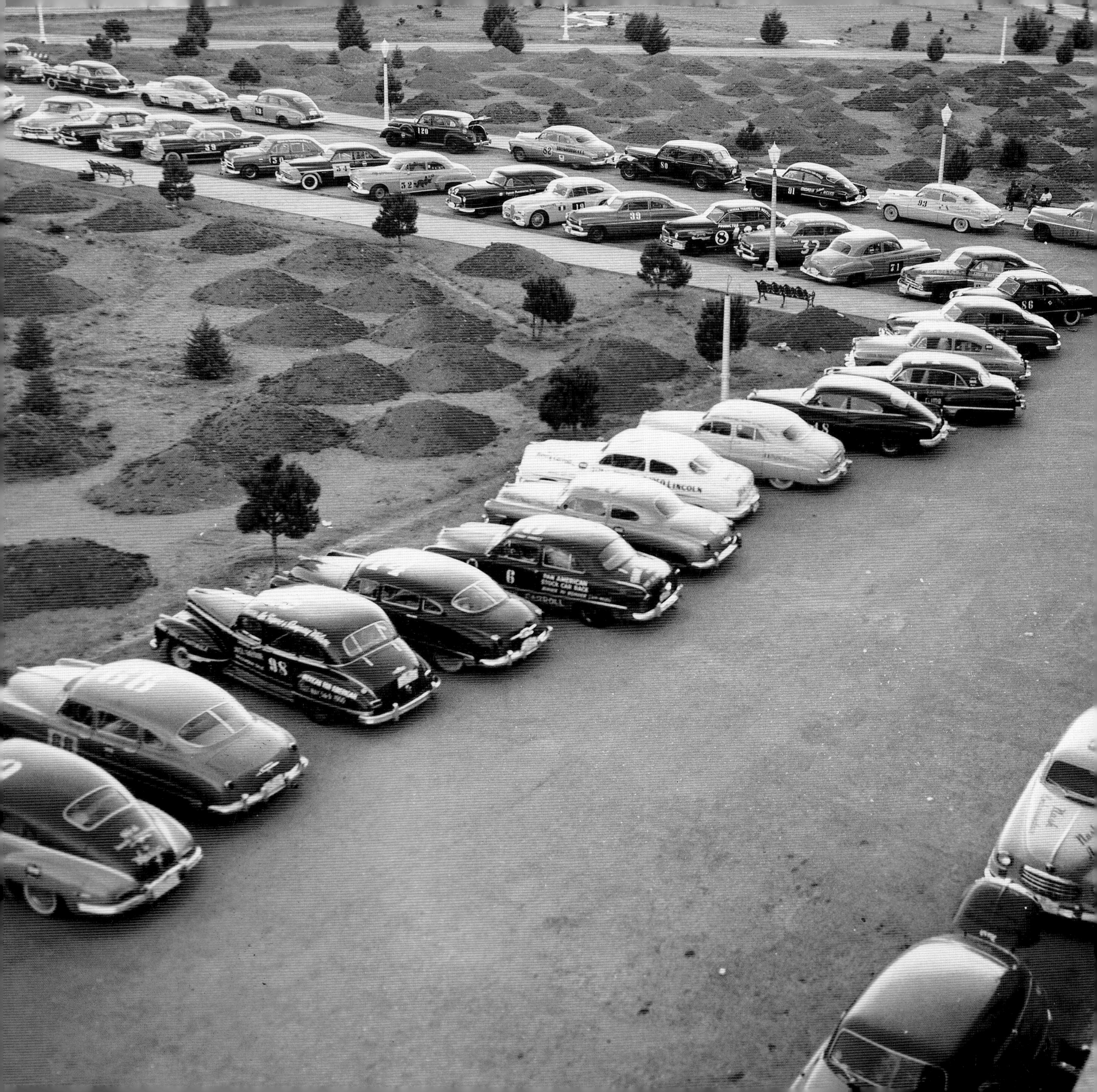
PAN AMERICAN
STOCK CAR RACE
LINCOLN

power-to-weight ratio made it an instant hit with stock car racers. Oldsmobile had won five of the eight National Association of Stock Car Auto Racing (NASCAR) Grand National races in 1949, and Olds driver Red Byron was National champion.

A drawing for starting positions for Carrera Panamericana was held in México City on April 29, 1950, and entrants began arriving in Ciudad Juárez on May 2 for inspection.

Entry fees were posted for 132 cars—fifty-nine by Americans, predominantly Californians and Texans.

Italian Formula One drivers Piero Taruffi and Felice Bonetto entered a pair of Alfa Romeo 6C 2500 coupes. Taruffi, whose specialty was road events, had been successful in the Mille Miglia (third in 1933, fourth in 1934) and the Targa Florio (second in 1939 and 1948) and was undoubtedly the most experienced road racer in the field. Other European competition came from Frenchman Jean Trevoux, who entered a Type 175 Delahaye.

The field was filled out by Mexican truck and taxi drivers equipped with little more than a desire to compete, along with a group of middle-aged gringo tourists who viewed the race as a chance to drive at speed across Mexico without the distraction of oncoming traffic.

Among the less serious racers were Marie Brookreson and Ross Barton in Brookreson's 1949 Lincoln Cosmopolitan. Marie lived near Wilcox, Arizona, and she had met Ross when the private airplane he was piloting was forced down on her ranch by weather. Both single and in their sixties, they fell in love and decided to get married if they finished the race.

Arthur and Marie Boone, a retired couple from New York City, entered their new Buick for a high-speed trip across Mexico, and Mrs. H. R. Lammons of Jacksonville, Texas, used the sides of her 1948 Buick as a billboard for advertising the brassieres she sold.

The oldest cars in the race were a 1937 Hudson driven by Ismael Alvarez of México City and a 1937 Cord 812 entered by Hugh Reilly of Chicago.

And then there was the Southern contingent—the boys from Thunder Road. Bill France was their ersatz leader. A racer since the first Daytona Beach race in 1936, France was denied sanction by the AAA Contest Board in 1947 to stage stock car events. The AAA was interested only in the open-wheel, oval track racing it had always controlled, so France had formed a dedicated group: NASCAR.

Accompanying France in Mexico as the codriver of a 1950 Nash Ambassador was consummate wild man Curtis Turner, a true original. Reformed moonshine drivers Bob and Fonty Flock from Atlanta, Georgia, entered a Lincoln. Fonty, who was called "the funniest man in racing" by his NASCAR buddies, would later gain notoriety as the only person ever to win Darlington in Bermuda shorts. And Johnny Mantz' codriver was California engine and chassis wizard Bill Stroppe.

Thomas A. Deal, a portly El Paso Cadillac dealer, tested all the cars at his lot and selected a 1950 four-door to enter, and Bill Sterling, a tall and lanky truck driver and amateur racer who was familiar with the roads of Mexico, was hired to drive a Cadillac for C. R. Royal, an El Paso Chrysler dealer.

Joel Thorne, whose Art Sparks—built Thorne Engineering Special had won the Indianapolis 500 in 1946 under George Robson, entered his personal 1949 Cadillac. Thorne, a full-time California playboy and sometimes millionaire, had also competed at Indy, finishing ninth in 1938, seventh in 1939, and fifth in 1940.

Pikes Peak Hill Climb champions Al and Ralph Rogers also entered a Cadillac.

The 132 starters assembled promptly at 6:00 am on May 5 and while waiting for the start, heard news of the race's first accident. A Mexican official, zealously speeding toward his post in Chihuahua ahead of the racers, failed to negotiate the only curve on the 233-mile leg and rolled his Pontiac station wagon. Unhurt, he was assisted by soldiers guarding the course, who righted his car and sent him on his way, a sadder but wiser driver.

Part of the starting field in the impound area at Ciudad Juárez the day before the start of the first Carrera Panamericana. Jack Cansler photo, Bruce Gross collection

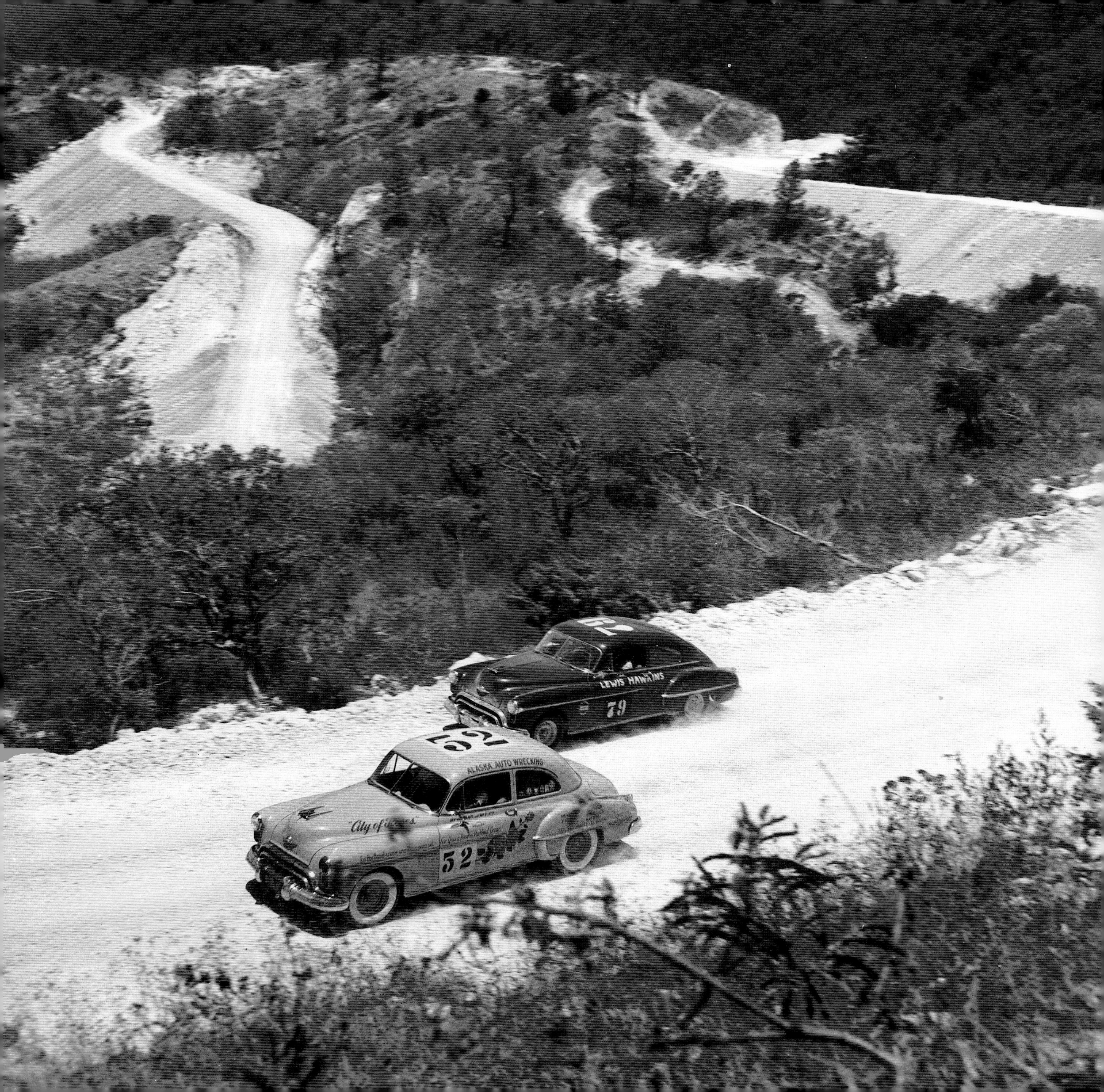

ALASKA AUTO WRECKING
52
LEWIS HAWKINS
79

Chapter 2

1950 Carrera Panamericana I
The Havoc Begins

After four hours of festivities and speeches, the governor of the state of Chihuahua waved the Mexican flag to start car number one, a 1950 Hudson driven by Luis Iglesias Davalos of México City.

The first section of the Carrera Panamericana was a high-speed run across a flat, hot desert, and tires began blowing like popcorn. Joel Thorne was not quite out of sight of the starting line when he wrecked his car. Another Cadillac, entered on behalf of the Mexican presidential staff, set the dubious record of crashing twice on the leg but bore bravely on, its top caved in, its windshield missing, and its driver's arm encased in plaster.

The only fatality of the race occurred 19 miles outside of Juárez when Guatemalan Enrique Hachmeister lost control of his Lincoln and crashed.

At Chihuahua, 113 cars were still in the running, and after the tabulations were gathered, Bill Sterling was declared leg one winner. He had made the run in 2:19:12, for an average speed of slightly over 100mph. One minute back was Anthony Musto of Chicago in another Cadillac, then Johnny Mantz in the Estes Lincoln. Herschel McGriff was seventh.

Piero Taruffi protested that no American stock car could sustain high enough speeds to average 100mph over that distance, and he was probably justified: *Motor Trend* had managed to coax only 95.44mph out of a new Cadillac in testing earlier that year. But most of the serious owners and drivers in the race were experienced hot rodders, race car preparers, and dealers, any of them capable of some "creative tuning." If they were cheating, it was at least honest cheating.

Of course, Taruffi's Alfa Romeo 6C 2500, which had a proclaimed top speed of 90mph, had averaged 89mph on the leg, so he grudgingly dropped the subject and hoped he could make up for the big sedan's slower speed in the desert with its agility in the mountains.

In any case, the next morning, Sterling's Cadillac had a new sign on its sides proclaiming that it held the World's Stock Car Record.

On leg two, a 186-mile run to Parral, the race moved into the foothills. Miraculously, no accidents occurred, and only three cars dropped out. The leg was won by George Lynch in a Cadillac at 95mph, followed by Mantz and Sterling.

The Bookkeeping Begins

At this point, everyone had to start keeping track of their leg times and positions as well as total elapsed times and standings in the

Herschel McGriff passes Lewis Hawkins on the torturous final leg in the mountains near Guatemala. As he crossed the finish line at El Ocotal, McGriff hit a dip in the road and ripped holes in the crankcase and fuel tank of his Oldsmobile. Jack Cansler photo, Tom Deal collection

Herschel McGriff and Ray Elliott never won any legs but stayed consistently high in the standings. Their average speed for the 2,135 miles was 78.421mph. Jack Cansler photo, Jean Ashley Stone collection

race. For instance, Bill Sterling, who had won leg one and was third on leg two, was leading the race in overall time, 1 minute ahead of Johnny Mantz. George Lynch moved into third, Bud Sennett was fourth, and Herschel McGriff was fifth.

Legs two and three were run on the same day, with a short mandatory layover in Parral. Tony Musto reached the finish line in Parral in good enough time to remain among the leaders but ignored the checkered flag and tore on through town toward the finish of leg three at Durango. He was summarily disqualified for failure to present his logbook and make the compulsory stop at Parral, but it was all academic, as he and his codriver were found sitting atop their wrecked Cadillac 12 miles short of the finish line at Durango some hours later.

Jean Trevoux moved his Delahaye Type 175 to thirteenth overall with a fifth-place finish. Piero Taruffi had tire problems that held him to twenty-eighth on the leg, and Alfa Romeo teammate Felice Bonetto finished thirty-first. Ismael Alvarez maintained last place in his 1937 Hudson and would be mercifully forced out on the next leg with transmission trouble.

More mountains, less speed, and numerous changes of position were recorded after the 110 survivors reached Durango at the end of the 250-mile leg three.

A National Event
Mexico was beginning to take notice of the race. Running commentaries on the radio and in the newspaper featured sensational—and often inaccurate—accounts of the events. "The

Johnny Mantz signals a third-place finish on the first leg of the inaugural race. Codriver Bill Stroppe looks over his shoulder. Jack Cansler photo, Tom Deal collection

1950 Model Factory Specifications

Model	Price	Engine	Ci	Hp	Weight	Top Speed
Alfa Romeo 6C 2500	NA	Dohc 6	149	105	3,080lb	90mph
Cadillac 62 2dr	$3,150	Ohv V-8	331	160	3,993	95
Ford Deluxe 2dr	$1,498	L V-8	239	100	3,026	NA
Hudson Super 2dr	$2,102	L6	262	123	3,555	NA
Lincoln 2dr	$2,529	L V-8	336.7	152	4,090	NA
Nash Ambassador 2dr	$2,060	L6	234.8	112	3,335	NA
Oldsmobile 88 2dr	$1,790	Ohv V-8	303	135	3,460	NA
Packard 2dr	$2,224	L8	288	135	3,740	NA

Not all the obstacles were found on the Pan-American Highway: evidence Harry Sents' 1949 Lincoln after it collided with a house. Jack Cansler photo, Bruce Gross collection

*Next page
Tire wear on the high-speed sections in the desert was a major problem for racers. Here, Francisco Ibarra Somohano makes a two-tire stop. Jack Cansler photo, Jean Ashley Stone collection*

Entry Rules Summary For 1950

Open to any make or model of closed automobile with five seats and without changes or special added equipment of any kind. Competing automobiles will use exclusively fuel of Mexican origin; specifically Super Mexolina, which will be supplied without charge. Entry fee 2,500 pesos ($290.75).

Car Preparation

Any 1949 and 1950 models may have a 0.030in overbore; 1948 and earlier models may have a 0.060in overbore. Shock absorbers may be replaced with stronger units, hub caps and fender skirts may be removed, and the rear seat may be removed for installation of a larger fuel tank. Stock air cleaners and mufflers must remain in place, and the car will be inspected for its roadworthiness. Fuel and oil will be furnished to all participants. Larger or extra fuel tanks will be permitted, and cars may also carry fuel in sealed containers.

General

No alcoholic beverages permitted in vehicle; cars must stay to the right, passing on left only. Cars will start from Juarez according to their race number at one-minute intervals with a five-minute interval between each twenty entrants; starting position on subsequent legs will be in the order of finish of the previous leg. Exceeding the maximum allowable time for each leg will result in disqualification. Unlimited time for maintenance is permitted between each leg.

Prizes

Placing	Prize
First	150,000 pesos ($17,442.00)
Second	100,000 pesos ($11,630.00)
Third	50,000 pesos ($5,815.00)
Winner of each leg	2,000 pesos ($232.60)
Winner of Léon-México City leg	3,000 pesos ($348.85)

Maximum Allowable Times

Leg	Miles	Time
1. Ciudad Juárez-Chihuahua	228	4:35
2. Chihuahua-Durango	485	9:45
3. Durango-Léon	341	6:50
4. Léon-México City	279	5:35
5. México City-Pueblo	86	1:45
6. Pueblo-Oaxaca	253	5:05
7. Oaxaca-Tuxtla Gutiérrez	345	6:55
8. Tuxtla-El Ocotal	160	3:15
Total	2,178	

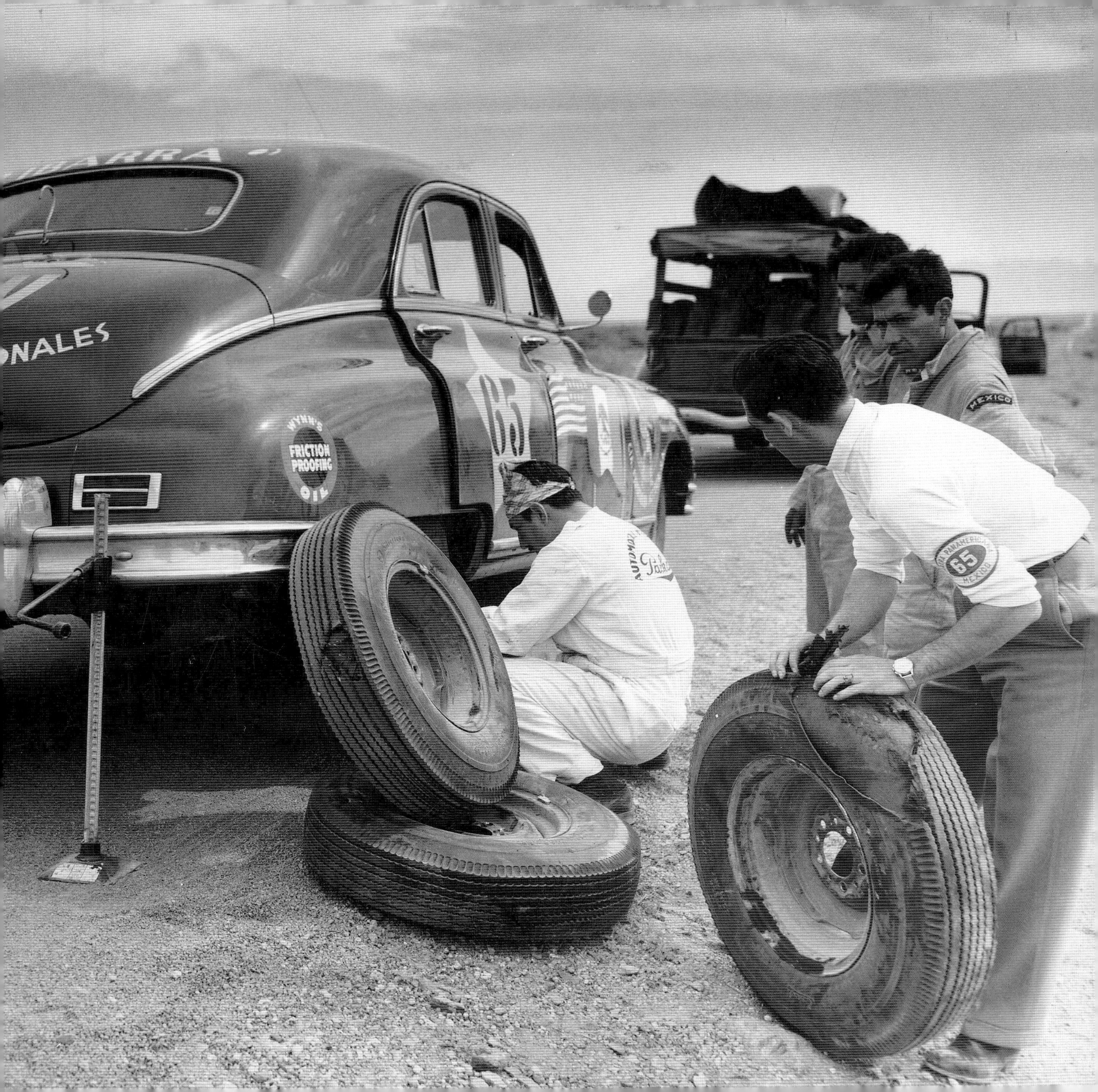
WYNN'S
FRICTION
PROOFING
OIL
65
MEXICO

A dejected Joel Thorne sits on the fender of his 1949 Cadillac after a rollover a few miles from the Juárez start. Jack Cansler photo, Bruce Gross collection

The race-leading Cadillac of Bill Sterling rounds a corner between Chihuahua and Parral. Jack Cansler photo, Bruce Gross collection

newspapers killed us on two successive legs on two successive days," complained Herschel McGriff.

With highways closed hours before the racers were to pass, spectators brought picnic lunches and lined the road. A crowd of 40,000 gathered a few miles from Durango and witnessed Bill Sterling—now nicknamed El Vaquero, The Cowboy—win the leg ahead of Johnny Mantz and of Tom Deal, who observed publicly for quotes, "I didn't know these guys were going to go so fast!" and privately to Sam Cresap, his codriver, "Let's get our butts in gear!"

Bill France and Curtis Turner in their 1950 Nash Ambassador moved up to third overall, with McGriff in fourth. Piero Taruffi finished nineteenth on the leg and was twenty-third overall.

When the third day dawned, 103 cars were ready for the longest grind of the race: 340 miles to Léon, then 278 more to México City. Texan Lonnie Johnson in a 1949 Cadillac won leg four, beating out Sterling and Mantz.

Jack McAfee had been plagued with fuel system problems in his 1949 Cadillac since the start and stopped twice on leg four with vapor locks. During the layover between legs four and five, he and codriver Ford Robinson effected hasty modifications to the reserve tank and set out to make up time. McAfee finished third into México City.

26

The real hotshot coming into the capital was Deal, who turned in a 93mph win to move into third for the race. The rotund Deal had also acquired a moniker: El Gordito, The Little Fat Boy.

Mantz had started the leg in front of Deal, but El Gordito passed him as they approached the finish line, and they came storming into the outskirts of México City with Deal's Cadillac two car lengths in front of Mantz' Lincoln.

It was exciting stuff to watch, but in reality, Mantz was already 8 minutes behind on the leg, even though he had moved into first in the race.

Sterling suffered two blowouts and finished the leg in sixteenth, dropping to second in the overall standings.

McGriff managed to keep his Olds in fourth in the race in spite of a dismal fourteenth-place finish on the leg. "An incident

Rodolpho Castaneda drove a Cadillac sponsored by the Mexican presidential staff and crashed twice before getting to Parral on the first leg. He still managed to finish the race 26th. Jack Cansler photo, Bruce Gross collection

27

The only fatality of the 1950 race occurred 19 miles from Juarez when Enrique Hachmeister crashed after losing control of his 1949 Lincoln at a grade crossing. Jack Cansler photo, Bruce Gross collection

south of Léon slowed us some," he explained. "A horse was standing on the highway—they do a lot of that—and a soldier patrolling the course threw a rock at it as we approached, trying to scare it away. The horse didn't move—it fell down! We barely brushed by it at about 90mph!"

The more favorable hazards of curves and hills allowed the Europeans to improve their standings, as Felice Bonetto and Taruffi finished eleventh and seventeenth on the leg.

After crossing the México City finish line, drivers turned in their route books at the edge of the city and proceeded with police escort to an impound garage in the heart of downtown. No one was prepared for the delirious reception that awaited them on the Paseo de la Reforma, the city's beautiful central boulevard.

Over 1 million people crowded the streets for a glimpse of the racers. Fifteen hundred police officers were no match for the crowd, and one driver noted that so far, the toughest leg of the race had been from the finish line to downtown México City.

Mexico's Revenge

Leg six, the 84 miles from México City to Puebla, was the shortest but hardest section for everyone but the natives. Razo Maciel won the leg in his 1949 Packard, followed by México City Packard dealer Jose Estrada Menocal in an identical car. "I've driven to Puebla so many times that I know every curve without having to look at it, the way you cross your living room in the dark and automatically avoid the chairs you cannot see," explained Menocal.

Jack McAfee finished third, followed by Johnny Mantz, who still held onto the race lead while widening the gap between himself and second-place Bill Sterling to 12.5 minutes.

Mantz may have been in first place overall, but his troubles were only beginning. Feeling

The marks trace Luis Davalos' path after he spun his 1950 Hudson on leg four in the mountains. Jack Cansler photo, Bruce Gross collection

Overheating on the over-10,000ft mountain passes between Léon and Mexico City was commonplace. Jack Cansler photo, Bruce Gross collection

Owen Gray flings his Olds four-door around a flat curve south of Léon while coddriver L. C. McMillan waves at the photographer. Jack Cansler photo, Bruce Gross collection

ill when he left México City, by the start of the seventh leg in Puebla, he was succumbing to the popular Mexican malady known as the Turistas, or the Mexican Two-step, convinced he'd have to start feeling better before he could die.

Mantz lost his brakes in the mountains and got sick, all at the same time. Codriver Bill Stroppe made a quick repair that allowed the Lincoln to run with front brakes alone, but he couldn't do much about the driver's health. After the impromptu pit stop, Stroppe took over the wheel, but in a few miles, Mantz decided that Stroppe's driving was worse than his own sickness and moved back into the left seat. The two dragged into Oaxaca sixty-ninth

"The last day/Tuxtla to Ocotal," wrote Tom Deal on this photo of the incredible twisting rock road on leg nine. The photographer's Nash is parked on the road at lower right. Jack Cansler photo, Bruce Gross collection

out of the remaining seventy-five cars and had dropped from first to ninth in the race.

Felice Bonetto won the leg in his Alfa Romeo and jumped to fourteenth overall. Tom Deal's Cadillac suffered from a clogged carburetor and stuttered in, in thirty-first place—still holding onto second place in the race because of Mantz' bad luck. Deal's misfortune, in turn, was Herschel McGriff's opportunity, and McGriff moved up to third, only 18 seconds behind Deal but 16 minutes back of the leader, Bill Sterling.

When Stroppe finished working on the Lincoln around midnight, he went to the hotel and found that Mantz had taken a turn for the worse.

"I went looking for a doctor," he recalled. "The police helped me round up one in a saloon, and he came over. He took out a hypodermic needle that looked big enough for a horse, and Johnny saw it and just fainted dead away. The doctor seemed to know what was wrong with him; the next morning I woke up

Lewis Hawkins cooks a flat turn. A Mexican Army communications tent is set up at right. Jack Cansler photo, Bruce Gross collection

and looked over at Mantz, expecting to find him dead, and there he was, sitting up and feeling fine!"

Sterling's bid came to an end on leg eight when he lost his brakes and plowed into a hillside hard enough to wreck his Cadillac's suspension. As Sterling limped the car back to México City to await the awards banquet, car

31

Roy Pat Conner's Nash was in a good position to win some money at the beginning of the last leg, so Curtis Turner decided to buy it, and almost pulled off an amazing upset. Note the masking tape covering the front of the Nash, a common practice that protected the finish of racing stock cars—most of which were sold by dealers after a race or a season. Jack Cansler photo, Jean Ashley Stone collection

El Pasoan George Ashley rolls onto Mexico City's Paseo de la Reforma in his Ashley's Mexican Foods Cadillac after the finish of leg four. An estimated 1 million spectators clogged the streets. Jean Ashley Stone collection

owner C. R. Royal accused his competitor Tom Deal of "paying Sterling more to lose than [Royal]was paying him to win"—an allegation he still stubbornly held thirty-five years later.

Leg eight started with 25 miles of straight, level highway, then turned into 125 miles of mountain roads up to 6,500ft high, and finally descended into the heat of 196 miles of flat and rolling country that dipped to near sea level and then roller-coastered back to the finish at a 2,500ft elevation.

Mantz took off in pursuit of a hopeless cause. He won the leg but was still 28 minutes behind first-place Deal in the race. Tommy Francis came in second on the leg in a 1950 Ford, Deal third. McGriff was now second overall. Piero Taruffi was ninth, and Bonetto eleventh.

Truth More Interesting Than Fiction

If the whole race up to this point had been handed to a Hollywood writer, the finish that

Bud Sennett's Oldsmobile 88 leads Tom Deal's Cadillac north of Mexico City as curious spectators watch the speeding cars from a few yards away. Jack Cansler photo, Jean Ashley Stone collection

The two Alfa Romeos in the first Carrera Panamericana were 6C 2500 models with nimble handling characteristics but modest speed. Felice Bonetto's, shown here, placed ninth; Piero Taruffi's fared better at fourth. Jack Cansler photo, Jean Ashley Stone collection

person would have created couldn't have been half as good as the real one.

What went on between Tuxtla Gutiérrez and El Ocotal was witnessed only by a few stray goats, assorted Indians, and a scattering of soldiers standing by the side of the road. Had it been filmed, it would have made one of the great racing movies of all time.

The cast of characters included Johnny Mantz, who had 160 miles of twisting mountain roads in which to make up 28 minutes on the leader; Tom Deal, the El Paso Cadillac dealer who just had to hold on and finish in a moderate time to win the race; Curtis Turner, who with Bill France in their Nash, was so far out of the money that he had to count on a miracle; Herschel McGriff, 8:42 out of first place but safely in second and 18 minutes ahead of the Rogers brothers, Al and Ralph; and Piero Taruffi, probably the best mountain driver in the world—driving probably the best mountain car in the world.

Mantz had seen all but the last 90 miles of the Pan-American Highway during his spring scouting trip with Bob Estes, and someone had told him that the rest of the course was paved with gravel, which was no problem to an old dirt-tracker like Mantz.

For half the leg, Mantz and Bill Stroppe roared along in great style, pulling further ahead of the field. Then, below them, they spotted a gleaming white road stretching across a valley.

"Got 'er made now!" Mantz yelled as they tore ahead. But, when they got to the white road, they found out that instead of gravel, it was paved with crushed rocks—each one the size of a man's fist.

In a matter of minutes, they had blown all four tires. They changed them and proceeded at a slower pace, but soon blew three more. By the time they reached El Ocotal, they had run out of spares and were driving on three tires and one rim, which had wrapped itself around the Lincoln's brake drum. Thirty-five cars had passed them, and they had dropped to ninth for the race. Their only consolation was about $800 earned in leg prizes.

Meanwhile, Turner and France had found out in Tuxtla at the start of leg nine that Roy Pat Conner—whose 1950 Nash Ambassador was in sixth place, 33 minutes out of first—had fallen ill. Being the enterprising fellows that they were, they simply bought Conner's car—along with sixth place—and drastically improved their odds.

So the stage was set. Leg nine was so treacherous that the cars were started at 4-minute intervals.

Turner, in the ill-handling, underpowered Nash with its 115hp six-cylinder engine, started 20 minutes behind the first car and 4 minutes back of Taruffi in his nimble Alfa. But Turner had no doubt that he would win.

And in the course of the next few hours, he not only passed the Italian, he passed everyone. France related years later that Turner said that when he tried to pass Taruffi on the narrow road, the Alfa driver wouldn't move over, so Turner just bumped him a few times Southern style until he yielded. Then Turner got sidelined with a flat tire, and Taruffi passed him back. Turner took off in pursuit, and actually had the Alfa in his sights when they crossed the finish line!

In elapsed time, Turner had beaten Taruffi by 3.5 minutes and Deal by 5 minutes to win—almost. A hasty conference of officials revealed that the rules specifically prohibited changes of crew in a car, so Turner was disqualified. To make things worse, his former partner France, who had kept campaigning their original Nash, ended up wrecking it in the mountains—although not seriously enough that they couldn't drive it home and campaign it the entire 1950–1951 season on the dirt tracks of the South.

McGriff had set out at Tuxtla to make up the time he needed to beat Deal out of first place. Knowing what the road surface was going to be like, he and Ray Elliott went shopping for some heavy-duty tires.

"We found some six-ply General Popo tires in Tuxtla," McGriff explained, "and the man who sold them to us said that we didn't have to pay for them if we won the race, so we felt obligated."

The road on the last 20 miles of leg nine was built with a high crown in the middle. "If you kept astride it, it was like being on rails, but if you got to the side of it, you couldn't control the car," McGriff related. "Right before the finish, there was a big dip in the road, and we hit it going about a hundred and the car bottomed out with a 'crunch.' An hour or so after we finished, I went to move the car and found out that it was out of gas and had no oil pressure—we had torn huge holes in both the fuel tank and oilpan; we couldn't have gone another hundred yards after the finish!"

Henry Bradley's Nash chases George Ashley's Cadillac on Leg Three near Léon. Jack Cansler photo, Jean Ashley Stone collection

Winner Herschel McGriff is presented the trophy and check by Miguel Aleman, president of the republic of Mexico. Jean Ashley Stone collection

Next page
Bill France, left, and Curtis Turner nearly had to hitch a ride back to Dixie after wrecking one car and disqualifying another. Jack Cansler photo, Jean Ashley Stone collection

Spoils to the Victors

Herschel McGriff and Ray Elliott had gone far enough and fast enough to make up almost 10 minutes on Tom Deal and beat him by 1:16 to win the first Carrera Panamericana. In third were the Rogers brothers, Al and Ralph, who had driven a smooth and careful race in their Cadillac.

At the awards ceremony in México City, there was hardware for nearly everyone and race money for the top three. McGriff pocketed $17,533, Deal $12,022, and the Rogers brothers $5,825, with another $2,700 in leg prizes distributed among twelve contestants.

Race officials decided that the trophy McGriff and Elliott were supposed to get should be awarded to the heroic driver of the presidential entry—the one that had crashed repeatedly. Although the move puzzled the Americans, McGriff decided not to complain to his hosts.

"That trophy was solid silver and about five-feet tall with a map of Mexico engraved on it—and the race route was traced in emeralds," McGriff remembered. "The one I got was only about three-feet tall—but it was silver, too."

McGriff's strategy of driving a conservative race had paid off. He knew that if he couldn't lead the race, he must stay within striking distance of the leaders and let them set the pace. His leg finishes were high and consistent throughout the race.

"General Motors wasn't exactly overjoyed that I'd won in one of their products," he related, "because they were selling all the cars they could make, and they said they really didn't need the publicity. But they did send us on an eight-day tour of eastern US dealers. I raced the Olds the rest of that season without doing much of anything but tuning it up, then I ran the inaugural Darlington race that year."

Carrera Panamericana, in retrospect, was kind of homey and a little naive. It was the first great adventure, an excursion into what was to become the ultrasophisticated specialty of winning in Mexico. Most of the drivers were woefully—if not criminally—inexperienced, the cars were not structurally prepared for endurance racing, and the officials were bureaucratic neophytes.

But, in spite of itself, the race was a success.

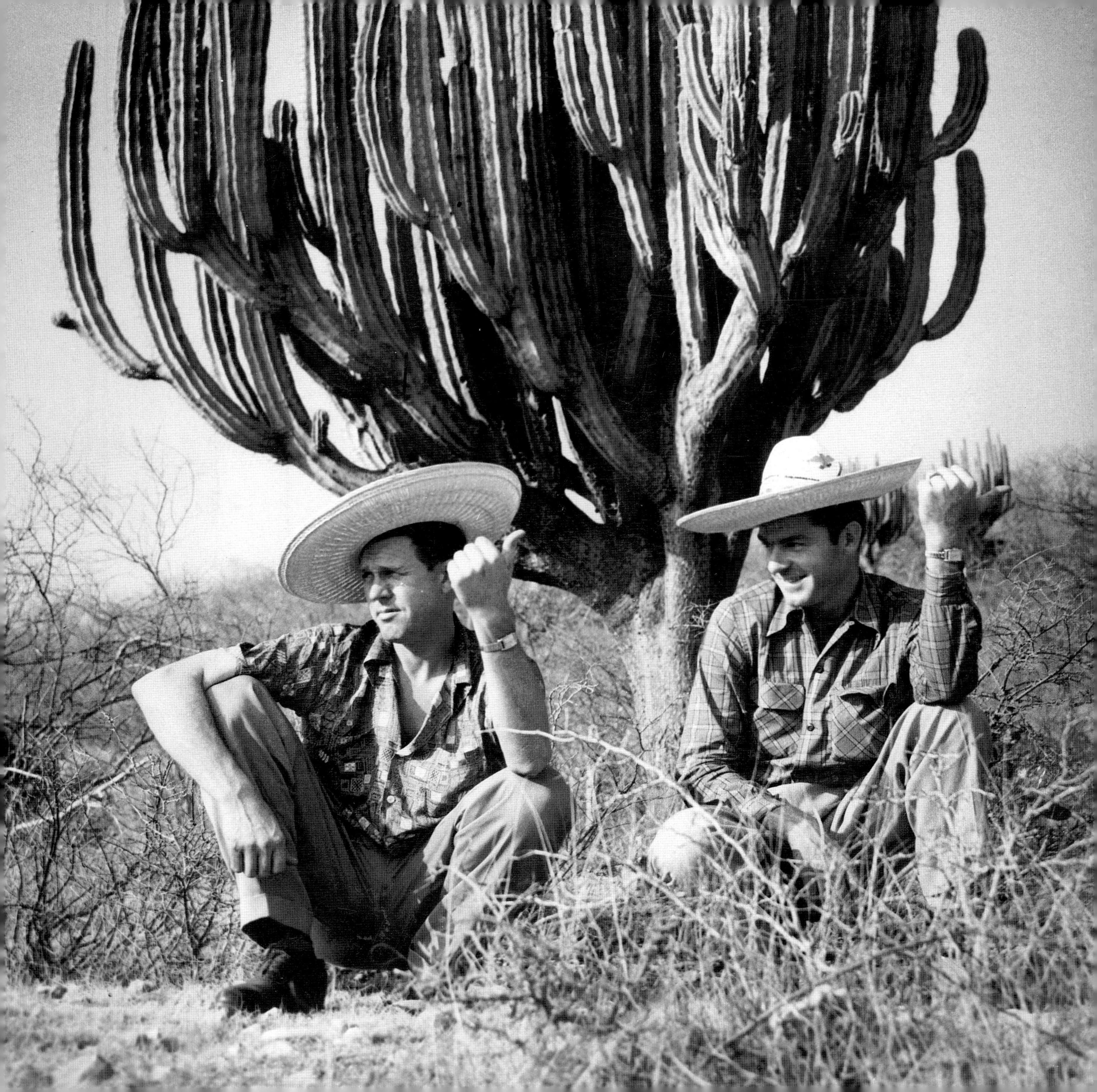

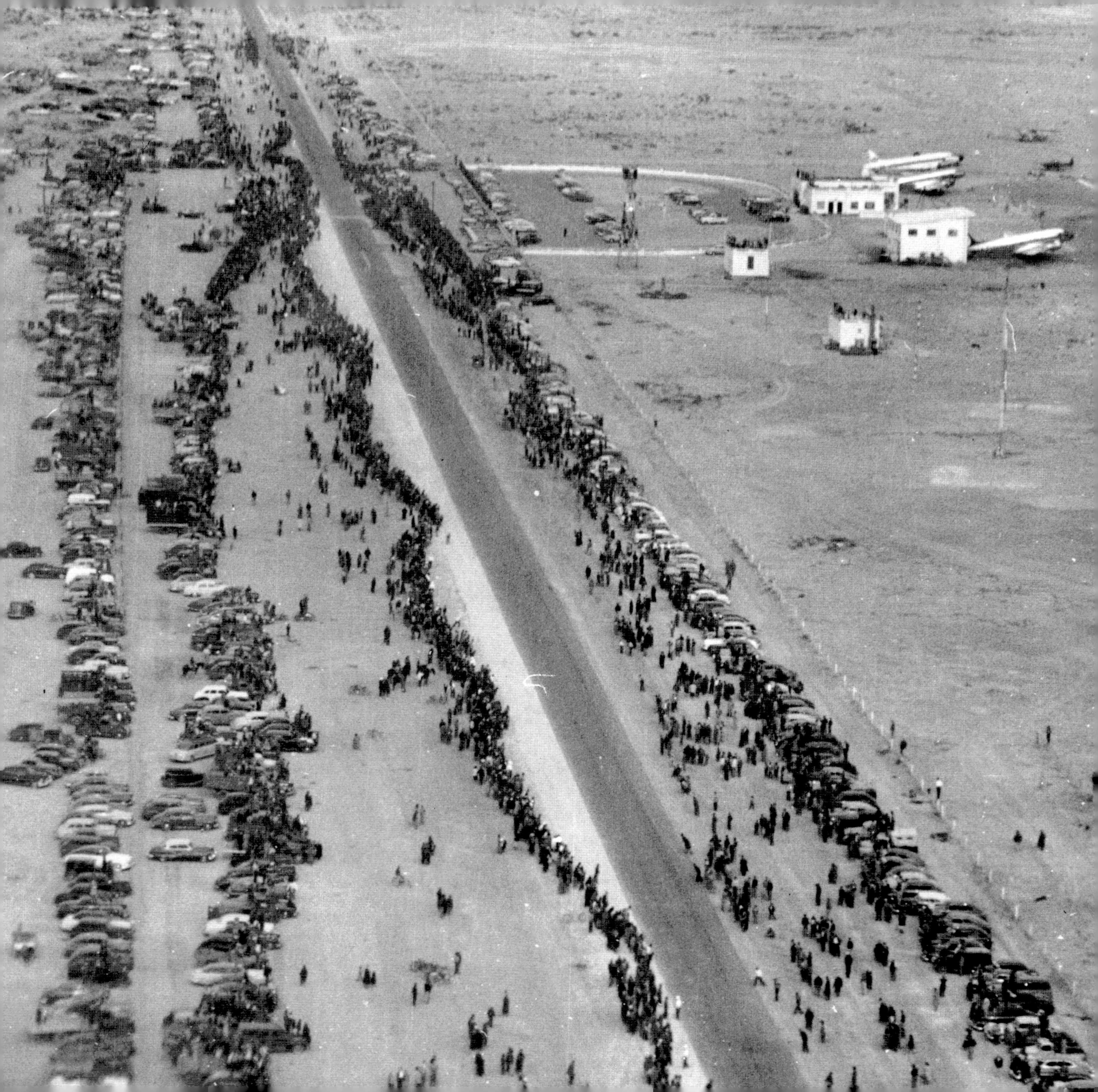

Chapter 3

1951 Carrera Panamericana II
The Sky's The Limit!

The world had discovered Mexico.

Piero Taruffi and Felice Bonetto returned to Europe after the 1950 race and spread the word, while American drivers began preparations for a return match armed with Detroit's finest. Race organizers, who initially had planned the Carrera as a one-shot event, saw the economic value in an annual edition and, in a move that was part procrastination and part genius, slid the race dates from May to November. As both European and North American racing seasons normally ended about Labor Day, the new date gave more teams a chance to compete—as well as being an overture to the FIA to place the Pan-Am on the international calendar as the venue where the World Championship could be decided.

The course was also reversed, starting near the southern end of the country at Tuxtla Gutiérrez—the end of leg eight in 1950—and finishing near Ciudad Juárez, across the International Bridge from El Paso. This plan eliminated the unimproved section of road near the Guatemalan border and also terminated the race in civilization instead of jungle—which not coincidentally ensured more media coverage.

The general rules were revised for 1951, and as long as a car was nominally a four-passenger closed model powered by its original engine type—unsupercharged—and a stock camshaft profile, it was eligible. Nearly every serious entry was being fitted with multiple carburetors and high-compression cylinder heads, roll bars and seatbelts were being installed, and chassis were being strengthened. Participants were now required to wear helmets, and after each leg, the cars could be worked on until the start of the next leg—but only by its driver or codriver.

The purse changed, too, making the race a viable economic exercise. First place paid 200,000 pesos (about $23,180), second 150,000 pesos ($17,385), and third 100,000 pesos ($11,590), with another 115,000 pesos ($13,328) divided among fourth place through tenth place, plus 5,000 pesos ($580) for the winner of each leg.

The Carrera would also have a pace car in 1951, a sporty Nash-Healey supplied by the Mexican Nash importer and driven by American race driver Charles J. Stevenson—who would become a Carrera competitor in 1952. The pace car's duty was to precede the racers by some distance, clearing the course and announcing the ensuing arrival of competitors.

In addition, organizers—fearing for the safety of drivers becoming airborne at railroad

The crowd gathers at the Ciudad Juárez Airport. The passage is narrowest at the finish line, top left center. Petersen Publishing

ALTITUDE CHART OF THE PANAMERICAN ROAD RACE

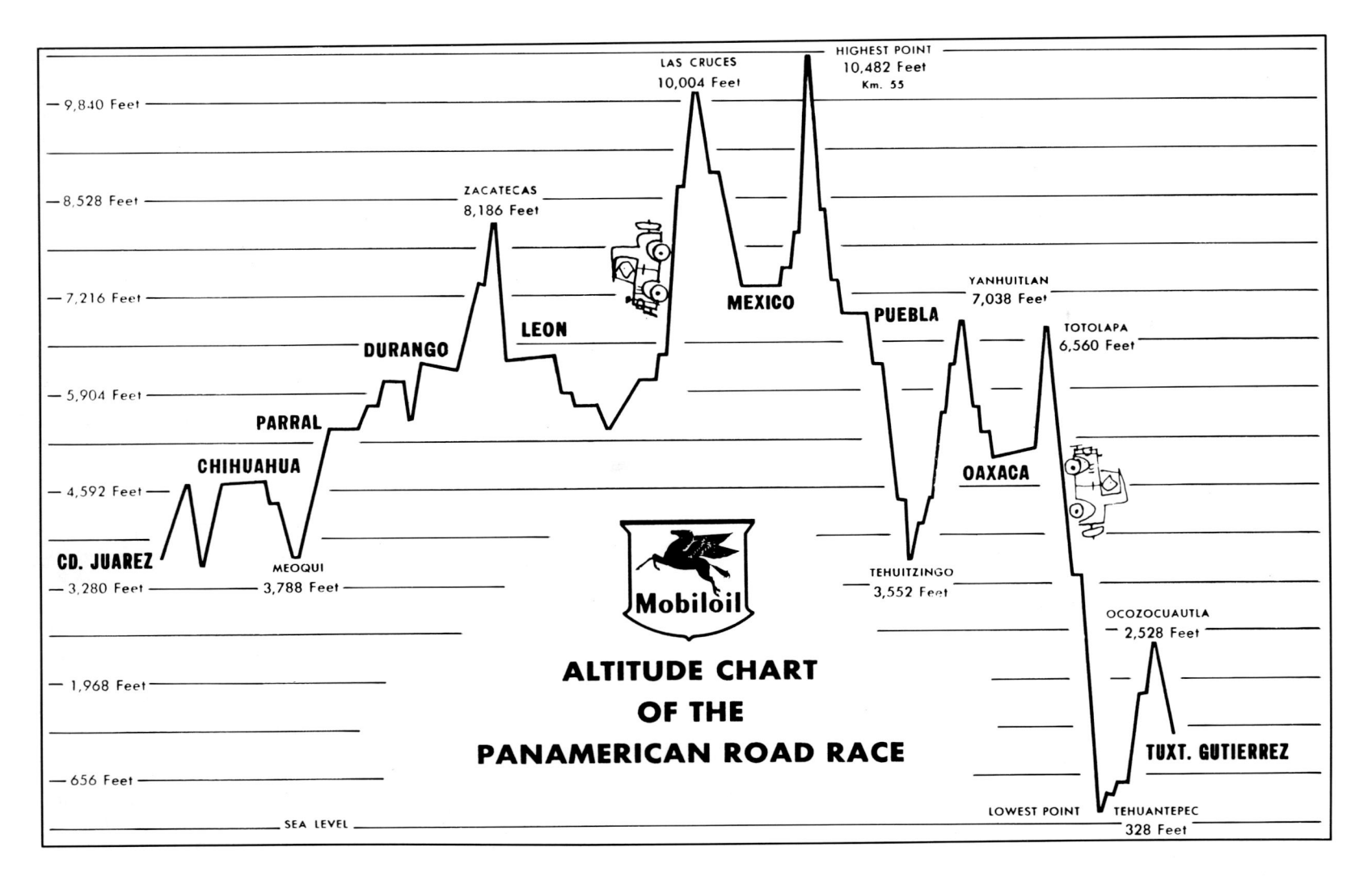

The Pan-Am course featured elevations from sea level to over 10,000ft, which tested the abilities of engine tuners as well as drivers.

grade crossings, the cause of the 1950 race's only fatality—decided to place a course commissioner with a signal flag 0.25 mile from each crossing to induce drivers to slow down, and a second signal 270 yards from each crossing would indicate whether drivers should stop. (It was not recorded if drivers paid any heed to the plan during the race.)

The second edition of the Carrera Panamericana drew a much more professional group of drivers than the first, but only 105 entries. The smaller number of cars resulted from an AAA boycott of the race as "irregular" because the Mexican rules were not compatible with those of the American sanctioning body. NASCAR, however, quickly jumped on the discrepancy and capitalized on it among its members.

A First Look at Ferrari

Piero Taruffi had promised he would be back, and when he returned in October 1951, he brought with him an awesome pair of Italian automobiles and a group of top drivers.

The cars were bright red Ferrari 212 Vignale Inter four-seat coupes with the Colombo-designed 2562cc 160hp V-12 engines with a single overhead cam per bank of cylinders. The marque was relatively new to racing in 1951, especially in North America. The first cars bearing Enzo Ferrari's name had been built in 1947 in the firm's Maranello factory. Even by 1951, the marque was only building about three cars per month.

With five Grand Prix wins plus two firsts at the Targa Florio and one each at Le Mans and the Mille Miglia, the prancing horse was virtually unknown to most of the competitors in Mexico, but the cars did possess impressive credentials. They were lightweight—at just over 2,000lb, nearly half the weight of some American stock cars. They were race bred on the mountain circuits of Europe and they had the long-legged gearing required for the flat desert highways in northern Mexico, where they could reach 140mph.

Taruffi would be sharing one car, chassis number 0163 EL, with 1949 Le Mans winner

Giovanni Bracco entered the Lancia B 20 GT Aurelia that he had driven to second behind Luigi Villoresi's Ferrari 340 America at the 1951 Mille Miglia. Petersen Publishing

1951 Model Factory Specifications

Model	Price	Engine	Ci	Hp	Weight	Top Speed
Cadillac 62 2dr	$3,436	Ohv V-8	331	160	3,993lb	95mph
Chrysler Saratoga 2dr	$2,989	Ohv V-8	331	180	3,948	102
Ferrari 212 Export	$9,500	Sohc V-12	156	165	2,100	124
Hudson Hornet 2dr	$2,543	L6	308	145	3,580	97
Jaguar Mk VII	$4,170	Dohc 6	210	160	3,700	101
Lancia Aurelia GT	NA	Ohv V-6	121	75	2,325	101
Oldsmobile 88 2dr	$1,815	Ohv V-8	303	135	3,585	92
Packard 200	$3,662	L8	327	155	4,115	93

Luigi Chinetti. The other coupe, 0161 EL, would be driven by thirty-two-year-old Alberto Ascari, second to Juan Manuel Fangio in the 1951 World Championship. Ascari's codriver was Luigi Villoresi, who had won the Mille in April for Ferrari. Villoresi, one of the most accomplished of postwar GP drivers, also had experience at Indianapolis, driving a Maserati to finish seventh in the 1946 race.

If all went according to plan, it was a foregone conclusion among the *cognoscenti* that Carrera II belonged to Ferrari.

The Late Lancia

One possible threat was from Lancia, which had hounded Ferrari all season long on the European circuits, and had now followed the circus to Mexico.

Sober and unspectacular, but quick and agile, the Lancias were potential world beaters. Giovanni Bracco had won the 2.0 liter class at Le Mans and would drive one of the B20 GT Aurelia coupes, with a 75hp 1991cc overhead-valve V-6, that had finished second to Luigi Villoresi's car at the 1951 Mille. Felice Bonetto—who had driven an Alfa Romeo to sixth in the same Mille Miglia—would be in another B20 GT. Bracco was a wealthy industrialist who generally bought his own cars to race, but Bonetto's only job was racing.

Bonetto's Aurelia was shipped to New York, and he enlisted the help of the infant *Road & Track* magazine in getting the car to the start at Tuxtla, in return for billboarding the magazine on the side of the racer.

"The car was flown to New York from Amsterdam via a KLM cargo flight November 12," recalled *Road & Track* staffer Bill Brehaut. "If it left New York immediately and was flown to Dallas, Bill Quin [another *Road & Track* writer] and I could meet it and drive it to Mexico in time."

At the time of the Lancia's scheduled arrival in Dallas, however, Brehaut and Quin learned that it was still in New York—awaiting a plan to load it on the airplane. Quin left for Mexico to tell Bonetto, and Brehaut suggested that the airline find ten men and simply *lift* the Lancia aboard.

On November 16, the car was on its way, but engine trouble forced the airplane down in Detroit, where it remained another day before continuing.

Race officials were persuaded to delay the deadline for checking in until November 19, and at 4:30pm on the 18th—some thirty-six hours before the starter's flag was to fall—Brehaut left Dallas for the 1,600-mile drive to Tuxtla. After getting lost in Monterrey and México City, he arrived at the starting line—

The four carburetors atop this Oldsmobile engine illustrate how far modifiers went to try to win Carrera II.
Petersen Publishing

Entry Rules Summary For 1951

Open to all four-passenger closed models with original engine type and stock camshaft profile—supercharging will not be permitted. Driver and codriver are required to wear helmets. Unlimited maintenance is permitted between each leg.

General
No alcoholic beverages permitted in vehicles; cars must stay to the right, passing only on the left. Unlimited time for maintenance is permitted between each leg.

Prizes
A total of 550,000 pesos ($63,583.72).

having averaged nearly 60mph and 23 miles per gallon on the endurance run.

Other entries included the 4455cc six-cylinder Delahaye Type 175—the one Jean Trevoux had driven to twelfth place in Mexico in 1950—entered for fifty-two-year-old Louis Chiron. Chiron was a veteran driver who had raced a variety of cars and courses for over thirty years and gathered ten Grand Prix wins for Bugatti and Talbot in addition to two Targa triumphs for Bugatti and a seventh at the 1929 Indianapolis 500 in a Delage.

American FirePower

In the stock-car camp, the new 331ci Chrysler V-8 appeared to be the one to beat. Its engine, called the FirePower, seemed to be stolen from the revolutionary Cadillac V-8 that had made its premier one year earlier. Its oversquare 3.81x3.63in bore and stroke were identical to the Cadillac's, but the one notable difference between the two was that the Chrysler engine had highly efficient hemispherical combustion chambers. With a 7.5:1 compression ratio and burning regular fuel, it pumped out 180hp.

And Bill Sterling, who had led most of the 1950 race in a Cadillac, was at the top of the Chrysler entry list.

Briggs Cunningham had prepared a Chrysler Saratoga V-8 for sports-car pilot Phil Walters. Cunningham, a sports car enthusiast and yachtsman who would later defend the America's Cup, had raced a stock Cadillac sedan and an unorthodox Cadillac-based road-

Clay Smith worked magic on the flathead V-8 in the 1948 Mercury driven by Troy Ruttman. The car, which represented only a $2,500 investment, attracted little attention at the starting line but would give the Ferraris a run for their considerable money. Petersen Publishing

At just over 2,000lb, the Ferrari 212 Inters of Piero Taruffi and Alberto Ascari weighed nearly half as much as the American sedans. They were race bred on the mountain circuits of Europe and had the long-legged gearing necessary to reach 140mph in the desert. Petersen Publishing

The heavier American cars, such as this Olds Super 88 of Venezuelan Magin Pastor, could often prove to be a handful when the roads became crooked. Petersen Publishing

ster called *Le Monstre* at Le Mans in 1950, which finished tenth and eleventh respectively.

Carl Kiekhaefer, soon to make Chrysler famous on the United States' ovals, signed reigning AAA National champion Tony Bettenhausen and road-racer John Fitch to drive a pair of Saratogas.

A total of fifteen of the new FirePower Chryslers would start the race. Even though the company's lightest model, the $2,989 club coupe, weighed in at nearly 2 tons, it had a better power-to-weight ratio than any other American stock car.

Defending champion Herschel McGriff led a parade of twenty-four Oldsmobiles—including the 1950 winning car, which he had campaigned the whole season and then sold to Bud Sennett. Fifteen of the Oldsmobiles were entered by Mexican drivers.

A swarm of Hudson Hornets was headed by the Teaguemobiles of Marshall Teague and NASCAR champion Red Byron. Hudson had been busy making its presence known on America's racetracks with its 308ci 145hp flathead six set in a low-slung "step-down" body that put a premium on handling. The combination had racked up twelve NASCAR wins during the 1951 season. El Paso Driver Swede Hansen drew starting number thirteen for his Hornet but assured everyone he wasn't the least bit superstitious.

Only three Lincolns were entered. Ford engineering had not kept up with the powerplant advances of General Motors and Chrys-

ler, and the best the company could offer so far was its tried-and-true long-stroke flathead V-8. Maybe in another year it could be competitive, but for now, Ray Crawford and AAA driver Walt Faulkner were the only American drivers to represent the company.

Crawford, a California supermarket owner and amateur racer, had entered the first Pan-Am only to go out on the last leg. "I had gone to Lincoln and told them it had been a helluva race the year before," he explained. "And if they'd prepare a car, they could win it! I thought I was going to get a car, but they wouldn't give it to me—so I bought my own."

Al and Ralph Rogers from Colorado Springs, Colorado, third in the inaugural race, were back in a new Cadillac, and another pair of Pikes Peak hill climbers, from Albuquerque, New Mexico, entered: Jerry Unser and his seventeen-year-old son, Bobby, would be driving a Jaguar Mark VII sedan.

The Used-Car-Lot Special

Then there was the entry of Troy Ruttman and Clay Smith. Ruttman, the young AAA Midwest Sprint Car champion, and Smith, a southern California engine builder, bought a 1948 Mercury club coupe off a Los Angeles used-car lot and modified it for the race.

"When I first saw it," Ruttman fondly remembered, "I thought, 'What a sled!' But Clay stripped it down to the frame rails, Magnafluxed each part, strengthened it, and put it back together with scientific thoroughness."

The engine was modified with a 0.125in overbore, Edelbrock cylinder heads and two-carburetor manifold, and Kong ignition.

While Smith worked on the car, Ruttman hustled parts and sponsors. When they were finished, they bought nineteen tires, saved the rest of their money for entry fees and the trip to Tuxtla, and left. On the way down, Smith made a rolling route map with speed and driving instructions for each curve and hill.

Ruttman was to drive, and Smith ride right seat, giving instructions. Ruttman handled the steering wheel, the gas pedal, and the brakes. Smith was in charge of the rest—including the horn. He had a manual spark control on his side to adjust the timing for the mountainous sections and for poor fuel grades, and a rev counter and vacuum gauge.

Their total investment had been $2,500, and when the Mercury arrived at the starting line, it attracted little attention.

Mexican Customs had barred thirty-five US racers from entering the country until they paid duty on the tires they were carrying—as many as eighteen in each car. Herschel McGriff led a group of protesters, and finally red tape was cut, and the spares allowed in—but only if everyone declared all the tires upon leaving the country after the race.

The Tuxtla start gave drivers 1,933 miles of asphalt stretching over all the terrains of Mexico. It also created a new strategy. The first race had started fast and ended in the mountains, where speeds were lower but handling was tantamount to winning. It didn't take a rocket scientist to figure out that gaining time

Carlos Panini, founder of Mexico's first scheduled airline, entered an Alfa Romeo 6C 2500 Super Sport with his daughter Tersita. The elder Panini was fatally injured in an accident between Oaxaca and Puebla. Petersen Publishing

The number 34 Ferrari 212 Inter of Piero Taruffi awaits the Oaxaca start. After the first leg, cars started in the order in which they finished the previous leg. Petersen Publishing

was the way to win the Pan-Am, and with a fast car, twice the time could be gained on the straightaways as on the twisty mountain roads.

Alberto Ascari and Piero Taruffi knew that their Ferraris had perhaps 20mph on any other car in the race, so they planned to carry just two spare tires, save rubber in the mountains, and not press the early leaders. After all, seconds gained at the expense of car and tire wear were not as appealing as minutes gobbled up on straighter roads. Their plan was simple: Keep up in the mountains, and then drive as fast as necessary in later stages to win the race.

On November 20, Carrera II began. Alongside race reports in the newspapers was a story from Korea that promised an armistice would occur by Christmas.

Abrasion and Abuse

The Ferrari plan was good—on paper. Unfortunately, most of the first leg was paved with asphalt made from the local volcanic rock, and it tore the tires to shreds. Piero Taruffi changed tires twice, and Alberto Ascari four times. Louis Chiron also had tire problems, finishing the leg in thirty-second place.

Within 4 hours, fully one-third of the starting field was either parked alongside the Pan-American Highway or scattered about the canyons of southern Mexico.

Herschel McGriff was among the first to go. He had passed a few cars and was breezing along when an unbalanced transmission set up a vibration that broke a fuel line.

"When the fuel hit the hot engine, it caught fire," McGriff explained. "We tried to get the fire out, but we didn't have any extinguishers aboard, so I drove into the ditch and jumped out. My codriver, Jim Thompson, was a lot of help; he stood there and took pictures!" The car was later recovered, and McGriff ran it successfully for the entire 1951 stock car season.

Jose Estrada Menocal, Mexican auto dealer and racer, had announced prophetically at the start, "I will win this race or die trying." His Packard tumbled 650ft into a ravine, and he and his codriver, Miguel Gonzales, were fatally injured.

John Fitch had mechanical problems in the lead Kiekhaefer Chrysler, and he was disqualified for not reaching the finish in Oaxaca within the maximum allowable time. A fuel line came adrift on Giovanni Bracco's Lancia, then tire problems slowed him down, and he finished the leg in fifty-fourth.

Felice Bonetto blew a head gasket on the *Road & Track* Lancia and cracked the block. He had to sell the car in Mexico, unable to afford to transport it back to Italy.

The Birth of a Legend

The winner of leg one was Jean Trevoux in a modified Packard, but the surprise was in second place: Troy Ruttman and Clay Smith in their Mercury, who blew into Oaxaca 7 minutes behind the Frenchman.

Douglas Ehlinger was third in another Packard, and US Air Force Captain Robert Korf was fourth in a Nash. Piero Taruffi could only manage fifteenth in the lead Ferrari, and Alberto Ascari was forty-fifth amid the sixty-eight finishers.

Also among the fallen on leg one was the pace car. Chuck Stevenson had started out with what everyone assumed was enough leeway to keep ahead of the pack, but speeds had increased so dramatically over those in 1950 that the lead car overtook Stevenson's Nash-Healey quickly, and in his haste to stay out of the way, Stevenson hotfooted into a curve and dumped his sports car over as the pack thundered by.

Swede Hansen's number 13 Hudson overturned but was righted and continued, limping to the finish line. Jacqueline Evans de Lopez wrecked her Chrysler, and Tony Bettenhausen burned out the brakes on his Chrysler.

Legs two and three were run on the second day with a half-hour layover in Puebla before the short run to México City.

The day began with tragedy. Ninety-four miles out of Oaxaca, an Alfa Romeo 6C 2500 SS driven by Carlos Panini and his daughter, Tersita, swerved into the Unser Jaguar as it attempted to pass on a narrow mountain curve. The Alfa Romeo crashed against rocks on the inside of the curve, and the elder Panini was killed.

"I was down to first gear and about to stop when my dad grabbed my arm," recalled Bobby Unser. "'Keep going,' he said, 'somebody else will stop.' He was a hard, realistic man who'd been around racing all his life, and he'd read in the rules that any car stopping during the race to assist another would be disqualified. I still blamed myself for allowing it to happen."

Sentiment ran high. When the death of Panini, founder of Mexico's first scheduled airline, was reported just one day after Menocal's, an official branded the race "an imitation of North American customs not suited to Mexican characteristics." *El Universal*, Mexico's national newspaper, suggested that "the second Pan-American race should be the last!"

It was later revealed that Carlos Panini suffered from epileptic seizures and did not even possess a driver's license.

While sports car buffs suffered over the poor showing of Ferrari and Lancia on the first leg, the hot-rod community swelled with pride

Even though Piero Taruffi, right, has just taken the lead in the race from him, Troy Ruttman congratulates the Italian driver. Petersen Publishing

at the accomplishments of Ruttman, who finished leg two in fifth and took the overall lead of the race from Trevoux. Ascari won the leg and moved into fourteenth; Giovanni Bracco was second on the leg in the surviving Lancia, and Taruffi third in the other Ferrari.

The Ferraris, whose Pirelli tires began shredding on the abrasive opening leg, switched to Mexican Goodrich-Euzkadis, which they kept for the remainder of the race. Ehlinger kept his Packard in the battle with a fourth-place finish that moved him to second overall, Louis Chiron brought the Delahaye in sixth, and Phil Walters retired when his Chrysler broke down. Chiron was disqualified for changing a tire on his Delahaye during the Puebla layover.

A Change in the Stallions' Gait

The 81 miles from Puebla to México City was an endless series of hairpin turns, but Troy Ruttman led Alberto Ascari nearly all the way.

"That is, until we reached the four-mile straight before the finish line," Ruttman remembered with a smile. "Then he came alongside, gave me a friendly wave, shifted into top gear, and beat us to the finish by a half mile!" Clay Smith was not as amused.

But the other Ferrari, driven by Piero Taruffi, had made spectacular time; starting third, 1 minute ahead of Ruttman, Taruffi had beaten Ruttman to México City by 7 minutes—breaking the course record at 86mph. Giovanni Bracco was second, and Jack McAfee in a Cadillac third.

Smith was worried; he did some quick figuring and decided that the Ferraris had a good 25mph advantage over his and Ruttman's Mercury—and 1,100 miles were left to go, most of them on much faster roads than they'd driven so far.

Ascari came roaring from thirteenth to fourth overall with an impressive 89mph win into Léon, and significantly, Taruffi was second, having clipped 11 minutes off Ruttman's time to take over the race lead. Ruttman was relegated to second, still leading Trevoux by 13 minutes and 16 minutes ahead of Ascari.

Bracco spun off the road near Queretaro as he was passing Bill Sterling's Chrysler and was forced out of the race, ending the Lancia bid. By this time, less than half of the starting field was left; car after car was breaking leg records, and the terrific speed was taking its toll.

While waiting for the start in México City, Walt Faulkner discovered a lack of oil pressure in his Lincoln. Driving across the starting line to remain qualified, he and his crew pulled the oilpan and went to work, but by the time the problem was solved, he was over the time limit and out of the race. That left only Ray Crawford to carry the Lincoln colors.

Third in leg four was the Cadillac of the Rogers brothers, Al and Ralph, who were in fifteenth overall. Fourth was captured by Tony Bettenhausen in the remaining Kiekhaefer Chrysler.

On leg one, Bettenhausen had lost his brakes and scrubbed off speed by broadsliding curves with no guardrails, and in Oaxaca, he stopped the car by bumping curbs. "It's taken me three days to get over being scared," he observed after leg four, noting that he was so far down in the standings that it might be smarter to quit.

Sterling finished leg four in fifth, followed by Marshall Teague and Jean Trevoux. Bud Sennett in the City of Roses Oldsmobile dropped out. The first seven cars had broken the 1950 leg record.

Run on the same day as leg four, leg five was won by Ascari at another blistering pace—98mph—but a surprising 47 seconds behind him was the suddenly motivated Bettenhausen, who was in thirty-second overall, 2 hours behind the Ferrari driver in elapsed time. Taruffi finished third and remained in the lead with an aggregate time of 15 hours, 26 minutes, 3 seconds; Ruttman came in second at 15 hours, 30 minutes, 40 seconds; and Ascari took third at 15 hours, 37 minutes, 7 seconds.

Carl Kiekhaefer signed reigning AAA National Champion Tony Bettenhausen to drive the new V-8 Chrysler. Even at a weight of 2 tons, this car with its 180hp Hemi engine provided a better power-to-weight ratio than any other American sedan. Petersen Publishing

49

The rolling hills and flat desert of the remaining 667 miles to Juárez would allow the Italian cars room to stretch their lead at a comfortable pace.

Following a full-day layover after the grueling 600-mile México City—Léon—Durango legs run on the same day, the two sections run on the fourth day seemed a breeze. Major maintenance and rebuilding had been accomplished, and both cars and drivers were fresher than they had been since the start.

Leg six was nearly a repeat for the top ten finishers of leg five, as Ascari won, followed 40 seconds later by the storming Bettenhausen, who had now moved up to twenty-second. Taruffi came 33 seconds later, then Trevoux, Sterling, Teague, and Ruttman. Ascari had made up enough time on Ruttman to take over second place overall; Sterling was in fourth, Trevoux in fifth, and Crawford in eighth after six legs. Swede Hansen's number thirteen Hudson finally ran out of luck and retired.

By this time, Bettenhausen had built his momentum and was trying desperately to catch someone. The contest was decidedly two races—the Ferraris in one, the remaining thirty-three cars in the other. The Italians' lead seemed insurmountable.

Formation Ferrari Finish

An estimated 200,000 people filled the road at the finish near Ciudad Juárez. When the first car was sighted by airplane, and the news radioed ahead, sirens wailed and whistles blew, and the crowd moved back a few feet to let the speeding racers pass, then surged back into the road until the next contender appeared to threaten them.

The first car they saw was Tony Bettenhausen's Chrysler, roaring across the finish at 130mph. He turned in a leg win at a record 112.681mph. Stepping from the car, he muttered, "I'm glad that's over!" In spite of his impressive late charge, Bettenhausen was a victim of too little too late: he ended up out of the money in sixteenth place for the race.

The next two cars were the blood red Ferraris of Piero Taruffi and Alberto Ascari, crossing the line in triumphant formation.

That they would win the race had been assumed for several days; who would be third was the burning question.

Both Bill Sterling and Troy Ruttman had become everybody's favorites: Ruttman because of his youthful good looks and underdog entry, Sterling because he was from El Paso and the archetypical Texan—tall, lean, and quiet.

The tiebreaker on the road was the horsepower superiority of Sterling's Chrysler. He finished the leg second and the race third, outdistancing Ruttman by nearly 5 minutes. Jean Trevoux and His Packard trailed in fifth.

After the finish, sixth-place Marshall Teague's only wish was for a drink of good water and a long sleep.

Taruffi and Ascari had won all the marbles. Of the $65,584 purse, $23,180 went to the winners. Sterling put $11,590 in his Levis for third and was proclaimed *El Piloto Mas Uniforme*, or The Steadiest Driver.

Ruttman and Clay Smith were happy with fourth. "When Clay and I rolled across the finish line, we had earned 50,000 pesos—$5,795," Ruttman said. "Then Lincoln-Mercury asked us to bring the car to México City for display, and they surprised us with another 40,000 pesos [$4,640] award. The Mobil people gave us another bonus, and we ended up with about $11,600!"

While the winners basked, the losers groused.

"They threw the rulebook away," grumbled Royal Russell, whose car finished out of the money in eleventh. "We thought this was strictly a stock-car race. Those Italian Ferraris are not stock cars—they're racing cars." Russell even accused the winners of using 100-octane fuel. His improbable logic: "I could smell it!"

Tommy Francis came to the foreigners' defense. "Look," he told reporters, "there has been a lot of scuttlebutt about the Italians. They said they teamed up, blocked the road, used 100-octane instead of Pemex, and had racing cars. Unless the race committee disqualifies them, everyone oughta keep their mouths shut. Taruffi and Ascari were perfect gentlemen."

Perennial Pan-Am competitors Jacqueline Evans de Lopez and Al Rodgers. Evans de Lopez raced in all five Carreras but never finished, while Rodgers completed all four that he entered—his best finish a third place in 1950. Petersen Publishing

Ruttman agreed. "The best car won," he said.

Taruffi had averaged 87.6mph, 8mph more than the driver of the winning Olds in 1950, and the race was run in 1 hour, 22 minutes, 15 seconds less than it took to travel a comparable distance in the longer 1950 Carrera.

"My victory was highly exalted by the press," commented Piero Taruffi some years later, "but it concluded the least hard-fought edition of the five Carreras in which I participated." Taruffi, who was popular in Mexico, had been given the nickname *El Zorro Plateado,* or The Silver Fox, and the people even coined a word in his honor: *tarufear* meaning "to drive fast."

As a result of the stunning victory, Taruffi's codriver, Luigi Chinetti, was appointed North American Ferrari distributor by his grateful old friend, Enzo Ferrari.

The two winning cars were sold on the spot, and they would appear next in the 1952 race in the hands of Mexican drivers. Competitors were assured that if a Carrera III was held, some kind of handicapping system would be used.

All in all, the second Carrera was a race unlike the first. The drivers were more serious and the cars were more serious, and the Carrera would be in the plans of more than a few factory teams in 1952.

51

Chapter 4

1952 Carrera Panamericana III: Sports Class

The Three-Pointed Star Invades Mexico

Pablo Aguilar drove the Ferrari 212 Inter in which Piero Taruffi won the 1951 race, and Paco Iberra, shown here north of Durango, was aboard Alberto Ascari's second-place 212 Inter from the previous year. Dean Batchelor collection

From its third year on, the Carrera Panamericana began to bog down under the weight of its own statistics. It had been easy to keep track of who was ahead in 1950 and 1951, but in 1952, two classes were created—one for stock cars and one for sports and grand touring cars. In 1953, the race would have four classes, and in 1954, five. That meant each of the eight legs would end with separate winners, separate second-place finishers, ad infinitum.

As Akton Miller observed, "If the race were still run, I'm sure there'd be classes for motorcycles—over and under 500cc—dune buggies, three-wheelers, ten-speed bicycles, and ultralight aircraft!"

But to the competitors, each of the main classes was a race in itself.

A World-Class Event

In just three years, the Mexican Road Race had become the world's premier road contest with its astonishing extremes of altitude, weather, and road conditions. At the time, it was compared with Le Mans, but that venue had large, well-appointed pits that were never more than 6 miles away from any point on the course. Every driver knew the Le Mans circuit intimately before starting the race, and crews relaxed and watched the event when not working on cars.

In Mexico, though, every mile was a new challenge. Assorted bird and animal life had to be watched for, and the heat and wind added a great deal to the tension. Crews had to pick up shop after servicing the cars, drive all night to the end of the next leg, catch a few hours' sleep, then start all over again.

The new sports car class was wide open—including supercharging—and any auto built between 1949 and 1952 that had two seats and a complete electrical system could compete, although the engine that started the race in each entry had to remain in its chassis. During the race, only the driver and codriver could repair the car; after each leg, however, mechanics were authorized to work on the vehicles with no time limits.

The Carrera was becoming a proper world-class event; it was getting big money, factory teams and famous drivers involved, and nearly everyone was figuring how to cheat and manipulate.

Mercedes-Benz and the Gullwing

In 1952, Daimler-Benz was making its first move into international sports-car racing since the war. Although its factories had been

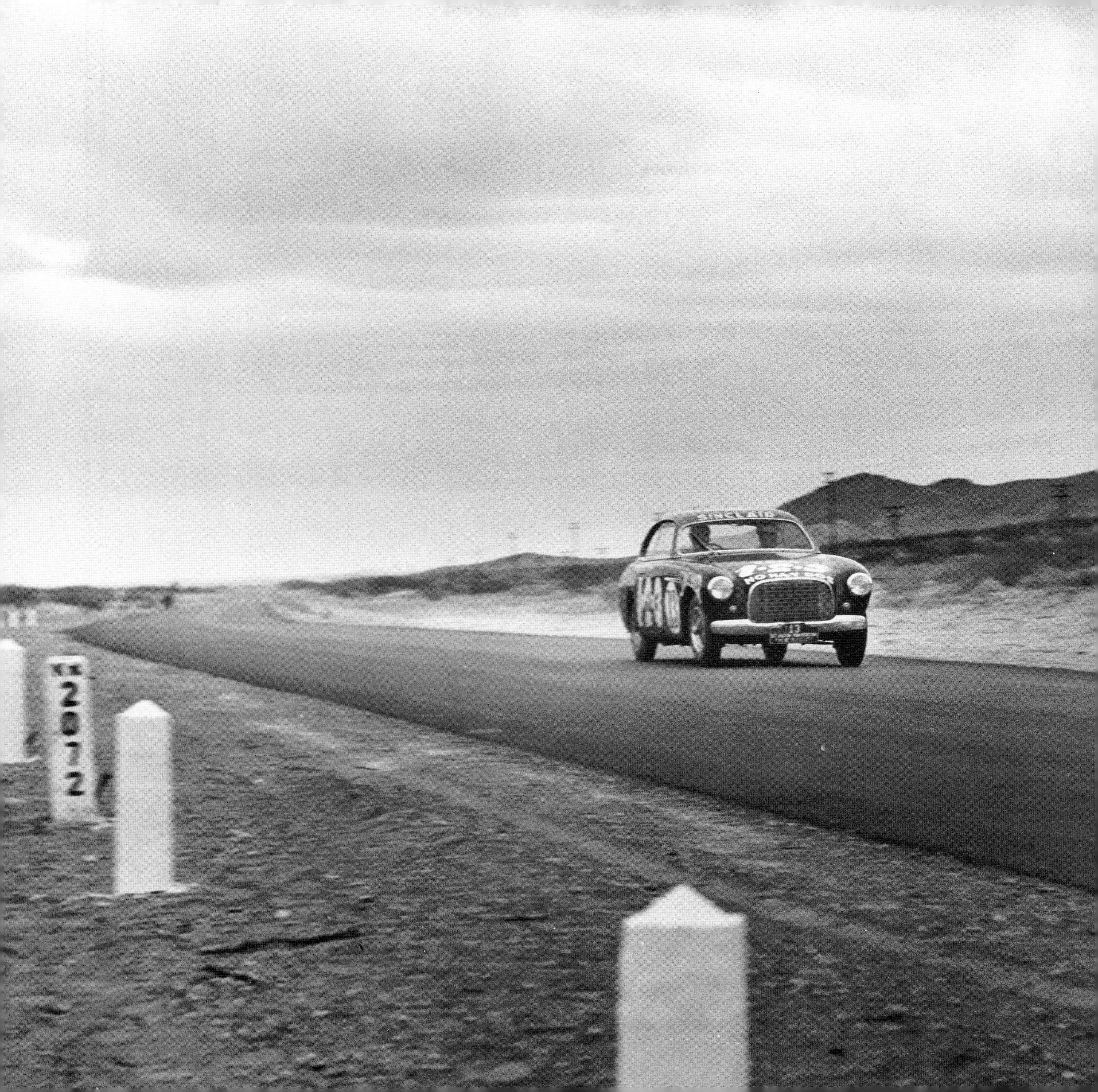
SINCLAIR
2072
13

Hans Klenk, left, and Karl Kling in Tuxtla Gutiérrez before the start of Carrera III. Before the end of the first leg, the 300SL had used more than its allotment of tires and had met with a low-flying buzzard, which broke the windshield and stunned Klenk. Road & Track

leveled during bombing, it was able to design a sports racing car largely from the existing parts inventory of its stately 300 sedan. With the addition of three Solex carburetors and other proper modifications, the 2996cc 115hp engine had been boosted to 177hp and rested partially on its side in the world's first true space frame, topped with a light-gauge aluminum body that kept the weight of the car under 2,000lb.

The Mercedes-Benz sports car had one unique feature that distinguished it from ordinary coupes. Because the space frame left no room for conventional door openings, engineers hinged the doors at the top. Even though its official name was 300SL, it was immediately nicknamed the Gullwing.

In the first outing of the 300SL in May at the Mille Miglia, three examples were entered: Karl Kling finished second in one behind Giovanni Bracco in a Ferrari; Herman Lang retired in the second; and Rudolph Caracciola finished fourth in the third. Two weeks later, in a sports-car race at Bern, Switzerland, Kling, Lang, and Fritz Reiss swept the first three positions in 300SLs.

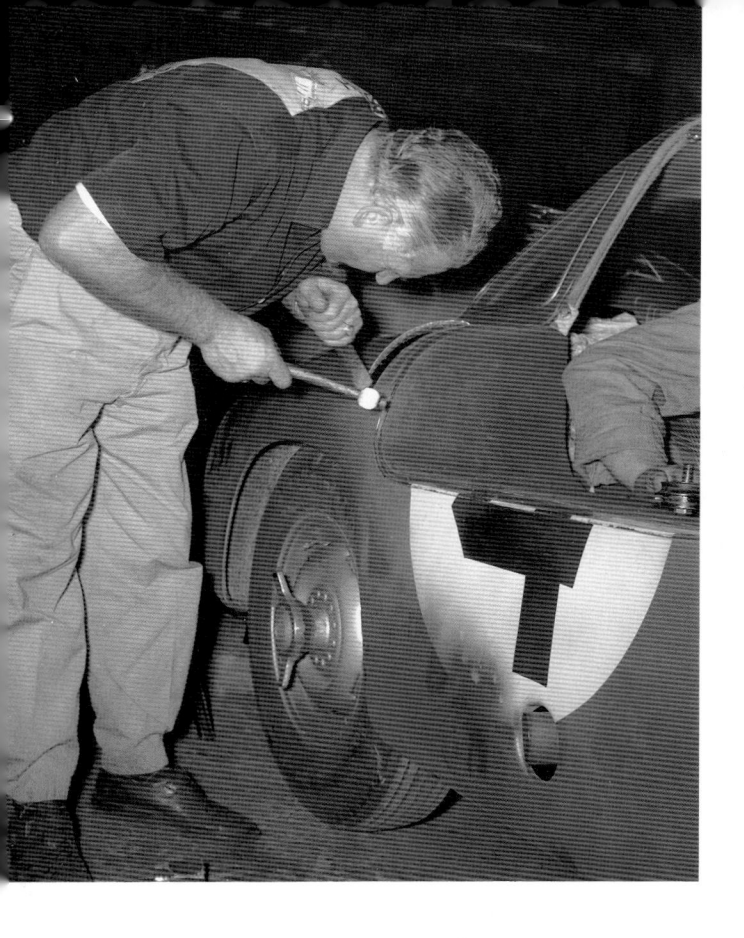

For Le Mans in June, three new cars were constructed. Lang and Reiss won in one, Theo Helfrich and Norbert Niedermayer were second in another, and the Gullwing of Kling and Hans Klenk retired in the 9th hour.

In its fourth showing, four cars were entered at Nürburgring, and a phenomenal one-two-three-four finish was achieved.

All told, the new model had captured nine of the first twelve positions in its only four races. Although the point of the program certainly had been proved, one last outing could not be resisted, and at the request of Prat Motors, S.A., the Mexican Mercedes importer, arrangements were made to field a team of three cars for the Pan-Am.

Kling and Klenk would drive their Le Mans coupe, number 0008. Lang—whose experience dated back to the 1939 Grand Prix championship in the Mercedes W.154—teamed with Edwin Gruff in a new coupe, number 0005, and American John Fitch and German Eugene Geiger would be in the Nürburgring roadster, number 0009.

The team prepared with Teutonic thoroughness. With borrowed 200 and 300 sedans,

Mercedes-Benz racing director Alfred Neubauer, right, with American team driver John Fitch. Petersen Publishing

Karl Kling cuts an opening in the rear fender of his 300SL in an attempt to duct cool air onto the troublesome Continental tires. Petersen Publishing

1952 Sports Category Model Factory Specifications

Model	Price	Engine	Ci	Hp	Weight	Top Speed
Ferrari 250S	NA	Sohc V-12	179	240	NA	155mph
Ferrari 340 Mexico	$16,000	Sohc V-12	250	280	1,980lb	174
Ferrari 340 America	NA	Sohc V-12	250	220	1,980	149
Jaguar XK-120	$4,039	Dohc 6	210	160	2,920	122
Lancia B 20	$5,800	Ohv V-6	121	80	2,425	115
Mercedes 300SL	NA	Sohc 6	182	177	1,900	NA
Porsche 356S	$4,284	Ohv O-4	91	70	1,675	96

Once the race began, the three weeks of practice paid off for the Mercedes-Benz team. At a scheduled tire stop between Tuxtla Gutiérrez and Oaxaca, Herman Lang's 300SL coupe and John Fitch's roadster, behind the coupe, are fitted with fresh rubber.
Road & Track

Instructions For Drivers 1952

"Aviation gasoline for sport class cars. Price: $0.88 centavos (Mexican currency) per liter. This is the official price which will be charged at all stops along the race route. The gas must be paid for in cash at the time of delivery. Checks or IOUs will not be accepted."

the drivers repeatedly drove each mile of the course, then drove it again in a spare 300SL practice car—on which 7,000 miles were logged in preparation for the race. In all, each driver had seen the entire course several times. Mercedes-Benz Team Manager Alfred Neubauer chartered two Douglas DC-3 airplanes to transport himself and his crews from one leg's starting point to the next, and he was later heard to say that although he felt well prepared, he would double the human resources and equipment if he were to return.

The Prancing Horse Stable

The Ferrari team and its drivers arrived just a few days before the start, and its mounts marked the first of the new, large-displacement designs that would set their style for years to come. Foremost were three coupes constructed especially for the Carrera—the 340 Mexicos. With 4.1 liter 280hp engines set in lightweight chassis and topped with streamlined Vignale bodies, the Mexicos could accelerate from 0-60mph in under 6 seconds and top out at an astonishing 174mph.

The coupes, prepared by Milan Ferrari dealer Franco Cornacchia's Guastalla Team and entered under the banner of Mexican oil and detergent distributor Industrias 1-2-3, were to be driven by three world-class drivers: in 340 Mexico chassis number 0226 AT were Alberto Ascari, reigning World Champion and second-place finisher in Carrera II, and Guiseppe Scotuzzi. In number 0222 AT was Luigi Villoresi, winner of the 1951 Mille Miglia, driving with mechanic Nino Cassani. And in number 0224 AT, Luigi Chinetti, winner of Le Mans in 1949, would pair with Frenchman Jean Lucas. American Bill Spear was slated to drive a 340 Spyder but had to cancel at the last minute.

Bracco was aboard the same car he had driven to a Mille Miglia victory in April when he beat Kling—the one-off 250S coupe, chassis number 0156 ET. This 250S had the first 3.0 liter engine ever installed in a Ferrari; at 2953cc, it offered almost exactly double the capacity of the original 1947 Colombo V-12 design on which it was based.

American West Coast Ferrari distributors Jack and Ernie McAfee would drive Tony Parravano's 340 America powered by the same basic Lampredi long-block 4.1-liter engine that was in the Mexicos. Although the America was down some 60hp from the Mexicos, the McAfees had prepared it to be competitive, including replacing its stock three-carburetor setup with six twin-choke Webers.

The two winning Ferarri 212 Inters from 1951 would be campaigned by Mexican drivers Pablo Aguilar and Paco Iberra. The talented American amateur Phil Hill, accompanied by Arnold Stubbs, would be in a 212 owned by Dallas diesel engine manufacturer Allen Guiberson.

Two Jaguar XK120s were starting, driven by Mexicans Santos Léona and Douglas Ehlinger, but their only hope for glory was if everyone else broke or crashed.

Lightweights in the sports class were two 1,300lb French-made T 15 S Gordinis driven by Jean Behra and Robert Manzon. These tiny cars had 2261cc 154hp six-cylinder engines and a tremendous power-to-weight ratio. In addition, they raced without mechanics aboard and with two spare tires secured to the rear.

Another new German marque appeared in Mexico in 1952. Prince Furst von Metternich and Graf von Berckheim persuaded their cousin, the Mexican Volkswagen importer, to sponsor their two personal 356 Porsches. Von

The Ferrari 4.1 liter 340 Mexico was purpose-built to win the Carrera Panamericana. Unfortunately, it was pitted against the Mercedes 300SL, which finished one-two. This example, now in a private collection in Japan, was driven in the 1952 race by Luigi Villoresi, who broke down near Léon. In 1953, the same car was driven by Phil Hill and Richie Ginther, who also did not finish. James Crandall illustration, Mitch Leland collection

Jack McAfee, behind the car, and Ernie McAfee prepare to leave Tuxtla Gutiérrez in Tony Parravano's Ghia-bodied Ferrari 340 America. Although the America gave away nearly 60hp to the similar 340 Mexico, the McAfees—West Coast Ferrari distributors—had modified its engine with six Weber carburetors. Petersen Publishing

Berckheim would drive his coupe and Von Metternich a cabriolet—the latter the first-ever Porsche with a synchronized gearbox.

Other sports competition would come from Umberto Maglioli, codriver on Bracco's second-place Mille Miglia the previous year, and Felice Bonetto, both in Lancia B20 GT Aurelia coupes with 2.0 liter V-6 engines. Maglioli's had a boost from Rootes supercharging, and so Lancia had high hopes, as it had swept the Targa that summer and placed eighth at Le Mans.

Mexican hot rodders made their bid for glory with an amazing variety of homemade machinery. The most thoughtfully designed model was a 1947 Cadillac that had a full-race engine with four Solex carburetors, as well as modified brakes and suspension. Another entry, modestly billed as *Supremo Especial*, ran a 1940 Mercury engine in a 1937 Lincoln chassis. The Del Campo Special was a 1934 Ford with a blown 1939 engine. The most eclectic—and eccentric—entry was a 1949 Cadillac modified to carry its crew in tandem underneath a war-surplus canopy off a North American AT-6 trainer.

First place in sports paid 150,000 pesos ($17,442), second place 100,000 pesos ($11,628), and third 60,000 pesos ($6,977).

The prize money went on through tenth place, which was worth 25,000 pesos ($2,907).

The government had decided to cut down its race expenses, and every driver was responsible for purchasing his or her own fuel and oil during the race—for cash. High-octane aviation fuel at 88 centavos a liter was used for sports cars, and Super-Mexolina, priced at 54½ centavos a liter, was for the stockers—that works out to 28 cents a gallon for avgas and 17.5 cents for regular.

A Long Road Ahead

Twenty-seven sports cars started at 7:00am, and within a few miles, the strain began to show. Robert Manzon's Gordini broke a rear axle; Alberto Ascari missed a curve and clobbered his Ferrari; Felice Bonetto wrecked the Lancia coupe but continued the race; and Herman Lang struck a dog and tore away the sheet metal beneath the grille of his 300SL.

Karl Kling met head-on with a buzzard, breaking the windshield and stunning co-driver Hans Klenk, who had removed his helmet at one of the numerous tire-changing stops and failed to put it back on. The huge hole in the front windshield created enough pressure that the 300SL's back window also popped out. The next morning, all three Mercedes appeared with "buzzard bars"—vertical steel tubes covering the windscreen. The press ate it up, and pictures of the cars with the bars were circulated around the world.

"You'da thought they were the only ones to hit a buzzard," laughed Oldsmobile driver Ak Miller. "Hell, everybody hit buzzards. They were just too slow on takeoff to get out of the way when we came by at 140mph!"

Both Kling and John Fitch had unexpected tire failures and had to stop before reaching the special tire depots Alfred Neubauer had spotted at strategic sites along the route. Continental had sent 300 special thick-tread Nuburg tires with the team, but in the mountains, the design was disastrous.

Ferrari had experienced the same problem the year before with Pirellis. This year, the Italian cars' problem was running-gear bearing; vibration; Luigi Villoresi's distributors shook loose, which held him up about 40 minutes, and he finished eleventh.

Jack McAfee awaits the start at Léon in his Ferrari 340 America. In the higher-speed sections, McAfee was beginning to have tire problems because of heat build-up in the car's Halibrand magnesium wheels. Road & Track

John Fitch averaged over 133mph on the final leg from Chihuahua to Juárez, but disqualification for a rules infraction prevented a one-two-three sweep for Mercedes. Dean Batchelor

The team of Luigi Chinetti and Jean Lucas placed the only surviving Ferrari 340 Mexico third behind the 300SLs of Karl Kling and Herman Lang. Dean Batchelor

Leg one of Carrera Panamericana was unlike any other race course in the world.

Nineteen cars arrived at Oaxaca, and the leader was Jean Behra in his Gordini, 5.5 minutes ahead of Giovanni Bracco in the first Ferrari. Behra's winning average was nearly 10mph faster than the old record. In spite of three stops for tires and one to revive his codriver after the buzzard incident, Kling was third, and Fitch and Lang were seventh and eighth in the other Gullwings. Umberto Maglioli placed the blown Lancia fourth but was by now alone to carry the company banner.

On leg two, the worst of the pumice surface was past, but the bends were trickier, and the mountains just as severe. Trouble showed up in the tiny village of Acatlan, whose main street had been closed during practice so that cars wouldn't tear up the loose surface.

Drivers slowed cautiously, but on frantic go-ahead signals from local *policia*, sped up. In the center of town, where the street curved between narrow buildings, car after car slid on the dirt and crashed into the curbing. Jack McAfee dented the rear of his Ferrari America, and Phil Hill lost valuable time replacing a bent wheel. Brakes, too, were a problem, especially at the end of the long, high-speed stretches.

Just outside Atlixco, the cars climbed to 7,000ft. In this violent section, Behra's Gordini was markedly superior—at least until he overshot a curve and catapulted into a ravine, suffering a concussion and fractured ribs. Luigi Chinetti also cut a double doughnut at

the same site but regained his footing and continued.

With Behra out, Villoresi stormed by to win the leg, although he had only climbed to ninth overall because of a poor first leg. Ascari's 1951 record was broken at 83.83mph. Graf von Berckheim's Porsche 356S retired with a broken gearbox.

After a brief rest in Puebla, the racers started for the capital on the incredible leg that had always managed to separate the adults from the children. In 1951, Piero Taruffi had astounded everyone with an 86mph trip; in 1952, Villoresi averaged over 100mph and shaved 8 minutes off the time! Bracco's car was second, followed by the three Mercedes in formation. Despite the one-two Ferrari finish, Bracco and the three-pointed-star team from Stuttgart occupied the first four positions overall.

The race's only fatality occurred just outside México City when Mexican driver Santos Léona plunged off the road in his XK120 and was killed.

While in México City, the Mercedes coupes were given the high-speed rear ends that Fitch's lighter roadster had been using from the start, and Alfred Neubauer confidently told reporters, "We are out of the mountains now; when we hit the flat, the race will be ours!"

Fitch described a team strategy meeting in México City: "During our discussion, Herr Neubauer was not concerned with the speed or capabilities of the other cars, and hardly ever

60

John Fitch and Eugene Geiger prepare to leave Chihuahua on their record-breaking run to the river. Note the tire inspection hole in the fender behind the door. Petersen Publishing

mentioned them. The whole team's energy was directed toward our own machines, anticipating the need for tires, parts, or special skills and otherwise arranging that our Mercedes would run as fast and dependably as they could, regardless of the competition. I thought at the time, Mercedes would rather bring the three cars to the finish than win the race, if it came to a choice!"

Also in México City, the racers were treated to a riot. Race day coincided with the forty-second anniversary of the revolution of 1910; 500,000 people jammed the area where the monuments to Mexico's heroes stood, and soldiers with fixed bayonets tried unsuccessfully to quell the crowd.

Then the cars climbed for 50 miles to Toluca—and into the fog. The mist did not slow them appreciably, but it was enough to cause a strain. Dropping down again to a more level terrain, the speeds increased.

By this time, drivers and mechanics had cut away rear fenders or installed louvers to direct air onto overheated tires. Road conditions had caused body damage, and some drivers were experimenting with tire pressures for minimum wear. The fenders of the Mercedes were badly scarred from flying tire treads, and Jack McAfee found that he blew tires on his Ferrari 340 at a constant 130mph, probably because of heat build-up in his magnesium wheels. Phil Hill suffered his only blowout of the race on leg four and dropped back.

Villoresi averaged a quick 112.8mph into Léon, 4 minutes ahead of Bracco, who remained first in the race. Behind Bracco was Chinetti in the orphan Ferrari 340 Mexico—so-called because it had been systematically plundered for parts throughout the race.

In fourth-fifth-sixth ran the Mercedes in close-order drill. Lang was still 7 minutes behind Bracco, but there were 1,001 miles left to the finish, and Neubauer felt his team's time had come. He unbridled his drivers and told them to go out and set the pace.

On leg five, Kling's somewhat battered 300SL roared to a win, with Bracco 1 minute

"The cars looked disreputable," observed John Fitch. "The paint was literally sandblasted away to base metal, the bodies were pocked by stones, dented by birds, and torn and bent by flying tire treads!" Petersen Publishing

back. Lang arrived 4 minutes later with Chinetti on his tail. And Villoresi failed to appear—he'd had terminal distributor failure and was out of the race.

Cars were wearying in the heated competition, and apparently no one had an edge on the field. Hasty repairs were made overnight. Fitch's car had developed 1.5in of toe-out; Hill's fuel lines had to be cleaned after a tank of dirty gasoline was ingested; Douglas Ehlinger's Jaguar had maladjusted carburetors.

Day four saw two dashes: Durango to Parral and Parral to Chihuahua. Both were over flat or slightly hilly terrain, except for the first 40 miles of what Hill called "goat trails." Since the last day of the race featured only one leg, anyone wanting to make a bid would have to make a move on one of these laps. Bracco was hoping his 7-minute lead over Kling was too much to overcome and was starting to take it easy in the Ferrari 250S.

Kling won the sixth leg at 106mph, followed by Lang. Chinetti was third, and Bracco fourth, but Bracco's lead had suddenly dwindled to 2.5 minutes, and his car was down on power.

The race ended for Bracco at Ciudad Camargo, 40 miles north of Parral, where two broken valve stems—which failed from constant overreving—put out the car that had led the race for 1,200 miles. He sat helplessly and watched Kling roar by and take the lead, knowing the only hope for Ferrari was Chinetti, unless Hill or McAfee could muster more speed.

Kling averaged 126mph on leg seven, even though he lost one of his gullwing doors at speed. Next was Chinetti, followed by Maglioli, respectively 39 and 47 minutes behind the leader in overall time.

Lang was fourth on the leg but moved into second place in the race. Fitch's alignment problems were still with him, and he blew three tires, finishing seventh on the leg.

At the start of the final run to the river, Fitch thought he had his problem solved and set out to make it a one-two-three sweep for Mercedes. He covered the 231 miles in a little less than 1.75 hours, averaging nearly

133mph, with Kling 9 seconds behind. But he had erred earlier, when a mechanic who didn't work for his team pitched in to help with the car's front-end problems. The rules stated that no outside help could be used, and Fitch was disqualified.

A German Victory

Karl Kling won the race at a 102.527mph average and broke Piero Taruffi's record by more than 3 hours. Herman Lang was second, 32 minutes back. Luigi Chinetti was third, followed by Umberto Maglioli, Jack McAfee, and Phil Hill—at least Ferrari had swept third through sixth.

The team from Germany had done a superb job against heavy odds, operating in unfamiliar territory far from home. They had scored the first victory for a Daimler-Benz factory entry ever recorded in the Western Hemisphere.

"The cars themselves looked disreputable," said John Fitch. "The paint was literally sandblasted away to base metal, the bodies were pocked by stones, dented by birds, and torn and bent by flying tire treads!"

The engines on the silver cars had been used in practice runs as well as in the race, and each had accumulated over 4,700 miles since arriving in Mexico. Service logs showed that Kling had never changed brake linings, whereas Fitch and Lang did; however, the winning car got a new clutch at Durango and rear shocks in Chihuahua.

After a few hours' rest, Kling and Hans Klenk climbed again through the gullwing doors into number 4 for the leisurely drive back to México City for the awards ceremonies.

The 300SL would have other jobs to do in the coming months, but its racing days were over. No other car in the history of motor racing had equaled its record of winning—and placing second—in four of five major races it entered.

For a simple car made of available parts by a company fighting its way back from obliteration, the Gullwing had done rather well.

In fifth place at Durango, Umberto Maglioli, left, contemplated improving his lot in the supercharged 2.0 liter Lancia B 20 GT behind the superior competition of the Mercedes and Ferraris.
Road & Track

63

Chapter 5

1952 Carrera Panamericana III: Stock Class

Dawn Of A Dynasty

Ak Miller and Doug Harrison in sombreros before the start at Tuxtla. Although they went out between Léon and Durango, their experience led to a unique home-built entry for the 1953 race. Petersen Publishing

Bill Stroppe and Clay Smith were really hot rodders at heart, banging around on Southern California's dry lakes with their home-built cars and developing their engine and chassis skills. But Stroppe had also made inroads in the burgeoning sports-car movement, building a successful MG TC powered by a Ford V-8 60 for amateur Phil Hill. Stroppe was becoming a noted driver as well as builder; in 1952, his short-wheelbase Kurtis 500S with a 200hp Ford flathead V-8 had been tearing up some sophisticated competition at some important sports car events.

Smith's reputation had never been higher either. The famous Smith Cams' cigar-chomping Woody Woodpecker trademark was appearing in more and more winner's circles—including the big one in Indianapolis in May, when Troy Ruttman won in a Smith-prepared car.

After his success in Mexico with Ruttman in the Mercury hot rod in 1951, Smith began thinking about mounting a full-scale attack on the Carrera. He got together with Stroppe, and they combined resources. Their partnership lacked only one ingredient: a backer that wanted to win in Mexico.

Lincoln-Mercury was the logical choice. It was introducing a hot new engine in the 1953 Lincolns, a 205hp V-8 unit to replace the new 160hp overhead-valve version that had been introduced earlier that year. Smith and Stroppe took their proposal to Dearborn, and Ford was interested. Within two months, the decision was made, and on July 30, 1952, Ford embarked on its official return to competition, its first since 1935—and the progenitor of all Ford racing programs since.

A 1952 Lincoln with a 1953 engine was available at Ford's high-altitude development center in Colorado Springs, so Smith and Stroppe picked it up, did a little tuning, and tested it on the salt at Bonneville, where it ran 118mph. Since it had not yet been introduced to the public, it was considered a prototype, not eligible for AAA records, but when it beat existing marks, private entrants began asking for examples. Eventually, instead of the three cars Stroppe and Smith scheduled for production, seven were built.

Dozens of changes had to be engineered to make the cars raceworthy and reliable at speed, and under the rules, the modifications had to be listed in the Ford catalog as options. So Ford rewrote the book, using as many existing parts from other Ford models—including trucks—as possible to speed up manufacturing and homologation.

108
RA PAN-AMERICANA
CARRERA PANAME
MEXICO
135
PILOTO
CO-PILOTO
AKTON MILLER
DOUG HARRISON
108
HARRIS MOTOR CO.
OLDSMOBILE
WHITTIER, CALIF.

Fernando Leeuw Murphy in his Mercury near Juárez on the last leg. The Mexican would drive for Lincoln in 1953 and 1954. Dean Batchelor

Chuck Daigh was Stroppe's main engine man, and Vern Houle—probably the world's leading authority on automatic transmissions—reworked the dual-range Hydra-matic transmissions. The cars used standard 3.31:1 axle ratios, heavy-duty shock absorbers, and scoops to direct air at the drum brakes. Under the hood, everything that turned was balanced, and the engines had four-barrel carburetors, Ford truck cams with solid lifters, and matched manifolds and ports. When they were finished, the "Stropped" Lincolns put out close to 300hp.

Ruttman was slated to head the Lincoln team, but owing to other commitments was replaced by Chuck Stevenson, 1952 AAA National champion and 1951 Mexican Road Race pace car driver, with Smith as codriver.

The old teammates from the first race—Johnny Mantz and Stroppe—were reunited in the second team car. AAA driver Mantz had won the inaugural NASCAR Darlington 500 in 1951 in a lightweight Plymouth 6 business coupe, besting the more powerful—and heavier—cars in the world's first 500-mile stock car race, collecting a $10,000 purse. The AAA fined Mantz $2,500, however, for driving in an "outlaw" race.

The third car of Lincoln's First Team was handled by Walt Faulkner, with Chuck Daigh

1952 Stock Category Model Factory Specifications

Model	Price	Engine	Ci	Hp	Weight	Top Speed
Cadillac 62 2dr	$3,542	Ohv V-8	331	190	4,174lb	109mph
Chrysler Saratoga 2dr	$3,187	Ohv V-8	331	180	3,948	106
Hudson Hornet 2dr	$2,543	L8	308	145	3,580	NA
Lincoln Capri 2dr	$3,549	Ohv V-8	317.5	205	4,165	98
Oldsmobile Super 88 2dr	$1,815	Ohv V-8	303	160	3,628	104
Packard 400	$3,797	L8	327	155	4,100	NA

The Lincoln tire stop 217 miles north of Tuxtla Gutiérrez. Tires are propped up in readiness for the arrival of team cars, air jacks are buried in the dirt, and air wrenches are used. Max Ellis collection

J. Garcia Torees, Mexico City Sales Manager, left, and Compania Comercial Vacuum S.A. (Mobil Oil) Vice President Howard Bird, Jr., present bonus checks to Johnny Mantz, Chuck Stevenson, and Walt Faulkner, the top three stock car finishers in the 1952 Pan-Am. Mobil Oil Corporation

riding shotgun. Accompanying them was a small army of cooks, mechanics, doctors, and factory engineers, with a large supply of spare parts under the care of John Holman (later of Holman and Moody). Besides a transporter for the cars, a sedan delivery truck towing a sleeping trailer completed the caravan.

Smith and Stroppe always managed to have a card up their sleeve, something that would give them an edge—within the rules. In 1952, they created the Lincoln Tire Depot.

The rules stated that no one but the driver or codriver could work on a car during the race—including the changing of tires—so Stroppe found a small soda pop stand at a wide spot in the mountain road where buses stopped. In the brush behind the shack, he hid six front tires, one pair for each team car. Then he dug a hole in the clearing and buried a cylinder of compressed air and hoses connected to a platform, along with air wrenches. When a Lincoln rolled into place, the driver and co-pilot would connect the cylinder, and the car would raise so that they could change the tires, of course aided by air wrenches.

The private-entry Lincolns that were prepared nearly identically to the factory cars were driven by Duane Carter and Ray Crawford—the latter ironically the highest-placed Lincoln finisher in the two years of the race, having come in eighth in 1951. Bob Korf's Cosmopolitan was a 1952 version prepared by Keikhaefer Motors.

Bill Sterling, who had finished last year's race just 15 minutes behind the winning Ferrari driver, gave up his Chrysler and returned to a Cadillac, this time backed by Tom Deal, the El Paso car dealer who'd placed second in the 1950 race. Jerry and Bobby Unser were back, in a Chrylser Saratoga for 1952, as was C. D. Evans. Jean Trevoux drove a Packard, and Marshall Teague brought his all-conquering Hudson Hornet—equipped with the 200hp "severe usage" engine option that had won twenty-seven of the year's thirty-four NASCAR Grand Nationals and had been eight-for-sixteen on AAA circuits, with forty-three cars in the first five places.

Defending champion Piero Taruffi was in a less exotic Oldsmobile Super 88 sponsored by the Mexican importer. Jim Rathmann—who had placed second behind Ruttman at Indy—and Herschel McGriff were also aboard Oldsmobiles, and Al and Ralph Rogers remained loyal to Cadillac for the third year.

Stocks paid 150,000 pesos ($17,442), 75,000 pesos ($8,721), and 35,000 pesos ($4,070) for the top three finishers and 5,000 pesos ($581.50) to each finisher placing sixth through tenth, plus leg prizes and an added purse from tire companies.

The Sweep Begins

Tuxtla Gutiérrez was charming, with earthquakes every morning, bird droppings in the rooms, and the beginning of digestive difficulties. But it always had its good point: it was the start.

When the dust had cleared after the 336 miles of the first leg, it was evident that Clay Smith and Bill Stroppe had done something right: Lincolns were in five of the top six spots, with less than a 3-minute spread among them. Walt Faulkner had squeaked out a 5-second win over Pat Kirkwood, in a Chrysler, followed by Bob Korf, Johnny Mantz, Chuck Stevenson, and Duane Carter. Bill Sterling was tenth, Hersh McGriff was fifteenth, and the rest of the field was peopled by some familiar names who had been considered real threats just a few hours earlier.

Nine drivers didn't make it to Oaxaca in the 6-hour, 15-minute limit. Ray Crawford arrived in 6 hours, 13 minutes, 19 seconds, in absolutely last place. It was going to be a long way to Juárez for some.

From Oaxaca to Puebla, Chryslers placed one-two, with Royal Russell in the lead, followed 6 seconds later by Tommy Drisdale. Russell had stormed up from thirtieth to try to improve his standing, but he was still over a half-hour behind Stevenson, the race leader. McGriff was only 6 minutes back.

Stevenson placed third on the leg; Mantz, Korf, and Faulkner were sixth-seventh-eighth; and Crawford appeared eleventh.

Piero Taruffi came from nowhere to win what he called "his" leg—the short, frantic 81-mile dash from Puebla to the capital. He took just 1 minute, 27 seconds longer in the Olds than he had the year before in the Ferrari.

Casualties on leg three included Sterling's car, Kirkwood's Chrysler, and Tommy Francis' Ford. The latter two were delayed by an accident and didn't finish under the time limit. Faulkner, Mantz, Stevenson, and Korf finished two-four-six-seven and maintained the top four spots overall for Lincoln. Carter had fallen off the pace at twenty-third, while Crawford stood thirtieth.

The five race leaders were the top five finishers on the 269-mile fourth leg. The Lincolns swept into Léon in a mob, all within 1 minute, 20 seconds, their aggregate times for the race all falling within a 1-minute spread, and Mantz and Korf in a dead heat for third overall. The close effort meant that if any of the four failed, three others would be there to take up the slack.

Reginald "Speed" McFee had been trying to keep his 1951 Chrysler Saratoga up with the Lincolns and had edged into fifth, but the team had been putting a larger gap between themselves and him on every leg. Speed was now 16 minutes behind fourth place, not quite 17 minutes out of first! Crawford retired on this leg, and Carter moved up slightly. Drisdale

The Oldsmobile of Felix Loza is beaten to the Puebla finish by the Packard of Fernando Razo Maciel. Mobil Oil Corporation

crashed north of México City, and Jerry and Bobby Unser were unable to start the leg.

Mantz broke Alberto Ascari's old record from Léon to Durango on leg five, paring 33 seconds off the time. McFee wedged his Chrysler into second ahead of three Lincolns. Taruffi finished eighth, and last place on the leg went to a Henry J. The Olds of Ak Miller failed, and mechanical problems sidelined both McGriff and Russell.

On the 252-mile sixth leg into Parral, Lincolns again dominated the top five, with McFee and Taruffi in sixth and seventh. Carter won the leg, but Mantz, who had been leading at the start of the day, fell slightly off the pace and dropped to third overall. Stevenson and Faulkner had picked up a minute on Mantz and took over first and second for the distance. McFee lost another 3 minutes on Team Lincoln. The gap was widening.

Lincolns filled the first four spots into Chihuahua on leg seven. Carter's engine let go north of Parral, and he was out. C. D. Evans placed his Chrysler fifth, McFee sixth.

"Three hundred yards from the finish," Evans recalled, "the crowd had moved onto the highway to gawk at something just as we came up! We had a choice—we could either kill half of Chihuahua, or we could go into the ditch! We picked the ditch."

The 1951 Tony Bettenhausen record of 111mph remained intact, as Stevenson won the leg at 110mph, followed by Mantz, who'd fought back into second for the race, 1 minute, 17 seconds ahead of Faulkner. McFee was closest to the Lincolns, and he was still 16 minutes behind the last one.

The annual crowd, estimated variously at from 10,000 to 100,000, gathered for the finish in chilly, windy weather. Some of the concessionaires took advantage of the cold, according to an El Paso paper, and charged the crowd the exorbitant price of 15 cents for a cup of coffee.

The Invincible Lincolns

After the first six sports cars screamed across the finish line, the stocks—the heroes of the masses—arrived. The only four Lincolns left in the race finished four in a row, led by Johnny Mantz, who had broken Tony Bettenhausen's catch-up record of the year before by over 2 minutes.

Chuck Stevenson won the class, beating out Mantz by only 31 seconds. Then came Walt Faulkner and Bob Korf. Speed McFee held onto his fifth place, beating out C. D. Evans by nearly 12 minutes.

The entire Lincoln team was protested by Carl Kiekhaefer, who had prepared Korf's fourth-place Lincoln. He accused Bill Stroppe of a multitude of sins, and the two men ended up shouting insults at each other before the governing body decided that the factory cars were within the rules as written. Clay Smith responded by asking if he could look at the powerplant Kiekhaefer had built.

After inspecting the engine on Korf's Lincoln, Smith smiled as he turned to Stroppe and said, "If they're going to use illegal valve springs, the least they could do is put them in right side up!"

Of the sixty-four starters in stocks, only twenty-nine were left at Juárez. The winning average was almost 91mph, just 12mph off the sports car pace. Stevenson collected 150,000 pesos ($17,442) from the total pot of over 727,000 pesos ($84,046).

The Lincolns were invincible. Smith and Stroppe were hailed by the racing fraternity. Lincoln-Mercury was publicly pleased, privately ecstatic! It was, indeed, the dawn of a dynasty.

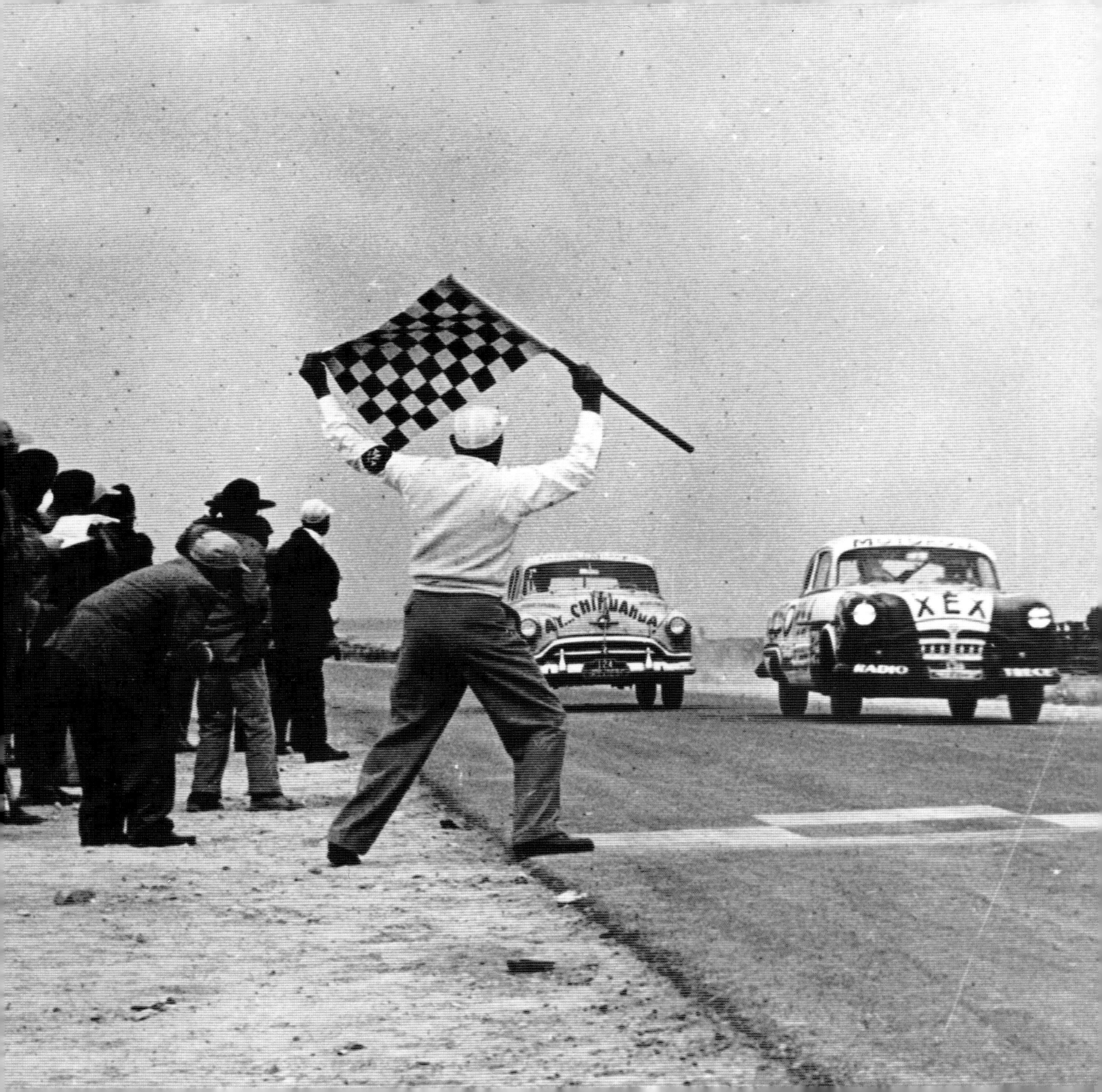
XEX
RADIO

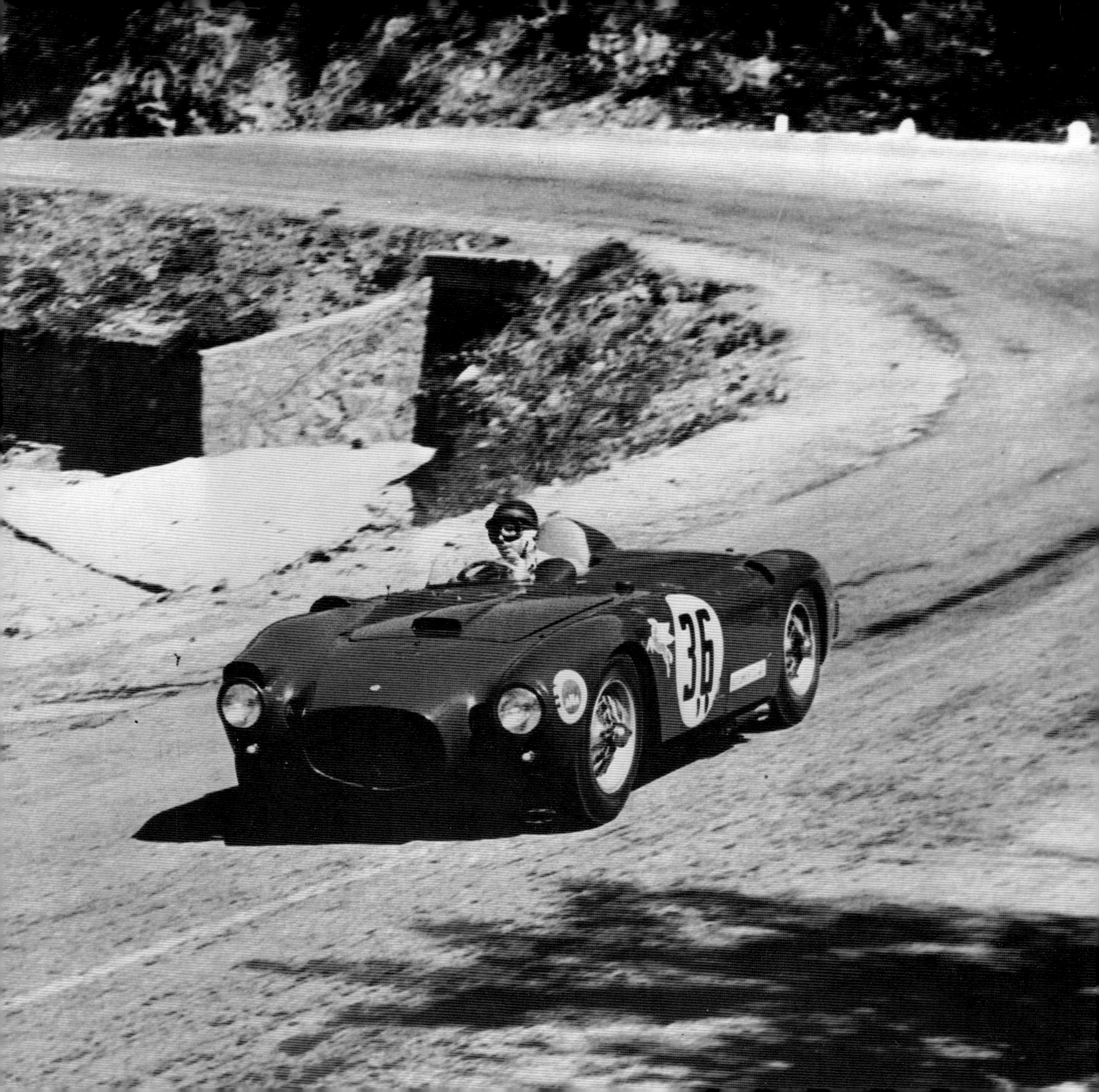
36

Chapter 6

1953 Carrera Panamericana IV: Large Sports Class

Lancia Continues The Legend

Felice Bonetto had managed a third-place finish in the April 1953 Mille Miglia for Lancia, with two other factory cars in seventh and eighth, and Umberto Magliolo's fourth-place finish in the 1952 Mexican Road Race with a supercharged B20 GT Aurelia had persuaded Lancia engineers to fit the D20 with a blower on a smaller 2963cc version of the V-6 for Le Mans in June of 1953. It was a disastrous decision, as the entire team not only failed to go the distance, but were slower on the straights than the Jaguars and Gordinis.

Before the next appearance of the D20, its supercharger was removed, its capacity was increased back to the original 3.0 liters, and it was fitted with lighter open bodywork. It was then designated the D23, and it won—for a while. It was later backed up by the D24, a 3.3 liter 265hp short-wheelbase version. Two D24s and a D23 failed at Nürburgring, and an entire four-car team broke down in the Supercortemaggiore Grand Prix.

At this point, with the enormous expense of specially built racing cars and a crowded program beginning to turn sour, Lancia had a fortuitous stroke of luck: it was the only works team to enter Carrera Panamericana IV.

Lancia entered five cars: three 230hp D24s whose four-cam V-6 engines had been cut from 3284cc to 3096cc for this one outing, plus two D23s at 2962cc and 220hp. The D24s were assigned to Juan Manuel Fangio, Felice Bonetto, and Piero Taruffi, and the D23s, less sophisticated and slightly less powerful, to Eugenio Castellotti and Giovanni Bracco.

Fangio had the distinction of being the only reigning World Champion to start the succeeding season without a ride. Alfa Romeo had retired from competition at the end of the season, so Fangio freelanced, driving Ferraris and winning Formula Libre events in South America. He failed to finish two races in the spectacularly unreliable BRM V-16s, and finally crashed at Monza and was sidelined for the rest of the season. When he returned in 1953, he won both the Italian and Modena Grands Prix; was second in the British, French, and German events; and finished second to Alberto Ascari in the championship. He also placed second in a private-entry Alfa Romeo at the Mille Miglia.

Bonetto had won the Targa for Lancia in 1952 and drove for the company in the 1951 Mexican Road Race. Taruffi was by far the most experienced Mexico driver, having raced the length of the country three times, finishing first, ninth, and tenth.

Lancia's main opposition was from

Juan Manuel Fangio in a Lancia D24 won Carrera Panamericana IV without ever winning a single leg. Mobil Oil Corporation

Jean Trevoux' special was based on a Packard 200 chassis. It had a Motto of Turin body and was powered by a 240hp Packard straight-eight engine that was modified by Howard's Automotive and could push the car over 135mph. Petersen Publishing

Maglioli in a Ferrari. Summer 1953 had seen the debut of the brutish 375 Mille Miglia with the 4.5 liter V-12 engine that had been developed for Ascari's 1952 Indianapolis 500 entry—which lasted only forty laps. Ascari and Luigi Villoresi set a race lap record at Le Mans in the 375 sports racing chassis, but the car retired with clutch failure, although it did win the 24 Hours of Spa and the 12 Hours of Pescara.

The four lead cars were 375MM Berlinettas plus a 375MM Spyder in which Ascari and Nino Farina had won the first Nürburgring 1,000km in August 1953.

The Ferraris had a slight speed advantage over the Lancias, but the latter were shorter and lighter. Ferrari used two mechanics for each car, one of whom rode. Lancia cars carried no passenger, and at overnight stops, the company allocated five mechanics for each car and a special truck with a hoist so that both the top and underside of the car could be worked on simultaneously within the new 3-hour time limit that the rules provided.

The engine in Maglioli's 375MM was a special short-stroke version of the V-12 with 84 x 68mm internal dimensions to displace 4522cc and produce 340hp at 7000rpm. His entry was supplemented by similar, but slightly less powerful 375MMs driven by Mario Ricci, Antonio Stagnoli, and Guido Mancini which had the stock 80 x 74.5mm, 4473cc engines of 310hp. A fifth Ferrari, a 375MM Spyder, was driven by Italian Luigi Chinetti

74

and codriven by the young Spanish marquis Alfonso de Portago, appearing in his first major road race.

American amateurs Phil Hill and Richie Ginther were aboard Allan Guiberson's 340 Mexico, which Villoresi had driven in 1952, and Mexicans Bush and Efrain Ruiz Echevarria in a 250 Mille Miglia Berlinetta rounded out the Prancing Horse defense.

Louis Rosier led the French contingent in a Talbot-Lago T.26 GS. Rosier had won Le Mans in 1950 and two Grands Prix in 1950–1951, in

Twenty-three-year-old Eugenio Castellotti, in a Lancia D 23, teamed with Juan Manuel Fangio, 1951 World Champion, and Piero Taruffi, Carerra II winner, in more powerful D 24s. Road & Track

1953 Large Sports Category Model Factory Specifications

Model	Price	Engine	Ci	Hp	Weight	Top Speed
Ferrari 250MM	NA	Sohc V-12	250	240	2,350lb	155mph
Ferrari 375MM	NA	Sohc V-12	276	340	2,530	180
Lancia D23	NA	Dohc V-6	179.2	220	NA	NA
Lancia D24	NA	Dohc V-6	187.3	230	NA	NA

Route map of the fourth Pan-American Road Race.

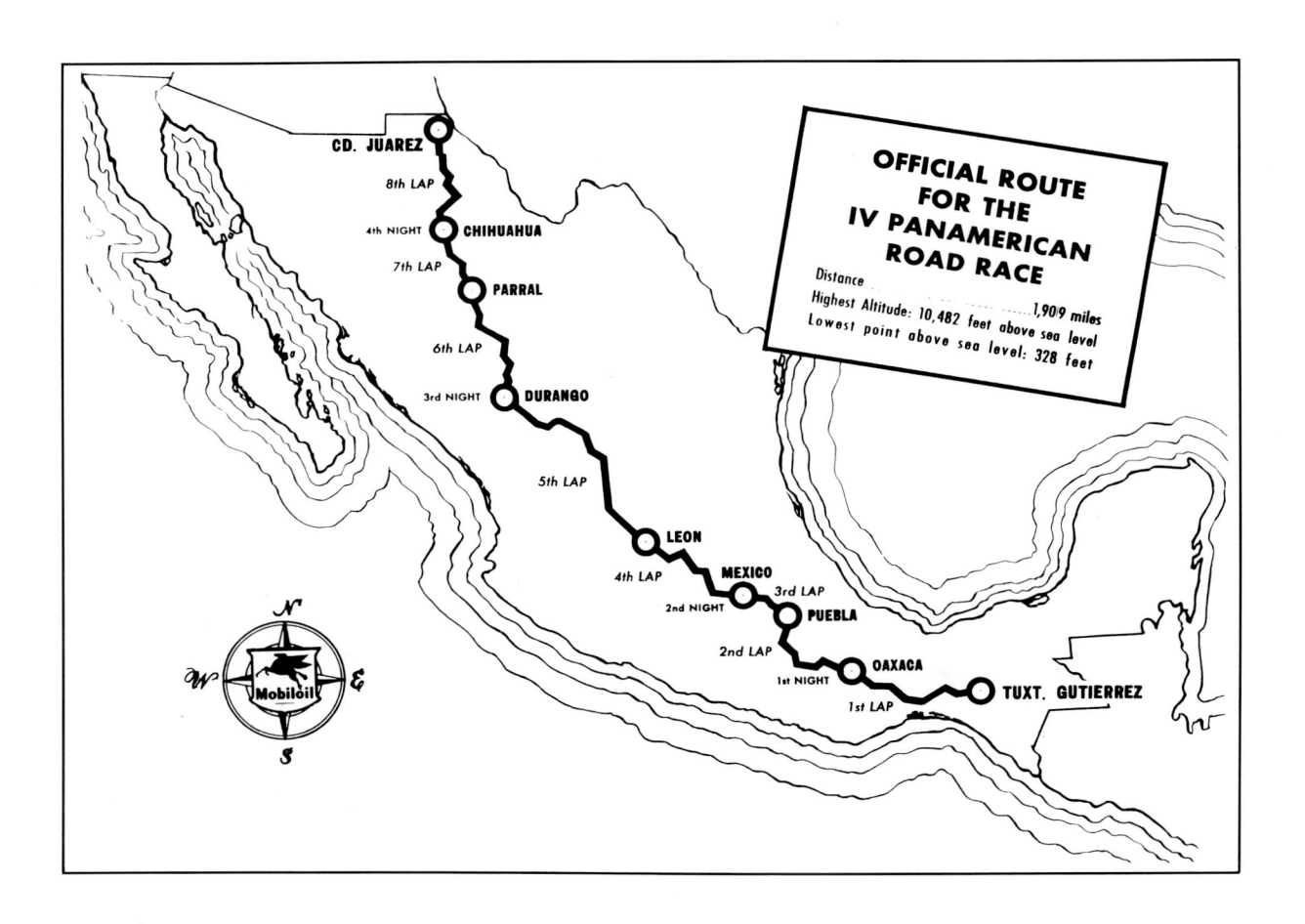

Entry Rules Summary For 1953 International Sports

Limited to fifty entries. Entry fee 5,000 pesos ($581.50). Any engine displacement, open or closed bodies with a minimum of two seats. Free modification, including supercharging and mixing makes of engine and chassis, although exchanging engines during race prohibited. Lights and fenders required, and must be in place during race. Cars will be sealed and impounded three hours after the completion of each leg. Regulation racing helmets are required; seat belts required only in closed cars.

Prizes

Placing	Prize
First	150,000 pesos ($17,442.00)
Second	75,000 pesos ($8,721.00)
Third	35,000 pesos ($4,070.00)
Fourth	15,000 pesos ($1,745.00)
Fifth	10,000 pesos ($1,163.00)
Sixth through tenth	Each 5,000 pesos ($581.50)
Winner of each leg	4,000 pesos ($465.20)

Maximum Allowable Time

Leg	Miles	Time
1. Tuxtla Gutiérrez-Oaxaca	329.3	5:00
2. Oaxaca-Puebla	252.9	4:00
3. Puebla-México City	79.5	1:20
4. México City-Léon	261.0	3:15
5. Léon-Durango	329.3	4:00
6. Durango-Parral	251.0	3:00
7. Parral-Chihuahua	186.4	2:10
8. Chihuahua-Ciudad Juárez	222.5	2:30
Total	1,912.0	

what were to be the French marque's last victories. He was sponsored by *Francia Amigos de la Panamericana*, which also provided a 3.0 liter 219hp Gordini T 24 S for Jean Behra and a 2.5 liter 174hp "cigar-shape" Gordini T 16 S for Jean Lucas.

The Iron Horse

The most unlikely competition for Lancia's exotics came from the backyards of Southern California.

After Troy Ruttman's performance in 1951 with the 1948 Mercury coupe, thirty-two-year-old Ak Miller of Whittier, California, became intrigued with the Mexican Road Race and prepared and campaigned an Oldsmobile in 1952, with his friend Doug Harrison. They lasted through Léon, but transmission trouble forced them out.

Miller had given thought to building his own creation for the race, and after running the event, was convinced he could construct a car that, although probably not an overall winner, could be competitive and go the distance. In true hot-rodder style, he scoured local junkyards with the help of Harrison, Ray Brock, and a host of friends. They spent six months of after-hours work building the entry.

And it was a classic. An Olds Rocket V-8 was coupled to a heavy, but armor-plated 1937 Cadillac three-speed transmission. To get the high speeds necessary for Mexico, a 1935 Nash overdrive unit was grafted on, which reduced

Lancia's huge support van was barely able to navigate narrow village streets but showed the team's preparedness. Petersen Publishing

77

IV
CARRERA
PANAMERICANA
MEXICO
Caballo de Hierro
PILOTOS: "AK" MILLER
"DOUG" Harrison
HOWARD'S CAMS
CATEGORIA
SPORT
INTERNACIONAL
11

engine speed by 30 percent at a given road speed. This mélange was dropped into a narrowed and shortened 1927 Ford Model T roadster body. Suspension was by 1940 Ford front axle, 1950 Ford rear axle and differential, Air-Lift bags inside coil springs, and 50/50 Houdaille shocks all around. Brakes were 13in units from a 1935 Chrysler Airflow, and a homemade 40-gallon fuel tank fed the monster.

The hood was built from two 1938 Plymouth rear fenders welded together, the grille was ½in electrical conduit, and stock Ford wheels carried 6.5x16in Firestone racing tires. In true hot-rodder style, Miller's ingenuity had kept the cost down to about $1,300, and *Hot Rod* magazine thought enough of the effort to more or less sponsor it, asking its readers to donate $1 each to the fledgling National Hot Rod Association for the team. And they gave it an appropriate name: *Caballo de Hierro*—the Horse of Iron.

The remainder of the large sports class was made up of more "specials," perhaps not as creative as Miller's but instead mostly 1954 Chryslers classed as such because their production numbers weren't high enough to qualify them as stock. Carl Kiekhaefer entered two for John Fitch and Reggie McFee, and Tony Bettenhausen would drive a Chrysler-Kurtis.

Jean Trevoux remained faithful to Packard, and for his fourth race, commissioned a car based on the 200 Series chassis. It resembled a Packard, but its sleek bodywork by Carrozzeria Motto of Turin was lower and shorter than stock. And its Howard's Automotive—built 234ci straight-eight flathead cranked out 240hp.

Joel Thorne, whose Cadillac had crashed 20 miles from the start of the 1950 event, decided to try again. In 1953, he entered the "Thorne Sport"—actually his reworked Indy car, in which he had placed ninth at The Brickyard in 1938, seventh in 1929, and fifth in 1940. Its power came from an Art Sparks—designed 337ci dual-overhead-cam Big Six built in 1937. In its original supercharged form, the engine developed 500hp on pump gas and powered the first car to exceed 130mph at Indy. Thorne had reworked the chassis and installed a two-seat body for the Mexican Road Race.

Jack Ensley rounded out the field of specials in a Cadillac-powered Kurtis, and a Mercury-powered Glasspar was entered by Mexican driver Fernando Duran Mejia. None of the homemade cars was expected to hold up to the grind to Juárez.

An Early Start and Stiff Competition

Tuxtla Gutiérrez was anxious for the race to start; over 1,000 drivers and crew members crammed into the city's 200 hotel rooms, and

A pensive Phil Hill before the start of the 1953 race. Hill was driving the 340 Mexico that Luigi Villoresi had campaigned unsuccessfully in the 1952 race. Dave Friedman

*Previous page
Ak Miller and the Caballo were popular wherever they went, particularly with senoritas, a point that is not lost on a smirking Ray Brock, right.*

PALMOLIVE EL MEJOR JABON
IV CARRERA PANAMERICANA MEXICO
CARRERA PANAMERICANA MEXICO
11
PILOTOS: "AK" MILLER
DOUG Harrison
CATEGORIA
SPORT
INTERNACIONAL

in addition to the nearly 200 cars participating, another 500 support vehicles were parked on the streets.

At 6:00am, the first car to leave was a Chrysler Special driven by Fernando Razo Maciel, followed by the Thorne Sport and then Texan Owen Gray in another Chrysler. Next was the first of the Ferraris, the 340 Mexico number 4 piloted by Phil Hill.

Antonio Stagnoli's number 14 Ferrari was near Juchitan—not quite 100 miles from the start—when a tire blew, and he crashed, killing his codriver, Giuseppe Scotuzzi. Stagnoli, who was rushed to an Oaxaca hospital in critical condition, died early the next morning.

Eight other sports cars either broke down or were sidelined so long that the 5-hour time limit was exceeded, including the Chryslers of Gray, John Fitch, and Reggie McFee, all out with transmission failures. Jack Ensley's Kurtis embarrassingly ran out of gas. *Caballo* survived, however, albeit in fifteenth place. Ak Miller and Doug Harrison discovered a flaw in the car's design: using the overdrive necessitated a low final drive ratio, and the high speed of the pinion gears was feeding more heat into its bearings than they could stand. The differential had begun howling even before they had reached the starting line.

Lancia swept into Oaxaca in the first four places: Felice Bonetto—Piero Taruffi—Juan Manuel Fangio—Eugenio Castellotti. The Ferrari of Umberto Maglioli, in the lead at the Tehuantepec checkpoint halfway through the leg, had split a radiator hose, which mechanic Nino Cassani had fixed by wrapping it with

Luigi Chinetti and Alfonso de Portago in the Ferrari 375 MM on the first leg near Tehuantepec. Lee Render photo, Dean Batchelor collection

*Previous page
Ak Miller's Caballo de Hierro—The Horse of Iron— had Oldsmobile power in a Ford Model T body. Despite being christened "the ugliest car in Mexico" by some of the European teams, it quickly became the fans' favorite entry.* Petersen Publishing

81

Giovanni Bracco was leading the race until entering the village of Silao, where his Lancia D23 hit a dip, and he was thrown against the side of a house, dying instantly. Dean Batchelor collection

Tony Bettenhausen awaits the starter's flag in his Kurtis-Chrysler at Tuxtla Gutiérrez. Dean Batchelor collection

friction tape. The repair stop plus several others to add water from a flask cost the team enough time that its car finished the leg fourth, followed by Jean Behra's Gordini, the other Lancia of Giovanni Bracco, and the remaining Gordini of Jean Lucas.

On the next leg, Taruffi's Lancia stormed into Puebla first, maintaining second in the race. Bonetto and Fangio followed, first and third overall. The Lancias were clearly the superior cars in the Pan-Am, and they were clearly driven by the best talent. Maglioli was standing fourth overall but already nearly 7 minutes behind third place. Luigi Chinetti's Ferrari broke a fuel line and retired, and Javier Razo Maciel's Glasspar-Chrysler failed to finish, but there were no accidents to mar the record-breaking pace set by Scuderia Lancia.

Tony Bettenhausen's Chrysler succumbed to the rigors of Mexico. Once again, at the end of two legs, he was already 2 hours behind the leader, much as he had been the year before. Despite the genius he showed on the ovals, Bettenhausen was baffled by the open road; this race was, he reckoned, not his favorite.

The Lancia onslaught continued with Taruffi reclaiming the Puebla-México City leg, erasing Luigi Villoresi's record of 48 minutes, 9 seconds with a 101mph run in 46 minutes, 25 seconds. Bonetto was second, Maglioli third,

and the Lancias of Castellotti and Fangio fourth and fifth, although the cars had been wounded—Castellotti's steering was damaged after hitting a dog, and Fangio's oil tank broke after he ran into a post.

Hill was the only dropout on leg three, after going off the road and hitting a tree 31 miles from México City. As he and Richie Ginther and a bevy of spectators surveyed the damaged 340 Mexico, a Cadillac spun off the road at the same spot, careened down the hillside, and came to rest on the other side of the same tree.

Only two specials survived at this point: Jean Trevoux' Packard Special in ninth and Miller's hot rod in eleventh place. Miller and Harrison were replacing their car's differential after each leg, and their crew was spending much of its time scouring Mexican junkyards for more Ford gears.

Tragedy struck Scuderia Lancia on leg four into Léon. Bonetto, leading the race, was momentarily distracted when he saw teammate Taruffi off the highway near Sialo. When he looked back at the road, he saw an unavoidable dip, which he hit at 150mph. The car was thrown against a house, and a protruding flower box caught the head of the fifty-year-old driver, who died instantly.

Taruffi lost 25 minutes straightening a bent steering arm before getting back into the race but was able to finish the leg in tenth. Bracco, sixth after México City, lost a wheel, and so much time that he was forced to retire.

"Unless highway conditions are improved," the distraught Taruffi said bitterly, "European drivers will not return in 1954!" Then, almost as an aside, he muttered, "This race will kill us all!"

Maglioli was first on the leg, over 4 minutes ahead of Fangio. Guido Mancini, in another Ferrari, followed in third, then came Castellotti and the Gordini of Lucas—who had misplaced his route book and was nearly disqualified. With the loss of the leading car, along with Taruffi's trouble, the front runners changed drastically. Fangio now moved to first, Maglioli was second, and the two Lancias of Castellotti and Taruffi were in third and fourth, with Mancini in his 375MM fifth.

The Ferrari threat turned out to be temporary. The three remaining Lancias swept into Durango leading the leg and the race, Fangio 8 minutes in front of Taruffi and 24 ahead of Castellotti. Maglioli burned out a wheel bearing north of the start and had to abandon his number 12 Ferrari. During the layover in Durango, he took the wheel of Mario Ricci's 4.5 liter car, which was in eighth, knowing it would be a miracle if he could catch any of the leaders; he sat 1 hour, 8 minutes behind third-place Castellotti.

Both Gordinis blew up and retired on the desert leg. They were fast but too delicate for the constant high speeds they had maintained to keep the torrid pace. Team leader Amedee Gordini put his two mechanics at the disposal of Louis Rosier, who had moved his 4.5 liter Talbot T.26 GS into the top five. Tenth at México City, Rosier was advancing simply from the attrition of the competition.

Lancia racing director Attilio Pasquarelli, sure of a victory, instructed his drivers to hold

Antonio Stagnoli and Guiseppe Scotuzzi in one of the powerful Ferrari 375 MMs between Tuxtla and Oaxaca. A few minutes later, the two were killed when a tire blew. Dean Batchelor collection

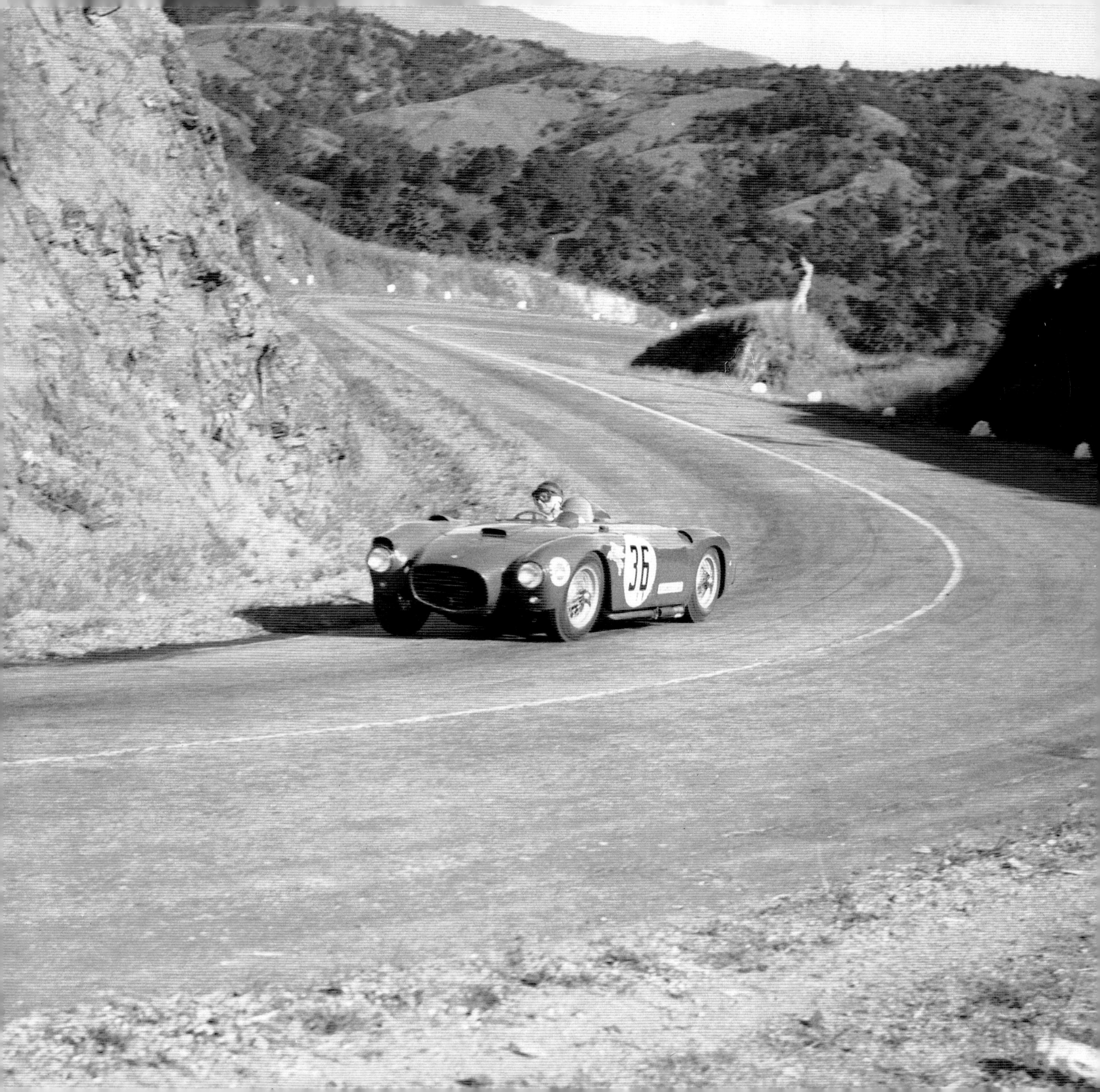
36

Piero Taruffi, winner of the 1951 Pan-Am, drove a Lancia D24 in 1953. Lee Render photo, Dean Batchelor collection

Newcomer Eugenio Castellotti rounds a curve near Oaxaca in his Lancia D23. Lee Render photo, Dean Batchelor collection

Phil Hill and Richie Ginther in their Ferrari 340 Mexico outside Oaxaca on the second day. The pair had finished leg one in 10th. Lee Render photo, Dean Batchelor collection

*Previous page
Juan Manuel Fangio, who had won the first of his five world championships in 1951, led the Lancia team in a D24.* Lee Render photo, Dean Batchelor collection

Jean Lucas' 2.5 liter cigar-shape Gordini T 16S. Dean Batchelor collection

The graceful-but-outclassed Talbot T.26 GS of Louis Rosier was able to finish fifth among large sports. Dean Batchelor collection

Driving a Lancia D23, Felice Bonetto won the difficult first leg in record time. Lee Render photo, Dean Batchelor collection

86

their positions. Taruffi and Castellotti could catch Fangio, but they were not allowed to pass him—Lancia wanted no more duels.

Maglioli proved the old adage that the driver rather than the car wins races. In Ricci's Ferrari—which had finished previous legs variously from seventh to fourteenth place—Maglioli won Durango—Parral section, averaging 109mph and breaking the Mercedes record. He finished 7 minutes ahead of second-place Taruffi but was up to only seventh for the race.

Trevoux' Packard packed up on leg six, leaving only one special—the Horse of Iron—in eighth place. Rosier stayed in fifth, 1 hour behind Mancini in fourth.

Maglioli repeated with a leg win into Chihuahua, making up 5 minutes, 6 seconds on leader Fangio but still a long way from a big-money finish at the river, now just 233 miles distant.

There were just nine survivors in big sports at this point: three Lancias, three Ferraris, one Talbot, one Jaguar, and Miller's

Louis Rosier's Talbot finished the first leg 16th out of twenty cars. Petersen Publishing

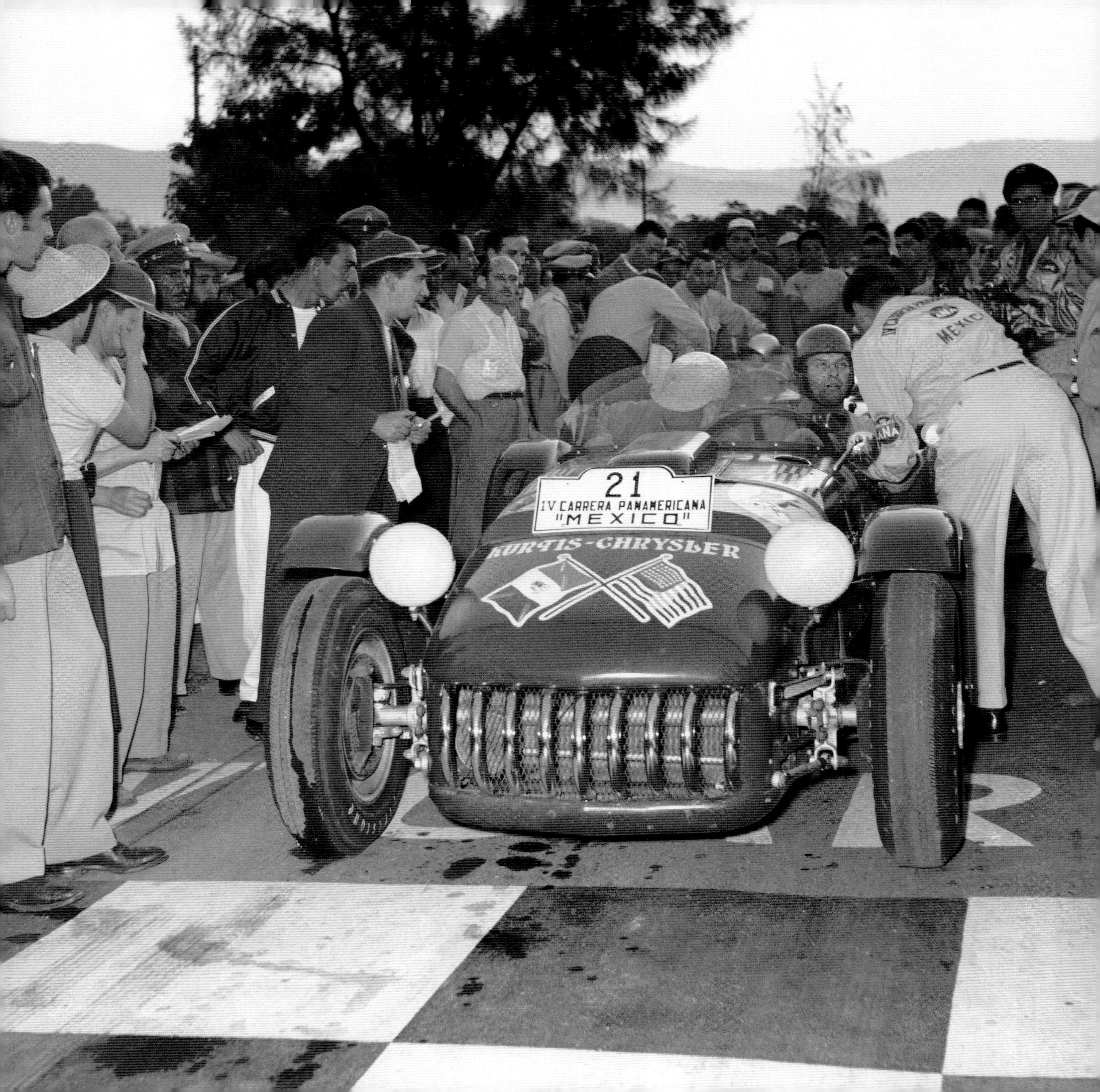
21
IV CARRERA PANAMERICANA
"MEXICO"
KURTIS-CHRYSLER
MEXICO

special. With an overwhelming lead in hand, the Lancia team truck left for Juárez preparing champagne for the celebration at the finish.

Maglioli finished with a flourish, covering the last section in a little over 1.5 hours at 138.311mph—a world record in open-road racing that still stood in 1992—but could do no better than sixth overall, disgusted that he was beaten even by the Talbot.

Castellotti, Taruffi, and Fangio showed up some 11 minutes after the Ferrari's blazing run. El Maestro had held his lead to win the fourth Pan-Am. Taruffi was second by 7 minutes, and Castellotti third another 6 minutes back. Mancini in his Ferrari was fourth, and Echevarria in another Ferrari seventh. Miller was eighth, ahead of Giullermo Giron in his Jaguar.

The Fangio Philosophy

Juan Manuel Fangio had driven one of his patented races. "You don't win a long race on

Guillermo Giron campaigned a Jaguar XK 120C. With its 3.4 liter 200hp engine, the C-Type was capable of 145mph. Petersen Publishing

*Previous page
Tony Bettenhausen prepares to start his Kurtis-Chrysler from Tuxtla Gutiérrez. Petersen Publishing*

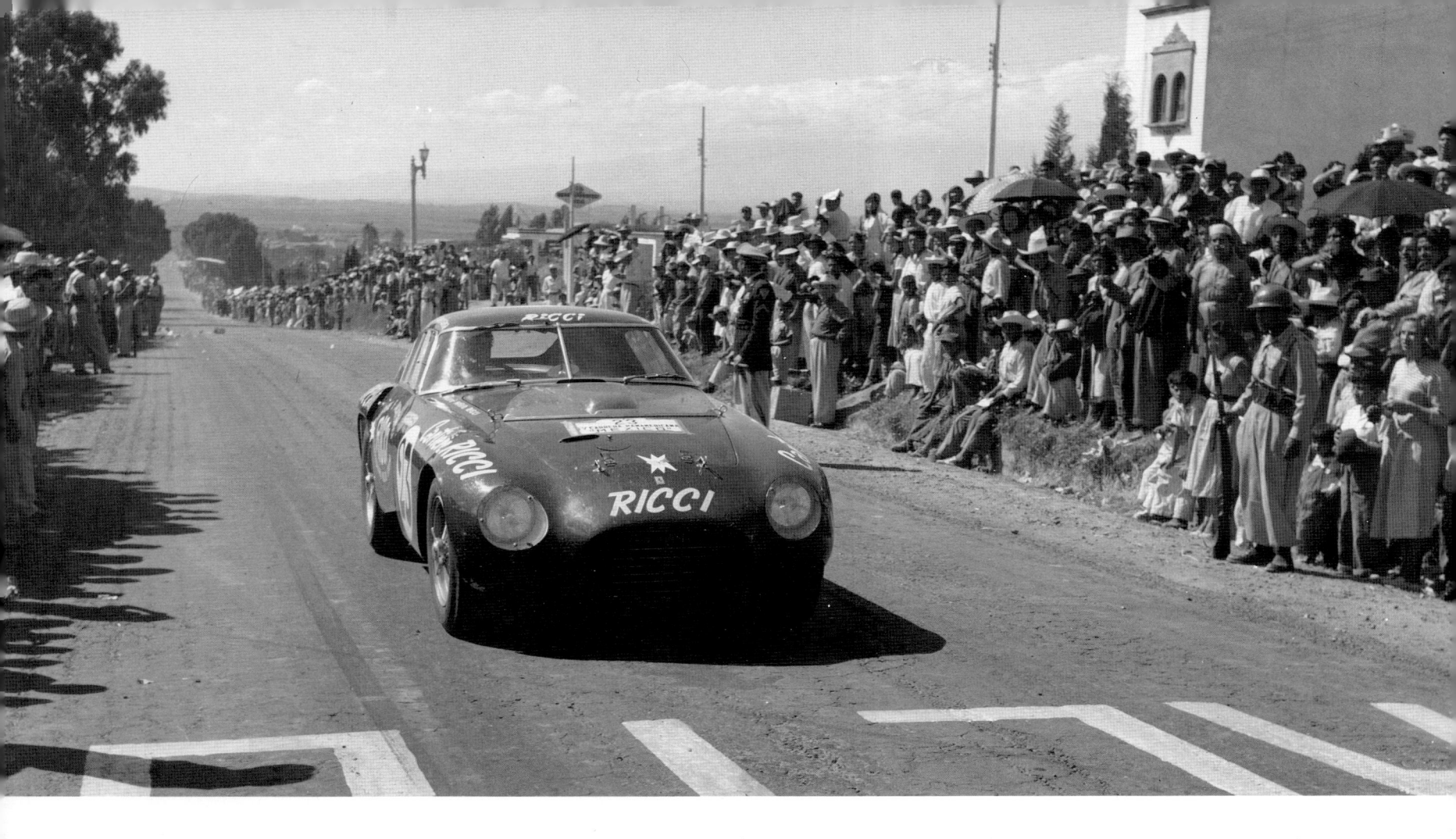

After a mechanical breakdown with his Ferrari while lying second in the race, Umberto Maglioli took over the wheel of Mario Ricci's 375 MM and proceeded to win the last three legs—including making a 138.31mph dash from Chihuahua to Juárez that still stood in 1992 as a speed record in open road racing. Despite the epic drive, he managed to place only sixth for the race. Petersen Publishing

The winning D24 on display at the Lancia stand at an unidentified auto show. Mobil Oil Corporation

Juan Manuel Fangio, center, compares the size of his General Motors award for winning the Carrera IV overall with the size of C. D. Evans' award for winning the light stock division in a Chevrolet. General Motors' Vernon Moore is at right. Dean Batchelor collection

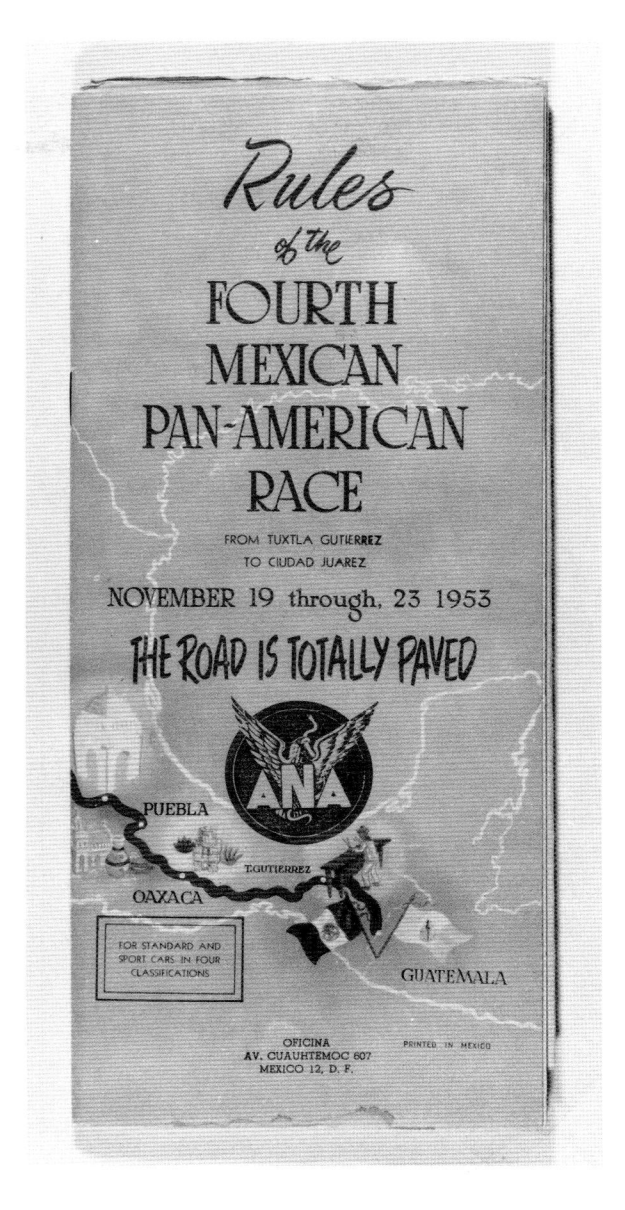

The 1953 rulebook.

the first day," he advised reporters. "It's a question of conserving your automobile and maintaining yourself intelligently in the best position possible."

The Fangio philosophy, which was familiar to many of his adversaries, was simply to drive fast enough to win, just like Herschel McGriff in the first Carrera. Fangio had never won a single leg but had stayed in the top five throughout the race, never more than a few minutes behind the leader, and he had taken over the lead on leg four, when his friend Felice Bonetto crashed.

"I am happy for having won," he said, "but sad for having lost my friend, who should have won."

As long as Fangio was in front, no one could make up time on him. As his Grand Prix teammate Stirling Moss said in later years, "I don't care how fast you went—he always went faster!"

Fangio accepted the 150,000 pesos ($17,442) winner's share for the team. The Lancia drivers had simply overwhelmed everyone: they led the entire race, broke most of the competition, and set a pace that was tough for the less-prepared to follow.

Umberto Maglioli had fought off Mercedes in 1952 in a Lancia, then switched to Ferrari in 1953 and was beaten by his old team. The twenty-three-year-old Italian driver vowed that 1954 would be his year.

MARCHA de NUESTRO SISTEMA
ASOCIACION GUATEMALTECA DE CAMINOS
152
152
IV CARRERA PANAMERICANA
"MEXICO"
MEXICO
CARRERA PANAMERICANA
ANA

Chapter 7

1953 Carrera Panamericana IV: Small Sports Class

And Then There Were Two

When the organizers of the Mexican Road Race decided to diversify, they created two classes in each division to add parity for smaller entries.

The differentiation in stocks was based on horsepower, in *Clase sport menor* on displacement at 1600cc—a convenient figure for Porsche and Borgward, two emerging German marques.

Borgward had raced its Isabella-based 1492cc pushrod sports racer successfully in Europe, with recent victories at Grenzlandring and at the Avus circuit by Hans Hartmann, whose past experience included driving on the 1939 Mercedes Grand Prix team. Hartmann and Adolph Brudes, who was third in the 1940 Mille Miglia in a BMW, would be driving a pair of five-speed roadsters in Mexico.

The Porsche marque was barely five years old in 1953, and the firm had just two years earlier completed only its 500th car. Porsche had won its class at both Le Mans and the Mille Miglia in 1952, although a failed top gear resulted in the Mille winner being driven the last 200 miles in third. The firm's only other major race in 1952 had been in Mexico, where Furst von Metternich placed eighth in the open sports class, twenty-fifth overall.

Ten Porsches were entered in the Pan-Am. The 1952 race winner Karl Kling and eighteen-year-old Hans Herrmann would drive the two official entries—550 Spyders with 1498cc 78hp pushrod engines, chassis numbers 03 and 04. Guatemalans Jose Herrarte and Jaroslav Juhan would have Spyder coupes serial numbers 01 and 02—the cars that had won their class at Le Mans and had been raced extensively in Europe (no factory ever gave its customers better cars than it kept for itself). The balance of the field was made up of 356s. Two were Gmünd models—lightweight aluminum-alloy-bodied coupes—the others steel. Jacqueline Evans de Lopez was making her fourth attempt to finish Carrera in her personal 356.

When the Porsche group arrived in New York from Germany on its way to Mexico, immigration officials detained Kling, suspecting that he was a Nazi general who had somehow escaped Allied prosecution after the war; it had only been eight years since the end of the war, and Kling's looks and manner resembled Hollywood's best portrayal of a Prussian Nazi. After two frustrating days, he was released.

Ernie McAfee entered a Siata V-8, a 1996cc Fiat-based 1,750lb sports racer. Frenchman Jacques Peron was campaigning an OSCA.

Fifteen drivers would be vying for a 30,000

IV CARRERA PANAMERICANA "MEXICO"

Ten Porsches and four cars of other makes started in the small sports class. Only this 550 driven by Jose Herrarte and a private 356 lasted to Juárez. Petersen Publishing

Fletcher Aviation, a licensed builder of Porsche engines in the United States, provided sponsorship—and air transportation for key crew members of the German team. Here, the company Navion poses with Karl Kling's Porsche 550 at the Tuxtla Gutiérrez Airport. Don Downie

pesos ($3,866) first prize from the class purse of 68,000 pesos ($11,000)—a *menor* amount for the *menor* category.

Survival of the Fittest

On the opening leg, Hans Herrmann squeaked out a 25-second win over veteran Karl Kling. Hans Hartmann's Borgward trailed Kling's car by nearly 10 minutes in third. Failing to reach Oaxaca in the allowable time were Jacques Peron, Adolph Brudes, Ernie McAfee, and perennial DNF Jacqueline Evans de Lopez; only the strong could survive leg one.

The race organizers—reasoning that these pocket racers with a fraction of the displacement and horsepower of some of the thundering stock cars would be significantly slower—had underestimated the small sports cars' pace. Placed behind the big stock cars at the start, Herrmann and Kling blew past the entire fifty-two-car stock class and finished 8 minutes ahead of the fastest Lincoln.

On leg two, however, the best-laid plans of Herrmann and Kling crumbled as Herrmann experienced steering failure and slid his car along a mountain face to avoid plunging off the road, and Kling suffered a failure of his right half axle. That left only Manfredo Lippman in a 356 to carry the colors against the privateers. Porsche racing director Fritz Huschke von Hanstein put the house mechanics at the disposal of the Lippman's Guatemalan team. McAfee retired the Siata V-8 after an accident, so the entire class was down to seven cars: six Porsches and a Borgward.

Karl Kling, 1952 Pan-Am winner, confers with photographer Don Downie on the best way to get from Tuxtla to Juárez after his Porsche broke on the first leg of the 1953 race. Don Downie

Jaroslav Juhan won leg two, 4 minutes up on Hartmann in his Borgward, but the overall pace had fallen when the two Spyders and their hard-charging drivers went out. Hartmann was keeping Juhan—his only competition at this point—in sight, but the German driver was smart enough to know that a lot could happen before this race was over.

The tortuous run to México City should have been easy for the Porsches, but Juhan finished first in just under an hour, further off the pace than before. Hartmann once again shadowed in second, with Guillermo Suhr, Fernando Segura, Jose Herrarte, and Salvador Lopez Chavez trailing. Juhan now led the small sports race by slightly more than 1.5

1953 Small Sports Category Model Factory Specifications

Model	Price	Engine	Ci	Hp	Weight	Top Speed
Borgward 1500	NA	Ohv 4	91.4	80	NA	NA
OSCA MT-4	$10,000	Dohc 4	90.9	110	1,280lb	124mph
Porsche 356	$4,284	Ohv O-4	90.8	70	1,675	109
Porsche 550	NA	Ohv O-4	90.8	78	NA	NA
Siata 208S	$5,350	Ohv V-8	121.8	125	2,460	120

The Porsche 356 of Salvador Lopez-Chavez inches through a crowd of fans and stock cars in Tuxtla Gutiérrez before the start. Dave Friedman

Entry Rules Summary For 1953 Sports up to 1600cc

Limited to 50 entries, factory-built "sports cars," of up to 1600cc displacement without supercharger, up to 800cc displacement with supercharger. Entry fee 3,000 pesos ($349.00). Open or closed body styles with a minimum of two seats are recognized. Electrical systems, fenders, and engine changes same as in International Sports class. Any fuel may be used. Approved racing helmets must be worn; seatbelts are required only in closed cars. No alcoholic beverages permitted in any car.

Prizes

Placing	Prize
First	30,000 pesos ($3,488.50)
Second	20,000 pesos ($2,326.00)
Third	10,000 pesos ($1,163.00)
Fourth	5,000 pesos ($581.50)
Fifth	3,000 pesos ($349.00)
Winner of each leg	1,000 pesos ($116.30)
Top Mexican driver	5,000 pesos ($581.50)

Maximum allowable times:

Leg	Miles	Time
1. Tuxtla Gutiérrez-Oaxaca	329.3	6:00
2. Oaxaca-Puebla	252.9	5:15
3. Puebla-México City	79.5	1:35
4. México City-Léon	261.0	4:15
5. Léon-Durango	329.3	5:15
6. Durango-Parral	251.0	4:00
7. Parral-Chihuahua	186.4	2:45
8. Chihuahua-Ciudad Juárez	222.5	3:00

minutes over Hartmann, with third place already nearly an hour behind!

Juhan and Hartmann led leg four into Léon. On leg five, the highway was flatter, and the Borgward driver became bolder, beating Juhan to Durango by 1 minute, 10 seconds, closing to within seconds of taking over the lead. Herrarte, Segura, Lippman, and Chavez followed.

On leg six, Hartmann began to get serious, pushing the Borgward to a 90mph average and finishing nearly 5 minutes ahead of Juhan, who had fuel system problems. Hartmann finally took over the lead. Chavez' Porsche expired, and now there were five.

From Parral to Chihuahua, the Borgward picked up an amazing 19 minutes over Juhan's Porsche, averaging 106mph. Hartmann was

The Porsche 550 Spyder, 550-02, of Jaroslav Juhan broke a distributor drive on the last leg of the race. Juhan had been carrying a spare in his pocket but discarded it before starting the leg. Dave Friedman

Adolph Brudes crashed his Borgward 1500 on the first leg between Tuxtla and Oaxaca. Dave Friedman

The winning Porsche 550 of Guatemalan Jose Herrarte was the first of the two surviving small sports cars. Mobil Oil Corporation

totally in command and had the momentum to run a record last leg and smash the Porsche opposition once and for all.

Roaring along in great style, bent on being the first of the small sports racers to Juárez, the Borgward faltered when its engine began running poorly. Hartmann stopped and changed the plugs, but the trouble persisted. Running on three cylinders, he charged at reduced speed, knowing that he had built up more than enough time to win. When he arrived at Juárez third behind two Porsches, Hartmann knew his accumulated time would place him nearly one and three-quarters hours

Ernie McAfee's Siata 8V Sport was powered by a 2.0 liter 125hp Fiat V-8 driving through a five-speed transmission. Petersen Publishing

ahead. But the maximum allowable time for the 222-mile leg had been set at 3 hours; he had finished in 3 hours, 7 seconds! He was disqualified.

A broken distributor drive put Juhan's Porsche out; he had been carrying a used gear in his pocket for several days but decided to throw it away the morning of the last leg. Lippman also had a breakdown, so that left just two cars running at the finish: Herrarte and Segura, declared class winner and runner-up respectively.

Herrarte, a Guatemalan coffee grower and amateur road racer who almost gave up the race in México City because of exhaustion, took top money of 30,000 pesos ($3,488), and Segura, an Argentinean architect living in Houston, netted 20,000 pesos ($2,230) for second.

Porsche Legends

It was ironic that the premier race for small sports cars ended in this manner. Intensely prepared factory entries driven by world-class drivers turned out to be not as reliable as cars in private hands.

The winning Porsche—a Spyder fitted with roof, number 550-02—later ran in a sports car race at Puebla and a 1,000km race in Argentina, then was retired to a place of honor at the Herrarte family estate, where it reportedly remained through 1992.

Fernando Segura's second-place 356 was the stuff of which Porsche made its legends: the owner had bought it new in New York, driven it to Mexico, and raced it with no more than a tune-up.

Jaroslav Juhan's Porsche in the impound area at Durango. Termed the "Spyder with roof," the 550 was a roadster with a special top attached for long-distance races. Dean Batchelor collection

99

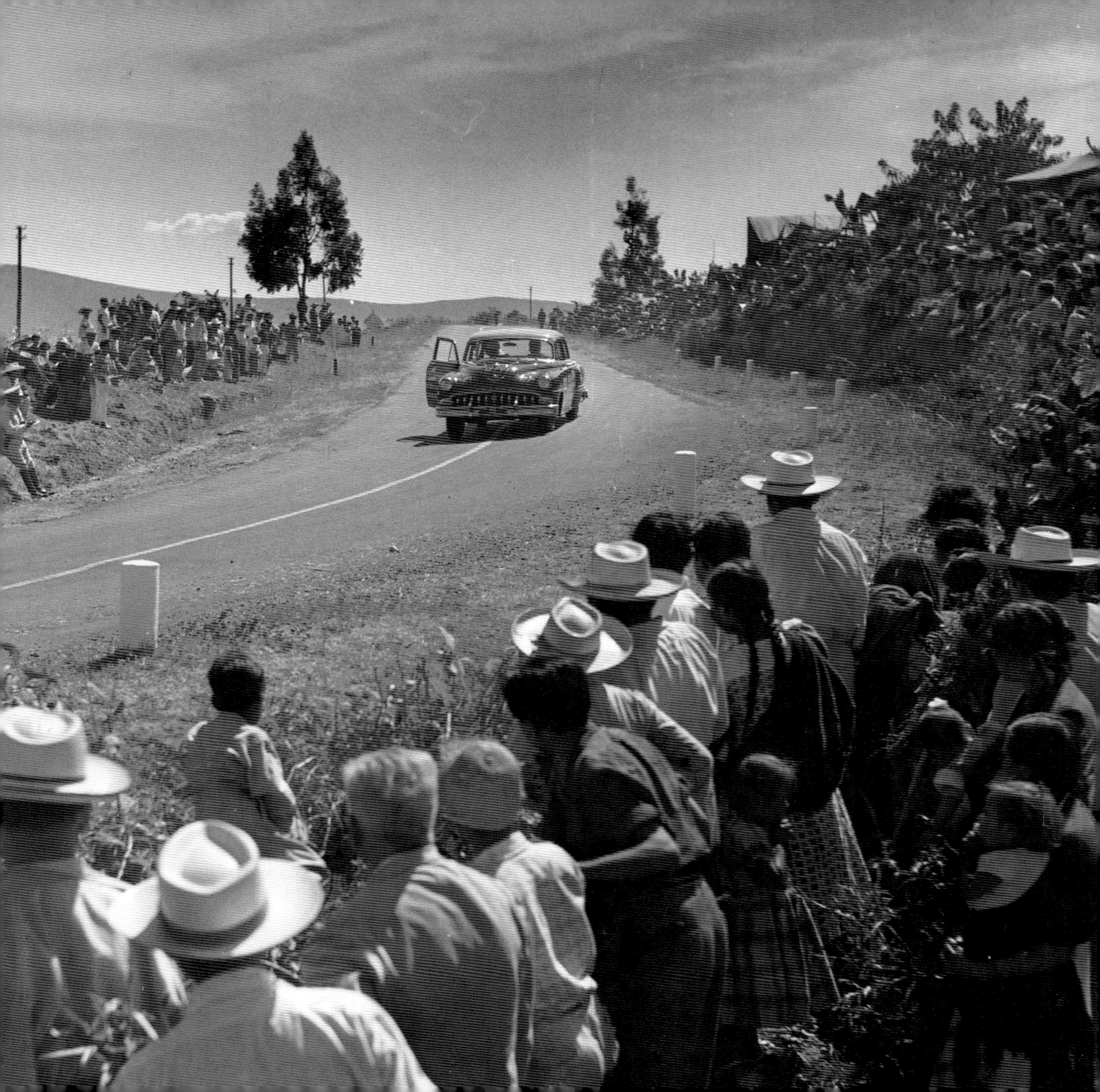

Chapter 8

1953 Carrera Panamericana IV: Large & Small Stock Classes

The Four Horsemen Of Dearborn

The Mexican Road Race was beginning to show the results of evolution. The first race was quickly organized as a one-shot event and was simply limited to strictly stock. A lack of experience made for scanty supervision, but the relatively slow speeds seemed to indicate an absence of serious speed modifications.

Carrera II was supposed to be a variation on the theme, allowing entrants some modifications to engine and chassis, but everyone had spent almost eighteen months sharpening the wits and finding loopholes in the rules.

By 1952, for Carrera III, all competitive foreign cars were separated specifically so that the Ferraris and their brethren wouldn't dominate the American stockers.

For Carrera IV, it was decided to divide each of the two extant classes into two more classes so that everyone would have a more or less even class in which to compete. It was becoming a volume business.

If you had a car with 115hp or less, then you would qualify for *turismo especial* and start at the back of the pack where you couldn't get in the serious racers' way. Everyone else would run in international standard (*turismo internacional*) and race up front with the big boys.

The modifications rules had taken twelve lines in the 1951 rulebook. Two years later, twenty pages were devoted to rules—and that was just for the large stock class! In addition, only current-year models were eligible, which prevented factories from introducing new 1954 cars not generally available to the public—a move that would prevent Lincoln in particular from having an edge over its competition.

One important rules change was that 3 hours after the cars finished each day, they would be impounded, sealed, and put under armed guard. Seals would remain unbroken until the cars crossed the starting line the next morning. No more round-the-clock engine and chassis rebuilds, no more cam upgrades and solid lifters, no port matching. After all, the reasoning went, the idea of road racing is to find out which are the best cars and the best drivers, not who has the biggest budget or cleverest team manager.

The course, which was always touted as 1,933 miles, was remeasured more precisely before the 1953 race and found to be some 21 miles shorter, so average speeds up to then had actually been slightly faster than published. For example, Kling's winning time of 103.56mph in 1952 could be corrected to 105.14mph if anyone cared. No one did. *Que sara, sara*—what will be will be.

The codriver of Roberto Balmar's De Soto helps slow the car as it nears the finish line at the end of a leg. Dave Friedman

LINCOLNS REPEAT
CLEAN SWEEP VICTORY IN MEXICAN ROAD RACE

second straight 1-2-3-4 win
again proves Lincoln King of the Road!

Lincoln rushed this brochure to dealers after the 1953 race to remind everyone that its product had swept the first four positions of the stock car class for the second time; seven of the first nine finishers were Lincolns.

Preparing Team Lincoln

If 1952 had been a good year for the Lincoln team, then 1953 was even better. Not only was the team loaded with experience and buoyed by the success of the previous season, but drivers Chuck Stevenson, Johnny Mantz, Walt Faulkner, Jack McGrath, Manuel Ayulo, and Bill Vukovich—fresh from his Indianapolis 500 victory—had driven nearly 10,000 miles in prerace practice, making sure they knew every hill and curve.

During weeks of practice, they rode three to a car, one driving, and the other two taking notes. When the passengers didn't agree with the driver on what he felt was a full-speed curve, they would write "flat out—JLS" or "100—JLM." The initials stood for "just lost Stevenson" or "just lost Mantz."

All the team Lincolns were marked for quick identification with a cartoon character on their hood: Faulkner was Woody Woodpecker; Stevenson, Jack the Bear; and Mantz, Popeye.

And the team would also have its own food and water supply, with a portable food wagon run by Gordon Smith. While in Mexico, every driver and team member was required to eat every meal and drink every drink from the food wagon, or face dismissal. Bill Stroppe remembered what had happened to Mantz in the 1950 race.

The Outsider

Once again "The Flying Grocer," Ray Crawford, was left out of the factory plan, but he was able to get a Bill Stroppe—prepared Lincoln.

"I picked up the new car for the race in México City two days before things were supposed to begin at Tuxtla, and I started to drive down," Crawford remembered. "I had this really cute girl with me. I'm making like a race driver—you know, impressing her. I came around this blind turn in the mountains, and I was on the wrong side of the road coming out at about 80mph. And there was this big rock. I swerved to miss it and spun, and we went off the side of that mountain backwards! We must have gone 150ft in the air and finally hit a whole grove of little saplings. The car crunched and bounced, it seemed like forever, and ended up suspended in the trees, right side up, about 12ft in the air."

Crawford and his companion carefully got out of the Lincoln and climbed down the tree. Surveying the damage, he found that apparently the only casualty was a broken front wheel.

1953 Large Stock Category Model Factory Specifications

Model	Price	Engine	Ci	Hp	Weight	Top Speed
Cadillac 62 2dr	$3,571	Ohv V-8	331	210	4,189lb	115mph
Chrysler New Yorker 2dr	$3,336	Ohv V-8	331	180	3,920	104
Lincoln Capri 2dr	$3,549	Ohv V-8	317.5	205	4,165	NA
Mercury 2dr	$2,244	L8	255.4	125	3,465	88
Oldsmobile Super 88 2dr	$2,253	Ohv V-8	303	165	3,634	109

1953 Small Stock Category Model Factory Specifications

Model	Price	Engine	Ci	Hp	Weight	Top Speed
Chevrolet 2dr	$1,761	Ohv 6	235.5	108-115	3,190lb	NA
Ford 2dr	$1,717	L V-8	239	110	3,136	NA
Hudson Jet 2dr	$1,933	L6	202	104	2,695	95mph
Kaiser 2dr	$2,459	L6	226.2	118	3,150	89
Plymouth 2dr	$1,707	L6	217.8	100	2,943	NA
Studebaker Commander	$2,089	Ohv V-8	232.6	120	3,055	NA

Clay Smith works on Chuck Stevenson's Lincoln during the 3-hour servicing period after the third leg into Mexico City. Smith was codriver of the class-winning car, which averaged 93.15mph for the distance. Dave Friedman

"Finally, a couple of those cartoon Mexican buses they have stopped, and the people all came down to where the car was hanging, and they got some ropes," he continued. "They started cutting down the trees with machetes. The car kept dropping down as they cut around it, and finally, just like a bunch of ants, they towed it back up on the road. I put a new wheel on it, and we were on our way!"

Crawford added that the trip to Tuxtla was at a more leisurely pace. He joined twenty-two other drivers with Lincolns, including private entries for Indy car drivers Duane Carter and Rodger Ward.

Entry Rules Summary For 1953 International Standard-Special Standard

International Standard

Limited to 100 entries. Entry fee 5,000 pesos ($581.50). 1950-1953 models with closed body, five-seat capacity, and measuring no less than 84in long and 54in wide (inside body dimensions), of which at least 5,000 units of the type entered for the race have been manufactured annually. Only factory-listed optional equipment can be utilized. Super Mexolina fuel must be used.

Special Standard

Limited to 50 entries. Entry fee 3,000 pesos ($349.00) for following 1950-1953 models at or under 115 hp: Henry J, Nash Rambler (closed), Nash Statesman, Willys Aero, Dodge Diplomat and Kingsway, Plymouth, Ford (six or eight), Dodge Coronet D-46, Hudson Jet and Wasp, Chevrolet and Pontiac Six. All rules established for International Standard category in respect to optional equipment applies.

Prizes

Placing	International	Special
First	150,000 pesos ($17,442.00)	30,000 pesos ($3,488.50)
Second	75,000 pesos ($8,721.00)	20,000 pesos ($2,326.00)
Third	35,000 pesos ($4,070.00)	10,000 pesos ($1,163.00)
Fourth	15,000 pesos ($1,745.00)	5,000 pesos ($581.50)
Fifth	10,000 pesos ($1,163.00)	3,000 pesos ($349.00)
Sixth-tenth	Each 5,000 pesos ($581.50)	Each 5,000 pesos ($581.50)
Winner of each leg	4,000 pesos ($465.20)	1,000 pesos ($116.30)
Top Mexican driver	15,000 pesos ($1,745.00)	5,000 pesos ($581.50)

General

After selection of tires and optional equipment, the vehicle must carry the same specifications throughout the race, with the exception of conforming factory-furnished carburetor jets or metering rods. No modification may be made to the original design, or to specified, cataloged parts. Valve angle or valve spring pressure cannot be altered, and where design calls for hydraulic valve lifters, there can be no change to mechanical lifters. Cylinders may be bored 0.020in in excess of original dimensions. Modifications permissible include suspension and shock absorbers, brakes, removal of mufflers without alteration to the exhaust manifold, reinforcement of the inside of the body, removal of rear seats to install additional, vented fuel tanks, installation of electric fuel pump, reinforcement or improvement of hood latches and installation of any type of stabilizer. Cars will be sealed and impounded three hours after the completion of each leg.

Maximum Allowable Times

Leg	Miles	International	Special
1. Tuxtla Gutiérrez-Oaxaca	329.3	5:33	6:00
2. Oaxaca-Puebla	252.9	4:30	5:15
3. Puebla-México City	79.5	1:30	1:35
4. México City-Léon	261.0	3:45	4:15
5. Léon-Durango	329.3	4:30	5:15
6. Durango-Parral	251.0	3:30	4:00
7. Parral-Chihuahua	186.4	2:30	2:30
8. Chihuahua-Ciudad Juárez	222.5	3:00	3:00

Bill Stroppe, left, waits for dinner from the team's cook. While in Mexico, every Lincoln team member was required to eat every meal and drink every drink from the portable food wagon. Stroppe didn't want a repeat of the digestive difficulties that plagued Johnny Mantz in the 1950 race. Dave Friedman

The only hope for stopping Lincoln came from the stables of E. C. Kiekhaefer, who fielded a team of four Chryslers, driven by Speed McFee, John Fitch, Frank Mundy, and Bob Korf. Fitch and McFee were forced to run in the sports class because of unhomologated transmissions that didn't meet the rule requiring 5,000 units having been built in 1953.

Douglas Ehlinger, who placed a Packard fourteenth in 1951 and a Jaguar tenth in 1952, returned with a Packard, and Indy car ace Jim Rathmann represented the dwindling number of General Motors entries in an Oldsmobile.

Al and Ralph Rogers—third in the first race, seventh in 1951, and sixteenth in 1952—were the first accident victims, although the mishap occurred a week before the race. Their parked Chrysler was hit in Juárez by a speeding car and damaged badly enough that the frame had to be straightened. And twenty-four-year-old competitor Guillermo Suahra wrecked his car at Tehuantepec on the way to the starting line.

Carrera IV drew seventy-four entries from Argentina, where stock car racing had always been popular. The great mobilization had been created by President Juan Peron, who granted to Argentinean participants a special permit that exempted them from paying customs duties normally charged on imported autos—

105

Mickey Thompson's Ford six before the start of leg one. Rounding a curve near Tehuantepec, Thompson saw people running onto the highway. Going too fast to stop, he deliberately drove over a small bank. His car fell on a crowd hidden below the road, and six spectators were killed. Dave Friedman

Independent Lincoln driver Ray Crawford autographs a program for a young fan while his mechanics do some last-minute fiddling with his Bill Stroppe-prepared car. Dave Friedman

in other words, the race made it possible to import large US cars at a fraction of the usual cost.

Same Song, Second Verse

Americans Johnny Mantz, Chuck Stevenson, and Walt Faulkner, and Mexican Fernando Carriles, all in Lincolns, were the first four stock cars to be flagged off on the 329-mile first leg. The team's pop stand pit stop had been improved with a lift that hoisted the entire car and allowed all four tires to be changed in record time. Just short of 4 hours after the start, Stevenson boomed into Oaxaca, breaking Faulkner's 1952 record by 12 minutes. Faulkner and Jack McGrath were in second and third, Mantz was fourth, and Frank Mundy in a Chrysler was fifth, 29 seconds behind the fourth Lincoln. Bill Vukovich lasted only 200 miles before his transmission let go—ironic because codriver Vern Houle had been in charge of building the team's transmissions.

The stage was set: the Lincolns seemed unbeatable, but the first leg had also always been a jinx—no leg one winner had ever won the race. Five cars broke, two arrived over the time limit, and Ramundo Corona's Packard and Speed McFee's Chrysler both crashed.

Stevenson won leg two, with Faulkner and McGrath again behind him, but Mundy captured fourth over Mantz. The Capris still occupied the three top spots in the race, and Mundy was 22 seconds up on Mantz for fourth. Ray Crawford finished sixth, and Felix Cerda Loza seventh. Lincolns occupied eight of the top nine spots!

Frank Davis' Plymouth Cambridge 208 and Tommy Drisdale's Chrysler New Yorker 66 clear customs at Ciudad Juárez on the way to the starting line. Both cars were sponsored by El Paso Chrysler-Plymouth dealer A. B. Poe. Dave Friedman

107

After repairs and servicing during the allowed 3 hours, each Lincoln team car was then washed. Each driver was assigned a cartoon character so that the crew could quickly identify its car. Note Panchito on the hood of this vehicle. Dave Friedman

Bill Sterling's Cadillac broke an axle as he rounded a curve and a wheel came adrift. The car's fender held the wheel in place, preventing the Texan from going over a cliff.

If there was any doubt about the Lincoln superiority, the dash to México City dispelled it; the first eight places again went to the Dearborn Freight Train. Mantz finally won the leg after trying for four years; his time was identical to Piero Taruffi's Ferrari time in 1951. Crawford was second, McGrath and Faulkner third and fourth. Second and eighth places were separated by only 39 seconds.

After three legs, first through fourth belonged to Lincolns, and when times were tabulated, Mundy in his Chrysler was fifth, followed by Crawford, Loza, Jim Rathmann, Tommy Drisdale, and Luis Leal Solares in a Lincoln.

More than 50,000 cars created the largest traffic jam in Mexican history as highways were closed for the race. And Bill Stroppe recalled the justifiable fear that most drivers had for the safety of the crowd: "Going into México City, the people would stand in the roadway, inches from the cars, and try to touch them as they went by at 120mph."

Chuck Stevenson south of Ciudad Juárez on the way to winning the stock car class for Lincoln. Dean Batchelor collection

C. D. Evans, left, with GM Mexico General Manager Vernon Moore and the 1954 Chevrolet that won the light stock division. The logo on the door reads El Abuelito—which loosely translates to The Flying Grandfather. Juan Guzman photo, Bruce Gross collection

Norm Patterson, left, and Bernie Shires pose with their Ford six after winning second in light stocks. The entry was sponsored by the city of El Paso. Eddie Neville photo, Bruce Gross collection

The Cadillac of Ed Stringer on the first day near Tehuantepec. Stringer placed 15th on the opening leg. Lee Render photo, Dean Batchelor collection

Cars, buses, and trucks were in a double line 40 miles long as spectators came home from the race. The traffic cleared by 4pm, but not before a woman reportedly gave birth to a baby girl in her car.

And in other news that day, Scott Crossfield had flown a Douglas Skyrocket to a new speed record of 1,320mph at Muroc Dry Lake in California. The space age had been conceived.

Back in Mexico, McGrath, Mantz, Stevenson, and Faulkner swept the run to Léon, breaking their own kind of record on the way. Loza and Crawford both retired, and for the moment, Rathmann and Drisdale moved up to sixth and seventh.

On leg five, the Four Horsemen pulled further away, winning the leg over Rathmann's Olds and increasing the gap to 27 minutes. Mundy's Chrysler strained itself trying to keep up, and he bowed out. Drisdale and Charlie Russell were sixth and seventh, and Sterling was having trouble. He had finished the leg seventh, only up to twentieth for the race.

In the closest finish since the one at México City, McGrath won leg six, with Faulkner, Stevenson, Mantz, and Rathmann shadowing him, the four separated by just 40 seconds. Rathmann had picked up about 2 minutes on fourth-place Mantz on the leg. Solares' Olds was the only casualty of the day.

Sterling wheeled his Deal Cadillac into fifth on leg seven—naturally, behind the Lincolns—with Drisdale and Russell again sixth and seventh. Rathmann managed eighth to maintain his overall fifth place. Only twenty-four cars were now left in the big stock class, out of fifty-two starters, and only one leg remained to go.

A pair of heater blowers in the trunk of the Stroppe-and-Smith-Lincolns. Petersen Publishing

William Sterling, left, was back for the fourth race, this time in a Cadillac codriven by Julius Colapret. Bruce Gross collection

111

OAXACA
MEXICO
OMEGA
ARGENTINA MEXICO
53
95
LINCOLN
BILL STROPPE

Fifty-five thousand spectators watched the finish from behind barbed-wire barricades at the Juárez Airport. A dust storm accompanied the first arrivals, hindering their visibility.

For the second year, Mantz broke the Chihuahua—Juárez record and won the final section at over 114mph. And also for the second year, Stevenson posted a race win for Lincoln, followed by Faulkner. McGrath edged out Mantz by 23 seconds for third.

Was it close? The spread between first and fourth after 20.5 hours of racing was less than 2 minutes!

Rathmann ended up watching the race from the roadside, as his Olds broke near the finish line, and El Pasoan Drisdale's Chrysler New Yorker followed the Lincolns home in fifth place. Sterling managed a fifth-place leg finish but wound up in eleventh for the distance.

No victory in Mexico had been as overwhelming as that which the Lincoln team turned in. It had swept its class for the second consecutive year—it had taken the first three positions on every leg, plus a fourth in all but one, a fifth in all but two. When the dust finally cleared, seven Lincolns were among the top nine finishers.

Stroppe and Clay Smith had done their job well. Besides the class win, they had placed their two-ton American luxury cars seventh through tenth behind the Lancias and Ferraris, and their nearest in-class competitor was over three-quarters of an hour behind them.

The team started looking forward to making it three years in a row as plans were formulated for 1954.

Small Stocks

For the first time, Carrera Panamericana gave a reasonable chance for the small, inexpensive automobile to compete in the Mexican arena. But along with the budget racers came inexperienced drivers. people whose total racing experience was usually on back roads or, at best, in unsanctioned forays.

Most prominent among *Turismo Especial* drivers was C. D. Evans, an El Paso midget racing promoter and participant in all three Pan-Ams, finishing sixth in 1952. An oval track racer in his younger days, Evans had driven six times at Indianapolis in the twenties and thirties and had finished fifth once and sixth twice. After a lifetime of driving on both road and track, he claimed he had never had an accident and modestly billed himself as The World's Safest Driver. For Carrera IV, he chose a Chevy six.

Mickey Thompson, pioneer California hot rodder, entered a Ford six, as did Norm Patterson and Frank Davis. Bob Barkimer entered his wife's Ford—presumably with her consent—and Scott Yantis a Chevy; the rest of the ninety-six starters were Mexican and Central American drivers.

Ford dominated the field with fifty-eight starters. The company had just introduced its overhead-valve six-cylinder engine in late 1952 to replace its venerable L-head six. The new powerplant had embarrassed the old flathead V-8, outperforming the very engine it was only supposed to supplement. The torquey six displaced 215ci and was conservatively rated at 101hp, whereas the V-8 was supposed to pump out 110hp.

Al and Ralph Rodgers, Pikes Peak Hillclimb champions, switched from Cadillacs to Chryslers for 1953, even though the former were still ahead in the horsepower race. Petersen Publishing

*Previous page
At the start of the second leg at Oaxaca, the four Lincolns of Chuck Stevenson, Walt Faulkner, Jack McGrath, and Johnny Mantz line up in their leg one finishing order behind the big-bore sports cars.* Petersen Publishing

*Next page
The Lincoln of Rodger Ward arrived in Puebla unceremoniously piled on its transporter, another victim of the Pan-American Road Race.* Petersen Publishing

113

Chuck Daigh studies the rolling route map that Clay Smith originated in 1951 when he drove with Troy Ruttman. Petersen Publishing

Bob Korf, a US Air Force captain, could have been the model for the Smilin' Jack comic strip. He drove a Carl Kiekhaefer-prepared Chrysler New Yorker in Carrera IV. Petersen Publishing

114

Before the start, the impound area at Tuxtla Gutiérrez was filled with shiny race cars and an air of optimism. Dave Friedman

Roadside vendors served the local specialties to the thousands of fans who gathered to watch the race roar through their country. Dave Friedman

Lincoln drivers Chuck Stevenson, stock division winner in 1952, left, and Walt Faulkner, third-place finisher in the stock division in 1952, right, visit with Lancia driver Piero Taruffi in front of Faulkner's car. Road & Track

Chevrolet was a natural for the Pan-Am—certainly not because of its performance image, but simply because so many examples were in Mexico. A confrontation with traditional rival Ford would be welcomed among owners of both brands, all of whom thought of their make as the faster. The Chevy engine was a splash-lubricated 216ci 92hp six in standard transmission form; the PowerGlide version was 235ci and 105hp with pressure oiling. Twenty-one were entered.

The balance of the starters were in Hudson Jets, Studebakers, Kaisers, Plymouths, a couple of Aero Willys, one De Soto 6, one Nash Rambler, and one Mercury. The small stocks posed only one threat to the faster cars: they

The Lincoln of Walt Faulkner and Chuck Daigh gets serviced after leg one. Dave Friedman

could get in the way. For this reason, they were given starting positions at the end of the field, behind sports, stock, and light sports racers.

Racing the Family Sedan

That leg one of Carrera Panamericana was not the place to race the family sedan became painfully obvious during the 329-mile trip from Tuxtla to Oaxaca. Seventeen of the field fell out of the race, including two who were involved in the most tragic incident in the race's history.

Bob Christie had failed to negotiate a curve near Tehuantepec, and his Ford plunged into the Tehuantepec River. As a crowd rushed across the road to spectate, Mickey Thompson rounded the curve. Unable to stop without hitting the massed spectators, Thompson deliberately drove his Ford over a small bank.

Bill Vukovich, right, and his support crew take a lunch break during practice for Carrera IV. Dave Friedman

117

Buick's newly introduced Fireball V-8 didn't live up to its billing in 1953. This 2-ton Roadmaster was driven to 19th by Ernie Hall and Louis Unser. Dave Friedman

After winning the first race, Oldsmobiles had fallen out of favor; only three were entered in 1953. The 88 of Ricardo Rivapalacio, shown here undergoing some field modifications, placed sixteenth. Dave Friedman

Unfortunately, another crowd was out of sight below the road, and Thompson's car fell on them, killing six persons.

Davis won the leg in a Plymouth, beating out Evans' Chevrolet by over 8 minutes. Malcom Eckart's Hudson Jet followed in third 5 minutes later. The great gaps of time between cars indicated that the class was grossly mismatched, and it might have served warning that it could be a boring five days before the race concluded. The winning average was 72mph, 11mph slower than that of the top Lincolns in unlimited stocks—about the same speed differential as the sports cars held over the big stock cars.

Patterson won the second go-round in a Ford, and race leader Davis retired with mechanical problems. No one in the top five on leg one was a contender in the second section, except Evans in fourth. Fourteen more cars dropped out: nine Fords, two Plymouths, one Studebaker, a Kaiser, and the lone Mercury.

Argentinean Guillermo Airaldi won the run to México City in 1 hour, 6 minutes, 35 seconds in his Ford. In the next 35 seconds came Enrique Paredes' Jet, Oscar Calaben's Ford, Evans' Chevy, and Patterson's Ford. The times—and the race—seemed to be tightening.

Evans' Chevy led the pack in accumulated time, 6 minutes ahead of Patterson's Ford, which in turn was 2.5 minutes in front of Eckart's Hudson. Nearly half the field was still running.

Eckart jetted into first on leg four with a 79mph run. Yantis followed him by 1 minute, 24 seconds, Oscar Calaben was third by 9 seconds, and Evans was fourth 12 seconds later. Seven more Fords failed, along with three Chevrolets.

The Lincoln of Johnny Mantz undergoes inspection after leg one. Dave Friedman

Chrysler's hemispherical-head V-8 put out 180hp, still utilizing a two-barrel carburetor. Here Tommy Drisdale airs tires on El Paso Chrysler dealer A. B. Poe's New Yorker prior to the start. Dave Friedman

Chuck Stevenson, left, and Clay Smith with their winning 1953 Lincoln. Mobil Oil Corporation

Yantis was beginning to reel in the leaders as he won leg five in his Chevy. After a disappointing first few legs, he had moved up to tenth by México City and fifth by Durango. Evans still headed the class and had stretched his lead over Patterson to 7 minutes, 11 seconds; Calaben was third, and Jorge Daponte fourth. Chevys finished one-two-three-four on leg five as a kind of low-dollar imitation of Team Lincoln.

As the road straightened out on leg six, the speeds began to increase—and so did the incidence of mechanical failures. Three more Fords folded, but Airaldi pushed his to an 81.8mph win, trailed by Patterson, Daponte, Yantis, and Evans.

Airaldi repeated with a win on leg seven into Chihuahua. He had been a dismal twenty-fifth at Durango, over 1.5 hours behind Evans. By virtue of his 92.4mph win in this leg, he moved to seventeeth but had only gained 10 minutes on Evans, who was still sitting comfortably in first overall.

Yantis won the last leg in his Chevrolet, averaging 91mph—no mean feat for a 90mph car!—and moved to fourth for the race. Eckart was second into Juárez, fifth overall.

The World's Safest Driver

Evans won the division, a little over 5 minutes in front of Patterson. Calaben placed third in his Ford. Evans had averaged 77.04mph for the distance and collected 30,000 pesos ($3,488) plus leg prizes for his trouble. Fellow El Pasoan Patterson pocketed 20,000 pesos ($2,326) for second.

A further surprise awaited Evans a few days after the race when General Motors' Ed Cole presented him a new 1954 Chevrolet Corvette—the thirty-ninth one made of the new model. Evans said later that he appreciated the gesture—the retail value of the Corvette was approximately equal to Evans' race earnings—but after Cole left town, he sold the prize, "because," he said, "I needed the damned money more than I needed the damned car!"

They were a noble experiment, those 100hp racers. With an attrition rate of approximately 75 percent, they were hardly testimony to the strength and endurance of the common man's automobile. Seventy-six percent of the fifty-eight Fords entered failed to finish, and 71 percent of the Chevys did not make it to Juárez.

But Evans was happy. He had raced Mexico four times, finished sixth once, and now had a class win. At fifty-four years of age, he was the oldest driver in the race. Maybe he should think of retiring while he still thought of himself as the safest driver in the world.

C. D. Evans, left, accepts new Corvette production number 39 from President Ed Cole of General Motors, a bonus for winning the light stock division in a Chevrolet. Sievers photo, Bruce Gross collection

121

Chapter 9

1954 Carrera Panamericana V: Large Sports Class

The Prancing Stallion Faces The Iron Horse

Umberto Maglioli rounds a left-hander outside Oaxaca on his way to winning leg two with an 87mph average. Mobil Oil Corporation

For the second year in a row, in 1954, Carrera Panamericana was the last of five International Championship races, and for the second year, Ferrari had the championship sewed up before it even set sail for Mexico.

Stirling Moss had tried to persuade Jaguar management to send a team of D-Types to Mexico but failed. It saw no reason to risk its equipment and its reputation against what it thought was a lost cause. This was a good management decision, but one that denied the Western Hemisphere witness to what could have been an epic confrontation.

Mercedes-Benz was tempted to make a reappearance in Mexico, as well. It was readying its awesome 300SLR, which was the 180mph follow-on of the 300SL and used the running gear from the firm's championship Grand Prix car. But development had slowed, and the car wouldn't be competitive until the spring of 1955, when Mercedes would run at Le Mans.

Ferrari Dominates the Entries

Carrera V would be a struggle among Ferrari drivers, who had entered nine cars. The two 4954cc 350hp 375 Plus racers were the most powerful and the fastest at an estimated 175mph. They would be driven by Umberto Maglioli and Jack McAfee.

Luigi Chinetti entered a 4.5 liter 375MM for its owner and codriver John Shakespeare, who was a manufacturer of fishing rods and reels. Phil Hill and Richie Ginther were again aboard an Allan Guiberson car, a 4.5 liter 375MM—the same car that had been driven with little success by Chinetti and de Portago in Carrera IV.

A Ferrari was also furnished for Giovanni Bracco, who had yet to reach Juárez in a race car after three tries. Bracco's car was a 750 Monza with the 3.0 liter 270hp double-overhead-cam four-cylinder engine Ferrari had developed for the 1952—1953 World Championship, which was campaigned in Formula Two cars. Another Monza was entered by the marquis Alfonso de Portago. Franco Cornacchia would drive a hybrid Monza powered by a 2963cc V-12 250MM engine.

Porfirio Rubirosa—famous Dominican playboy and husband of heiress Barbara Hutton—would race his 500 Mondial with Ernie McAfee as codriver.

The Ferrari list was completed by Argentinean Roberto Bonomi aboard a 4.6 liter model.

122

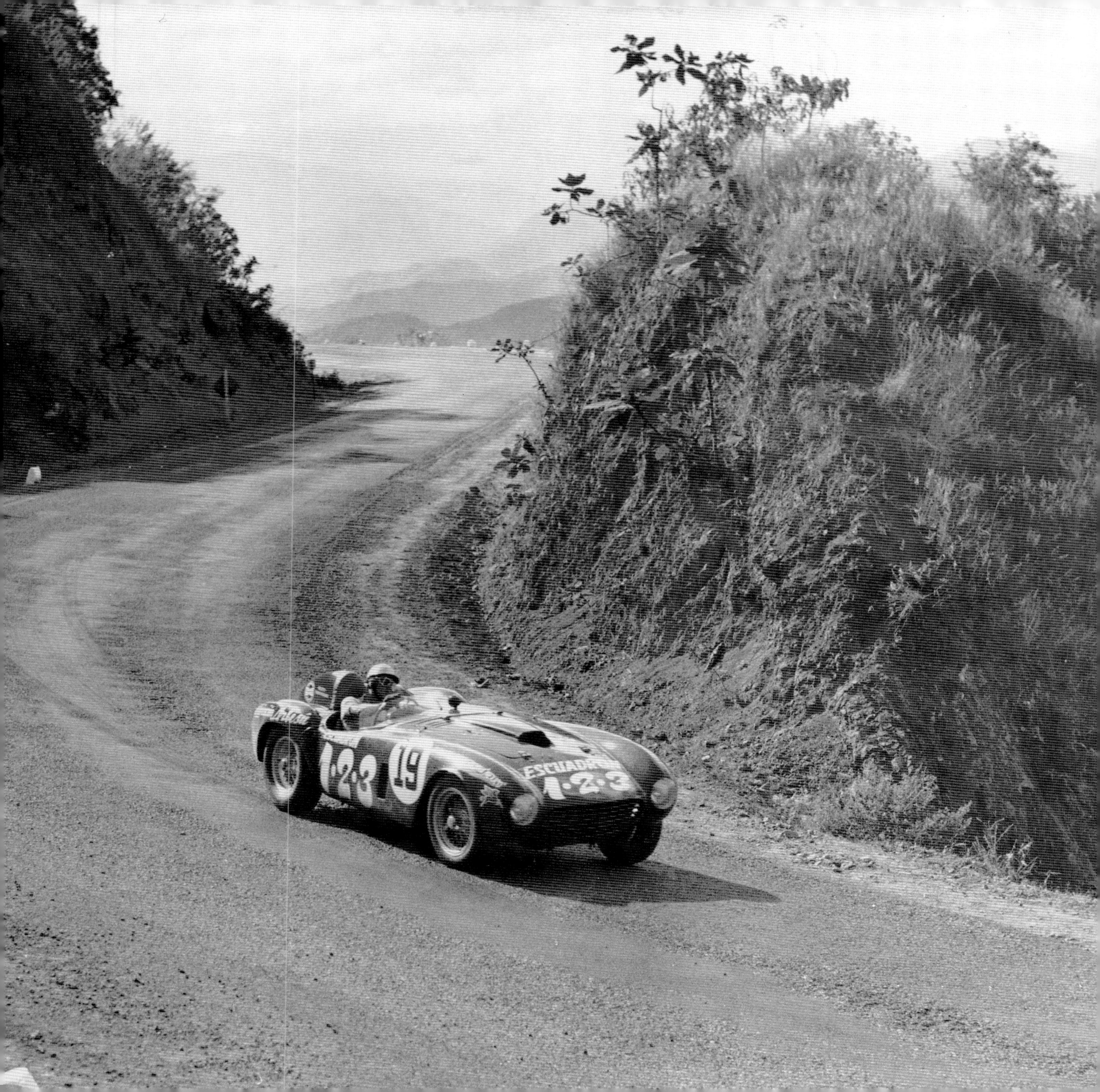
1·2·3
19
ESCUADR
1·2·3

Porfiro Rubirosa, at the wheel, reflects the gentleman racer's fashion of the day—scarf, polo sweater, and kid gloves—as he and his American codriver, Ernie McAfee, prepare for the dawn start of Carrera V. Petersen Publishing

A Pegaso, manufactured in the old Hispano-Suiza works in Barcelona, was entered by Joaquin Palacios under the auspices of President Rafael Léonidas Trujillo Molina of the Dominican Republic. The complex Z102BS roadster featured a Rootes-supercharged 3.2 liter 285hp four-cam aluminum-head V-8 coupled to a five-speed transaxle. Palacios showed up with the Pegaso rigged to run on its usual mixture of 75 percent 100-octane gasoline, 15 percent methanol, 10 percent benzene, and a touch of castor oil but was dissuaded, hastily modifying the engine for 80-octane Pemex, the more mundane but official race gasoline.

Austin-Healey sent a modest two-car team of 100S roadsters—100 models with lightweight bodies and the basic 2660cc four-cylinder Austin engine pumped up to 130hp with Weslake aluminum cylinder heads. A streamlined version of the 100S had set an international record of 192.74mph at Bonneville during the summer, and Carroll Shelby drove a specially prepared stock-bodied 100S to an average of 157.92mph to break 25km to

Although Marquis Alfonso de Portago's Ferrari 750 Monza carried no codriver, he nonetheless was able to secure a stylish assistant for the Mexican Road Race. Petersen Publishing

200km records. Shelby and Lance Macklin were to drive in Mexico.

Jean Trevoux was back with his Packard Special, and Jack Ensley, 1954 Sports Car Club of America (SCCA) B sports racing champion, and Duane Carter, Indy 500 ace, drove Kurtises.

And in its first international competition, Americans Bill von Esser and Ernest Pultz entered the newest sports car on the world scene: a fiberglass-bodied, six-cylinder Chevrolet Corvette.

The Garden-Variety Hot Rod

Ak Miller was back with *Caballo de Hierro*, except the Mexicans had given it a new name: *Ensalada*, or *Salad*. No other title seemed as

1954 Large Sports Category Model Factory Specifications

Model	Price	Engine	Ci	Hp	Weight	Top Speed
Austin-Healey 100S	NA	Ohv 4	162.2	130	NA	140mph
Chevrolet Corvette	$3,523	Ohv 6	235.5	150	2,705lb	NA
Ferrari 500 Mondial	NA	Dohc 4	121	170	1,760	NA
Ferrari 750 Monza	NA	Dohc 4	183	260	NA	164
Ferrari 375 Plus	NA	Sohc V-12	299	350	NA	175
Jaguar XK 120C	$5,860	Dohc 6	210	200	2,128	145
Pegaso Z102	$29,500	Dohc V-8	194	280	NA	160

Carroll Shelby suffered a fractured arm when his Austin-Healey 100S crashed south of Puebla. By the time an ambulance arrived, ol' Shel had killed the pain—along with a great deal of beer and tequila proffered by interested bystanders. Don Downie

appropriate for this garden-variety mixture of practically every make of American car.

Miller had spent the year rebuilding the *Caballo* with the knowledge he'd gained in Carrera IV. The 5.6 liter (340ci) Olds V-8 sported four Stromberg 97 carburetors, a 12-quart oil sump and developed about 285hp, and the differential had been replaced with a late-model Lincoln unit courtesy of Bill Stroppe. Even though one of the sponsors of Stroppe's Lincoln team was a lubricant manufacturer, Stroppe suggested that Miller might want to use the combination of castor bean oil and white lead he was employing to lubricate the gears in his cars. Miller chose Lincoln wheels for the car because Stroppe had suggested that he might scrounge through the Lincoln tire supply after each leg to take the best of the used 8x15 Firestones for his next day's racing—if he didn't get caught by John Holman.

Enchanted by the American hot rod's contrast to the sleek and expensive Ferraris, the Mexican press asked the aristocratic Ferrari driver Porfiro Rubirosa to pose for pictures in Miller's car.

"Rubirosa wouldn't even sit in *Caballo*," Miller remembered, "let alone have his photo taken."

As race time approached, the annual last-minute hysteria about arrivals and entries erupted. It wasn't until the night of November 16, barely two days before the start, that the cargo ship carrying most of the big European sports cars arrived in Vera Cruz. And in the El Paso papers, news of the race shared page one with reports on the start of the Sam Shepherd murder trial in Cleveland.

Tragedy and Triumph

Lincoln had set up its first advance base 217 miles north of the start at Tuxtla, and exactly 2 hours after the first car—the Ferrari 275 Plus of Jack McAfee and Ford Robinson—was waved off, it was reported by radio to be 5 minutes out. But McAfee and Robinson never arrived. Going into a deceptive right hander at 120mph, their white number 1 Ferrari slid across the road and overturned in the brush. McAfee was only shaken up, but his friend and codriver, Robinson, died instantly of a broken neck.

Immediately behind McAfee's car were two more Ferraris, the blue and white number 20 of Phil Hill and the red number 19 of Umberto Maglioli, up front, incredibly, so soon.

Giovanni Bracco, the wild mountain driver and the only one other than Hill with a chance

---

Entry Rules Summary For 1954 Large Sports Cars

Limited to 50 entries. Entry fee 7,000 pesos ($560.00). FIA sports cars over 1500cc. Supercharging permitted, pump fuel is mandatory. Engine may not be replaced, but unlimited time between each day's run is allowed for servicing and repair. Approved racing helmets must be worn, and seat belts are required in all closed cars. No alcoholic beverage allowed in vehicles. Competitors must drive on the right, pass on the left.

Prizes

Placing	Prize
First	200,000 pesos ($16,000)
Second	100,000 pesos ($8,000)
Third	40,000 pesos ($3,200)
Fourth	20,000 pesos ($1,600)
Fifth	15,000 pesos ($1,200)
Sixth through tenth	Each 7,000 pesos ($560)
Winner of each leg	5,000 pesos ($400)
Top Mexican driver	20,000 pesos ($1,600)

Maximum Allowable Time

Leg	Miles	Time
1. Tuxtla Gutiérrez-Oaxaca	329.40	5:00
2. Oaxaca-Puebla	252.95	4:00
3. Puebla-México City	75.13	1:20
4. México City-Léon	261.03	3:15
5. Léon-Durango	329.40	4:00
6. Durango-Parral	251.09	3:00
7. Parral-Chihuahua	186.47	2:10
8. Chihuahua-Ciudad Juárez	222.51	2:30
Total	1,908	

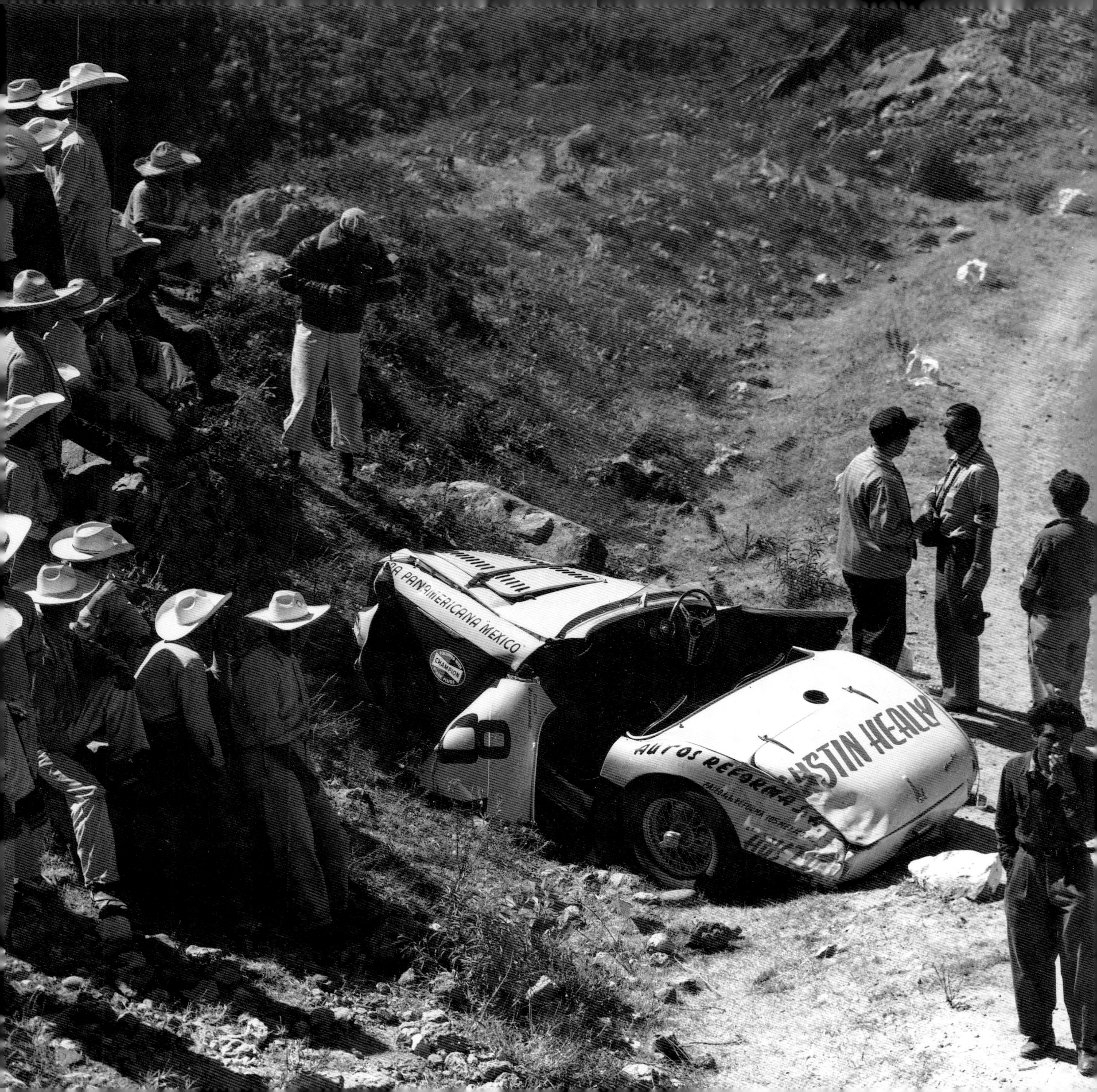
PANAMERICANA MEXICO
CHAMPION
AUTOS REFORMA

Accompanied by a photo plane, Carrera V winner Umberto Maglioli flashes across the finish line at Ciudad Juárez at 140mph just inches from the crowd. Don Downie

to beat Maglioli, should have been fast behind the pair, but his Ferrari was one of the nine cars already either out of the race or limping badly from the grind.

The casualty list was impressive: the number 2 Ferrari of Alfonso de Portago suffered a broken oil line; the number 3 and number 4 Ferraris of Porfiro Rubirosa and Roberto Bonomi broke; the number 7 Healey of Lance Macklin lost a condenser and finished overtime; Carroll Shelby's number 9 lost its front shocks but continued on to finish sixth; the number 8 and number 17 Kurtises were sidelined (the Oldsmobile engine in Duane Carter's

Kurtis cracked a piston); and a rod punched through the side of Bill von Esser's Blue Flame engine block and the fire died in his Corvette.

Ten miles from the start, Ak Miller saw Rubirosa's Ferrari at the side of the road, its radiator steaming. As he sped past, Miller said, he paid back the nobleman's earlier rudeness with a one-fingered American wave.

Hill beat Maglioli to Oaxaca by 4 minutes, 9 seconds and Franco Cornacchia by over 30 minutes, for a one-two-three Ferrari sweep, with Miller in fourth. The *Caballo* was fast becoming the favorite of Carrera fans, who, like fans everywhere, loved the idea of the little folks sticking it to the factory teams. The sports class was already down to eleven competitors.

"Don't clobber the hay bales at Atlixco," a friend had warned Hill. The route through town took a 90-degree right followed by a 90-degree left and was lined with hay and spectators who were having a field day watching as one car after another slid into the bales. Hill made it safely through, but Maglioli soon caught him and stormed into Puebla leading by over 3 minutes, with Cornacchia in third. Joaquin Palacios and his Pegaso finished fourth, Miller fifth, and Luigi Chinetti in the other Ferrari sixth.

Shelby crashed his Healey and suffered a fractured arm. Years later, he recounted: "At first I didn't realize I had a broken arm. I just sat there at the accident site for 6 or 7 hours, hoping that an ambulance or an organization car would pick me up. Two American tourists passed and gave me a beer, then came some Mexicans who offered me a bottle of tequila, so when the ambulance arrived, I was three sheets to the wind."

The Puebla–México City leg was always as fierce as it was short. On each side of the

Giovanni Bracco's four-cylinder Ferrari 750 Monza—shown leaving Tuxtla Gutiérrez on leg one of Carrera V—crashed before reaching Oaxaca. Don Downie

129

Ak Miller and Doug Harrison in Caballo de Hierro—the Horse of Iron—before the Tuxtla start. Ak Miller collection

Ak Miller and Doug Harrison await the starter's flag at Tuxtla. Their homemade hot rod surprised the sophisticated competition, placing fourth on leg one behind three Ferraris. Ak Miller collection

highest point in the race—10,486ft Puerto d'Aire—long flat-out straights terminated in vicious adobe-walled right-angle turns through villages.

Hill gained the race lead back by beating Maglioli to the capital by a scant 39 seconds. At this point, the Ferrari team manager was pleading with the young Maglioli to take it easy; with his three major competitors out of the race since the first leg, it was vital that Maglioli not be drawn into a duel with Hill. Maglioli's car was at least 20mph faster than Hill's, and the only thing that could hurt his chances was a mechanical breakdown.

The Pegaso had surprisingly moved up to fourth overall, its supercharging a plus in the rarified air, but the real leadfoot of the leg was Louis Chiron in a 1.5 liter OSCA MT-4—he had passed everyone in small sports *and* large sports except for Hill and Maglioli.

An accident at Rio Hondito, 25 miles north of México City, affected competitors in several classes on leg four. Karl Bechem spun his Borgward and wrecked while leading small sports. As first aid personnel rushed to help the injured driver, Palacios lost control of his Pegaso at the accident site and flipped several times. Although the driver was thrown free, the car continued into a field, where it struck and killed a soldier and burst into flames.

While the wreckage was still smoldering, driver Frank Davis missed the curve and flipped his small stock Dodge into the field, although he was able to effect some repairs and continue racing.

Maglioli: In Front to Stay

Umberto Maglioli regained the race lead in the mountains near Léon. Phil Hill, realizing that he'd lost on the winding roads where he had his only chance, resigned himself to maintaining a safe second; his only hope for winning was a mishap or breakdown of the lead car.

Ak Miller's carburetors iced up in the mountains, and he had to chip them free with a screwdriver. He and Doug Harrison finished the leg in sixth and kept fourth place overall, much to the frustration of those behind them. Most annoyed was Luigi Chinetti, whose Ferrari had chased the hot rod since the beginning of the race and still trailed it by 6 minutes.

"Chinetti was really upset that he couldn't catch us," Miller said. "He called our car a 'shitbox.' Oh, well, at least we were noticed."

A Hollywood movie company had been on location in Durango for two weeks when the race arrived. Actor George Montgomery was starring in a film called *Robber's Roost*. On the day of the race, the entire company took a holiday, probably, as *National Speed Sport News* editor Chris Economaki put it, "to prevent the unexplainable embarrassment of having screaming race cars roaring by in the background of a movie which was set in the early 1800s!"

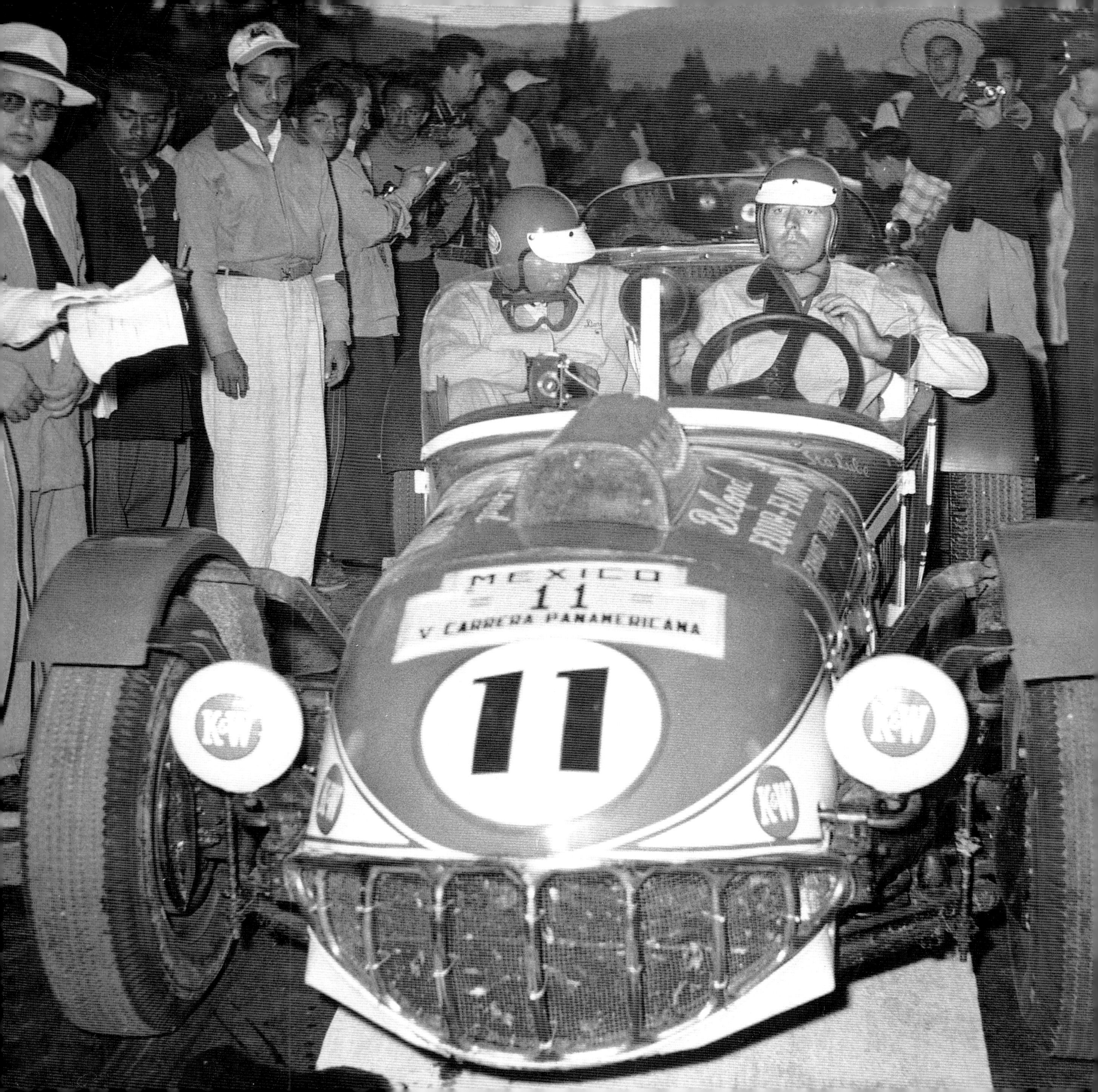
MEXICO
11
V CARRERA PANAMERICANA
11

Caballo was probably the most famous entry ever in the Pan-American Road Race series. Its distinctive shape and homemade charm made it the favorite of fans, many of whom contributed money through sponsor Hot Rod *Magazine for its construction.* Ak Miller collection

Franco Cornacchia's Ferrari 750 Monza flashes across the finish line in Oaxaca at the end of leg one, third behind the Ferraris of Umberto Maglioli and Phil Hill. Don Downie

From Léon to Durango, the overall race leaders remained Maglioli, Hill, and then Hans Herrmann in the Porsche, but Franco Cornacchia in the 2.9 liter Ferrari finally moved up and passed the balance of the 1500cc cars to secure fourth place, while Miller continued to show more speed on the straights than anyone thought he had a right to.

At Léon, Ensalada was refueled and the two rear tires were changed, but no one thought to check the air pressure. One of them was only carrying 22lb instead of the normal 45lb. "I had to keep it under 110mph just to stay on the road," Miller recalled. The oversight dropped Miller and Harrison to fifth, and they were holding just a 28-second lead over Chinetti when they arrived at Durango and joined the other racers at a party the movie studio threw.

Jack McAfee's Ferrari 375 Plus slid off the road 200 miles north of the start at Tuxtla Gutiérrez. McAfee was shaken up, but his codriver, Ford Robinson, died in the crash. Petersen Publishing

The entry of Jack Ensley, SCCA B sports racing champion, was a Kurtis-Cadillac, despite the Nash logo on the hood. Petersen Publishing

Phil Hill waits to start at Durango, where he sat second behind Umberto Maglioli. Hill drove the Ferrari 375 MM of Allan Guiberson, a Dallas businessman, which had been campaigned—briefly—in the 1953 race by Luigi Chinetti. Petersen Publishing

Umberto Maglioli crosses the finish line at Juárez as the winner of Carrera V. He had won five of the race's eight legs and set a record pace of 107.955mph. Petersen Publishing

*Next page
The world's newest sports car, the Chevrolet Corvette, made a debut in Mexico, but a thrown rod put Bill von Esser out early.* Petersen Publishing

von Esser's SPEED-
EQUIPMENT
Chicago, Ill.
CHAMPION
MEXICO
= 12 =
V CARRERA PANAMERICANA
ALID

Looking for all the world as if he were enjoying a Saturday night in his hometown of McKinney, Texas, Carroll Shelby sits atop his Austin-Healey 100S in Oaxaca, watching the traffic and awaiting the start of leg two. He had finished sixth on the first leg. Petersen Publishing

At the Chihuahua finish line, Ray Brock, right, tells Ak Miller and Doug Harrison that they have slipped to fifth place behind Luigi Chinetti. Petersen Publishing

*Next page
Luigi Chinetti and fishing tackle manufacturer John Shakespeare coast to a stop in their Ferrari 375MM after they have been passed by Ak Miller and his hot rod, for fourth between Durango and Parral.* Petersen Publishing

The next day, leg six provided straighter roads for Maglioli, and he stretched his lead over Hill to 10 minutes. Hill was secure in second with a 1.5-hour lead over Cornacchia. A pumped-up Miller regained fourth from Chinetti.

At Parral, a 30-minute layover awaited the finishers, then the seventh and next-to-last leg began—leaving only about 400 miles in the run for the river.

Maglioli scorched the road between Parral and Chihuahua with a 131mph run, erasing his record of the year before. On the way, the metal tonneau cover over his empty codriver's seat came loose. Maglioli grabbed it, holding onto it with one hand while driving with the other. The errant part nearly made the whole

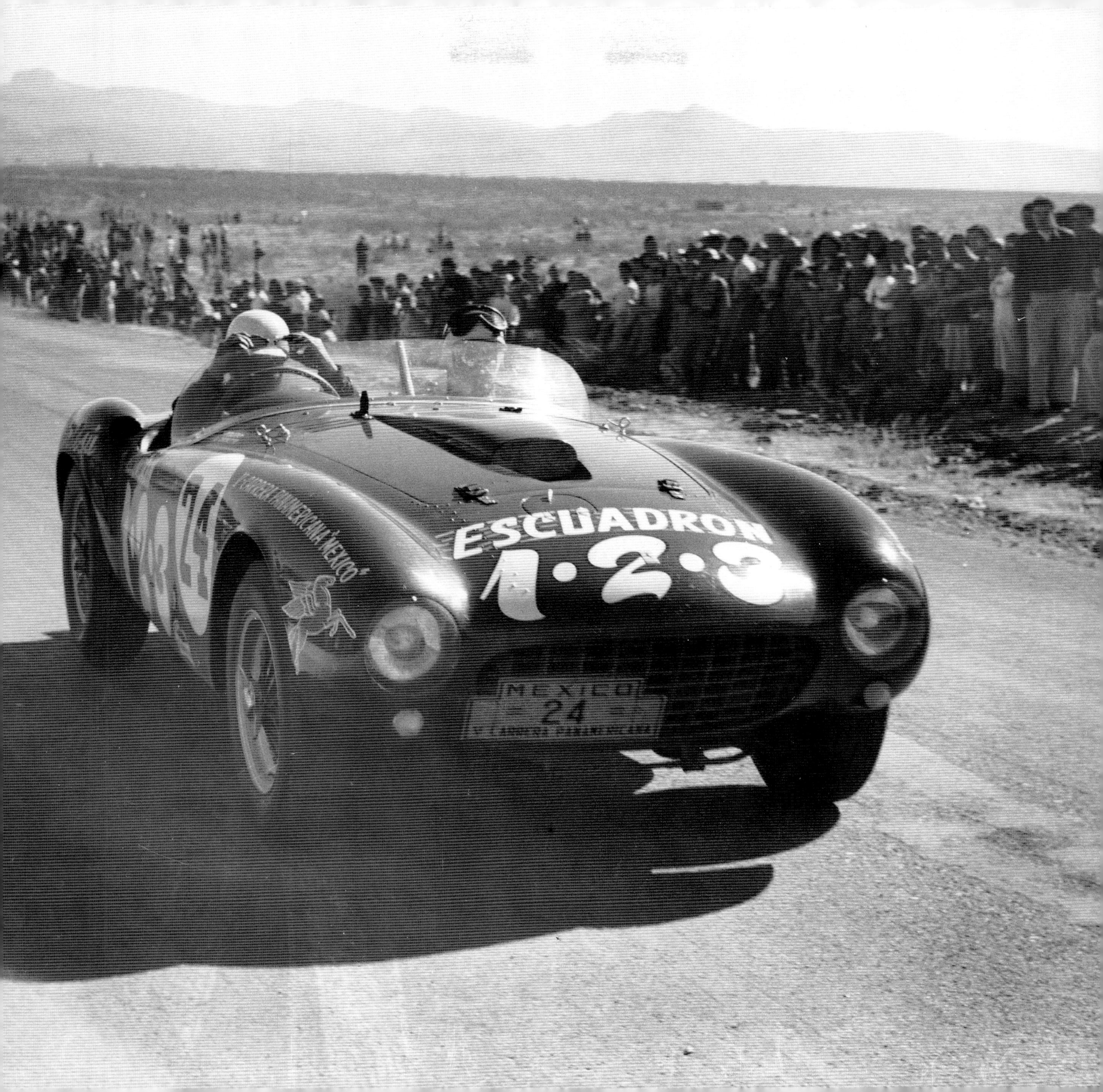
ESCUADRON
1·2·3
MEXICO
24

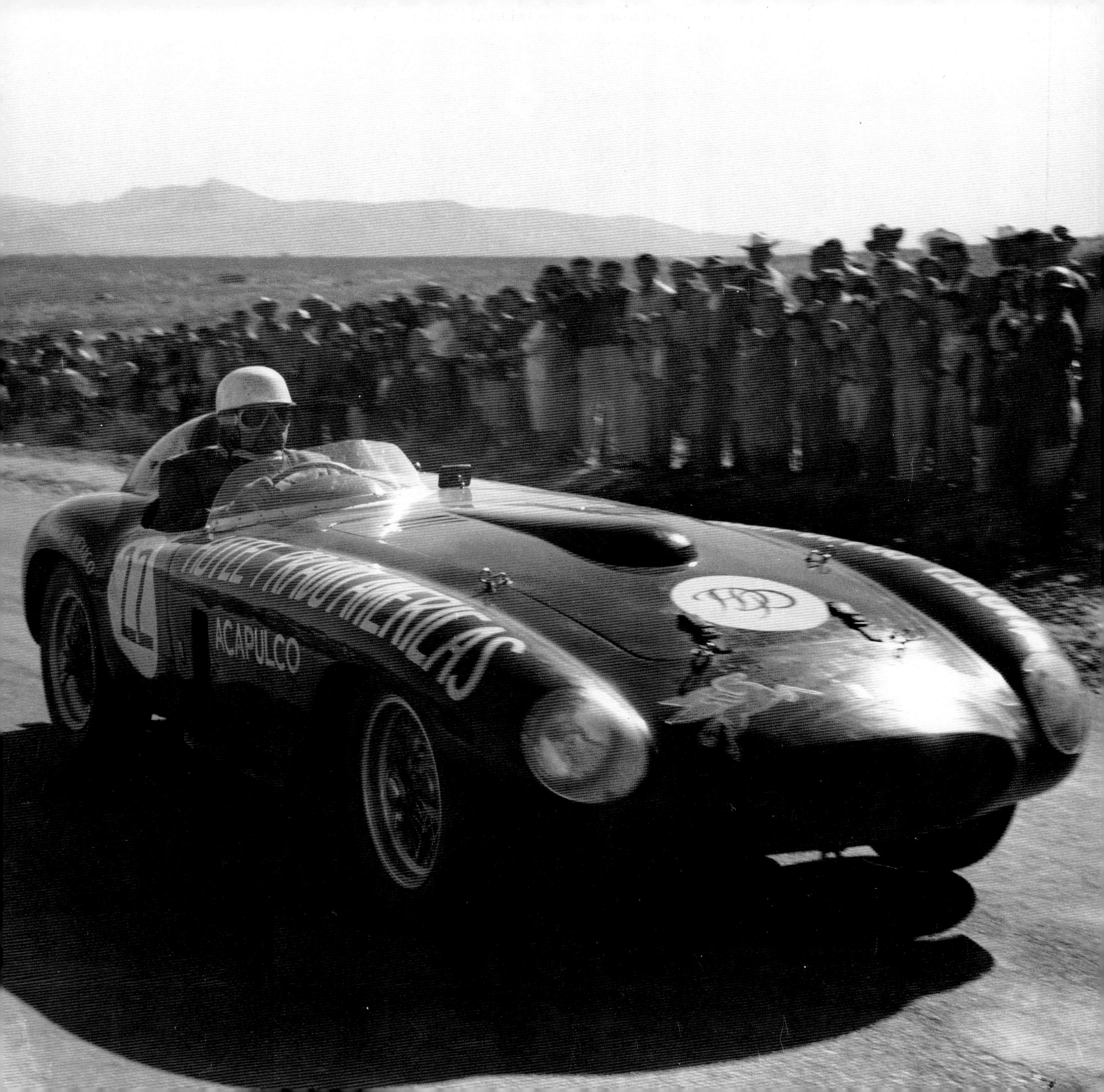
ACAPULCO

Previous page
Franco Cornacchia's Ferrari Monza was a hybrid, powered by a 2963cc V-12 from a 250 MM. Petersen Publishing

The battered Ferrari 375 MM of Phil Hill and Richie Ginther finishes in Léon after relinquishing the lead to the Ferrari of Umberto Maglioli. Petersen Publishing

Franco Cornacchia, Ferrari dealer and team leader, finished third in a Ferrari 750 Monza, nearly 2 hours behind winner Umberto Maglioli. Road & Track

Next page
Caballo slows down after the finish at Juárez as a crowd of well-wishers and photographers moves toward the car. Petersen Publishing

trip, but Maglioli's arm tired, and he let it go overboard a few miles from the finish.

Hill ran out of gas and was out of first place by 25 minutes; Chinetti took second on the leg and finally found the speed to pass Ensalada to take over fourth place in the race.

The Last Day of the Last Race

It was dawn outside Juárez; the usual fanatical faithful were bivouacked by the thousands so as not to miss the finish. By mid-morning, the annual mob was crowding the finish at the airport. Private planes were the first to pick out the red of Umberto Maglioli's Ferrari followed immediately by the blue and white of Phil Hill's.

139

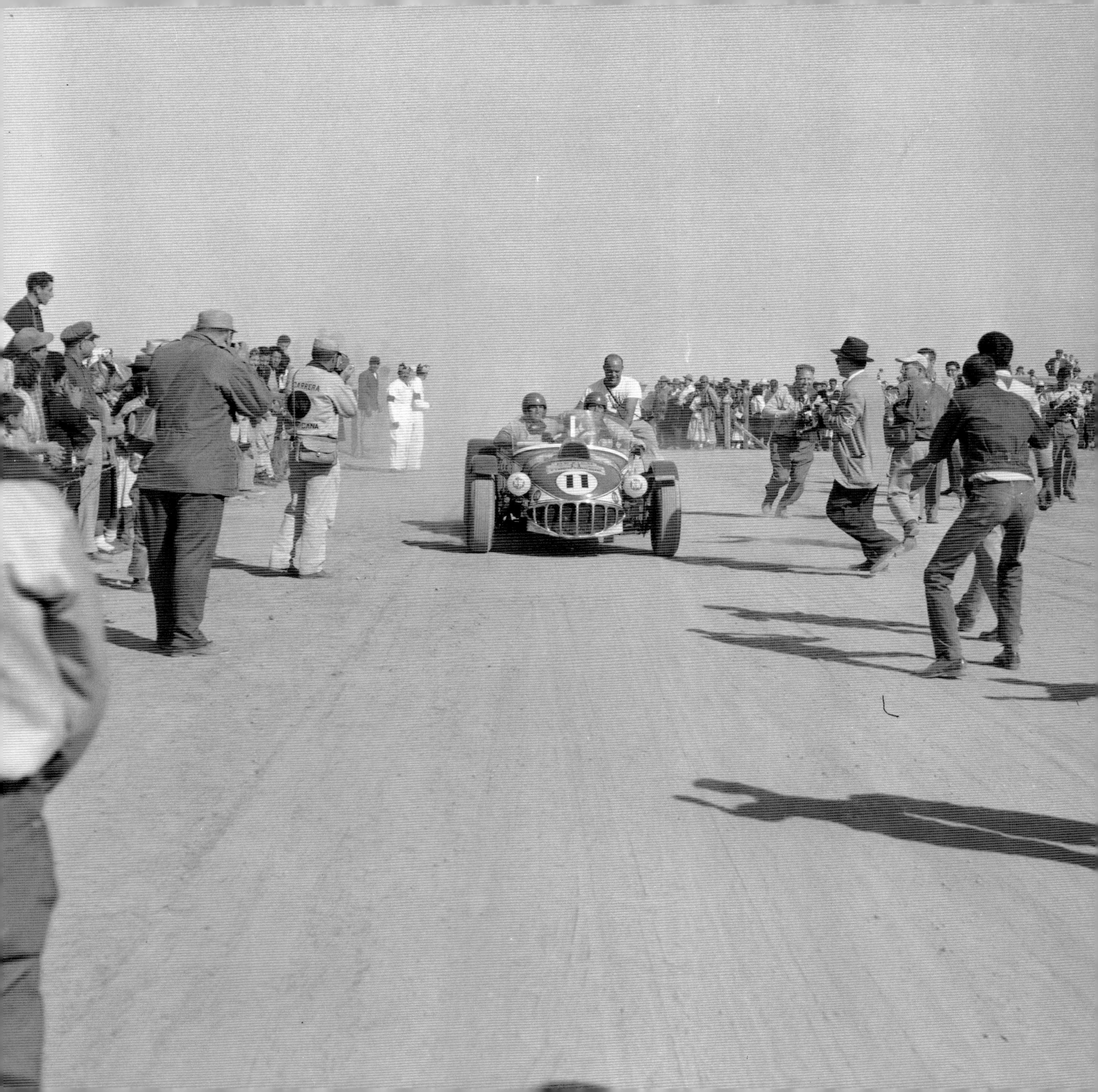
CARRERA
11

Hill won the final leg, but Maglioli had won the race by a 24-minute margin. He had averaged 107.9mph for the entire 1,908 miles, bettering Juan Manuel Fangio's 1953 time by 30 minutes. Franco Cornacchia swept by next, third in large sports but fifth overall. Hans Herrmann and Jaroslav Juhan in their Porsches flew by in formation for three-four overall and one-two in class, and then came Luigi Chinetti.

All eyes turned southward as Ak Miller approached the finish line to a waving and

Richie Ginther hands the route book to an official as he and Phil Hill finish a leg. Petersen Publishing

141

The 1954 rulebook.

wildly cheering crowd. His easy-going personality and incredulous homemade racer had won the respect and admiration of nearly everyone.

"We were really pleased with the finish," Miller remembered. "Just to be there was a thrill—to last the distance was exciting, and to get all that recognition . . . phenomenal! We even made a little money from prizes, but the great thing was that it opened doors we'd never got through before. It gave us credibility—not so much us as the sport. The hot rod sort of came of age there. The next year, we were invited to race in the Mille Miglia."

Winner Maglioli accepted the accolades of the press and his competitors, then, after a 3-hour rest, left for México City and the awards banquet. He collected about 225,000 pesos ($18,000) for his efforts, and the car left immediately for the Bahamas so that its owner, Erwin Goldschmidt, could drive it in a race there.

Hill and Richie Ginther had finally broken into the top ranks of racing. Neither had ever been classified as a pro: Hill was described as a "technical advisor to a film studio" while Ginther's occupation was listed as mechanic. Both men, of course, went on to bigger and better things, ironically getting started with Chinetti, Ferrari's American importer. Hill would be World champion for Ferrari seven years later; Ginther was second in the 1963 championship and won his only Grand Prix, and Honda's first, in 1965—in Mexico.

Plans were made for 1955: it would be the biggest, longest, and toughest road race in the world.

Duane Carter's Kurtis-Oldsmobile aims at Oaxaca on leg one. Unfortunately, the engine failed before Carter reached his goal. Don Downie

Chapter 10

1954 Carrera Panamericana V: Small Sports Class

Porsche Comes Of Age

The Porsche of British-born Mexican actress Jacqueline Evans de Lopez featured a memorial portrait of Eva Peron, the wife of the Argentine dictator who had died in 1952. Dave Friedman

After the less-than-perfect Porsche victory of 1953—when the private entries of Jose Herrarte and Fernando Segura were the only survivors in a fifteen-car class—Porsche made careful preparations for 1954 that would ensure its cars' lasting reliability. Leading the way was the new four-cam engine of 110 DIN hp (132 gross SAE hp), which had class wins at Le Mans, Mille Miglia, and Silverstone already to its credit.

The Spyder that Karl Kling had retired last year in Mexico, 550-04, would be driven by Hans Herrmann under the sponsorship banner of Fletcher Aviation, a Pasadena, California, manufacturer with production ties to the Stuttgart company. Fletcher would also supply Porsche's 190mph single-engine Navion and pilot-journalist-photographer Don Downie to fly support for the race team.

Two new Spyders, numbers 05 and 06, were entered by Jaroslav Juhan and Segura. During the past twelve months, Juhan had sold his 550-01 to Salvador Lopez-Chavez with its original pushrod engine, and Lopez-Chavez entered it under sponsorship of his company, the largest shoe manufacturer in Mexico.

In addition, three 356 coupes backed up the team, including one driven by Jacqueline Evans de Lopez, who had purchased the Gmünd coupe driven previously by Joaquin del Castillo; the Porsche group was close-knit.

Rounding out small sports were the OSCAs of Louis Chiron, Roberto Mieres, and Manfredo Lippmann. The MT4-1500s were proven giant killers: an OSCA owned by Briggs Cunningham and driven by Stirling Moss had won the Sebring 12-Hour Endurance outright earlier that year by three laps over a Lancia—besides topping the Index of Performance—and three more OSCAs came in fourth, fifth, and eighth, so the make had to be considered a serious contender. Its 1.5 liter double-overhead-cam four-cylinder engine produced 120hp at 6300rpm, and at 1,280lb, the Spyder could exceed 125mph.

The Borgward RS 55s of Karl Bechem and Franz Hammenick posed a threat, as well. The Hansa-derived 1500cc engine had been replaced by a new powerplant with Bosch direct fuel injection, 115hp, and again five-speed transmissions.

A total of 175,000 pesos ($14,000) was set aside for the purse in *Clase sport menor,* and the group had been moved from its former starting position behind the big stocks to a more judicious spot after the big sports cars.

Lopez-Chavez led the small sports starters on leg one from Tuxtla. Porsche—which was

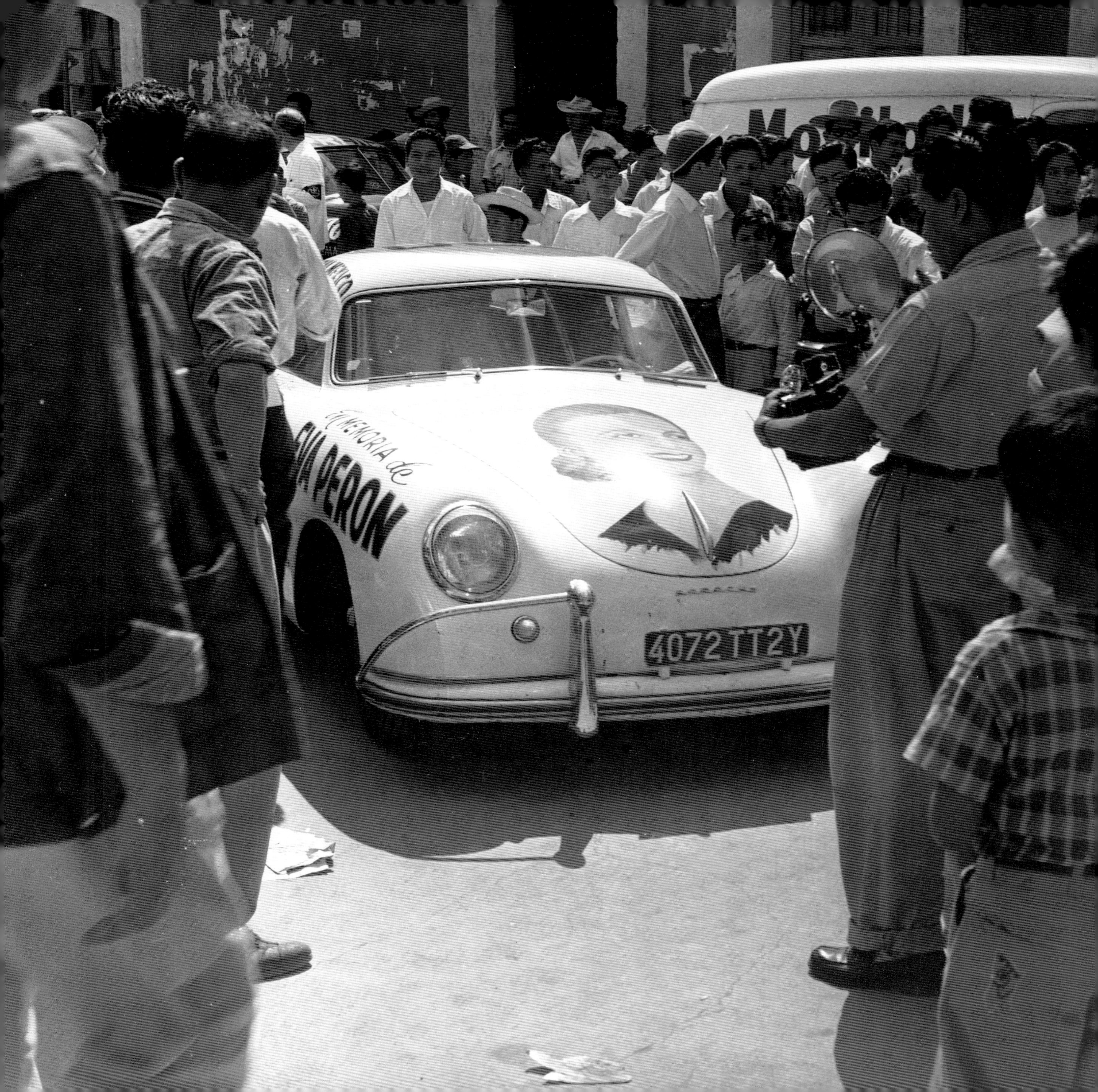

MEMORIA de
PERON
4072 TT2Y

The victorious Porsche team poses after the finish at Juárez with the 550s of Hans Herrmann and Jaroslav Juhan. From left, relief driver Herbert Linge, Herrmann, Juhan, mechanic Werner Enz, Fernando Segura, and mechanic Sigmund Muyerlien. Don Downie

worried more about the OSCAs than the Borgwards—had underestimated the competition. Bechem's Borgward beat Juhan's Porsche to Oaxaca, both hot on the heels of the Ferraris of Phil Hill and Umberto Maglioli. Bechem had bested Kling's 1953 class time by 7 minutes. Segura, who finished sixth, hit a dog as he crossed the finish line and damaged his Porsche. Herrmann lost time changing two Dunlop tires by himself, and drove the last 45 miles with one treadless tire.

At the completion of each leg, all cars received 1 hour for refueling, repairs, and tire changes, then were sealed and impounded for the night.

The second day, Bechem kept Borgward's hopes alive by winning leg two from Oaxaca to Puebla and increased his lead over Juhan to 7 minutes, 18 seconds. Herrmann went to work closing the 26-minute gap between himself and the leader as he advanced from fifth to third in class.

Bechem's teammate Hammenick flipped his Borgward and suffered a broken shoulder. Lippmann's OSCA was out, and the field had already shrunk to nine.

The comparatively short downhill run of 81 miles to México City was duck soup for the Ferraris, but the class act was Chiron, his OSCA finishing just 3 minutes behind the overall leg winner, Hill. Chiron had eclipsed the light sports record by nearly 9 minutes and stood fourth in class, sixth overall in the race.

Bechem still led the class, despite hitting a dog and demolishing his left front fender, but Juhan chopped the distance between them to 1 minute, 30 seconds. Herrmann, still third, now trailed Juhan by 19 minutes, which meant

The Borgward RS 55 of Karl Bechem crosses a river near Tehuantepec—the lowest point on the 1,908-mile course. The 1500cc fuel-injected sports racer led the light sports cars until crashing north of Mexico City. Don Downie

1954 Small Sports Category Model Factory Specifications

Model	Price	Engine	Ci	Hp	Weight	Top Speed
Borgward RS 55	NA	Ohv 4	91.1	115	NA	NA
OSCA MT-4 1500	$10,000	Dohc 4	90.9	110	1,280lb	124mph
Porsche 356S	$3,495	Ohv O-4	90.8	70	NA	120
Porsche 550	NA	Dohc O-4	90.8	110	NA	140

Jaroslav Juhan waits to start in his Porsche 550 at Tuxtla Gutiérrez. The Spyder, chassis number 05, was one of the two equipped with the new four-cam engine. Don Downie

Entry Rules Summary For 1954 Small Sports Cars

Limited to 50 entries. Entry fee 3,500 pesos ($280.00). Cars up to 1,500cc displacement (750cc with supercharger). Pump fuel is mandatory. Engine may not be replaced, but unlimited time is allowed between each day's run for servicing and repair. Approved racing helmets must be worn, and seat belts are mandatory only on closed cars.

Prizes

Placing	Prize
First	50,000 pesos ($4,000)
Second	35,000 pesos ($2,800)
Third	20,000 pesos ($1,600)
Fourth	13,000 pesos ($1,040)
Fifth	10,000 pesos ($800)
Sixth through tenth	Each 5,000 pesos ($400)
Winner of each leg	1,500 pesos ($120)
Top Mexican driver	10,000 pesos ($800)

Maximum Allowable Times

Leg	Miles	Time
1. Tuxtla Gutiérrez-Oaxaca	329.40	6:00
2. Oaxaca-Puebla	252.95	5:00
3. Puebla-México City	75.13	1:35
4. México City-Léon	261.03	4:15
5. Léon-Durango	329.40	5:00
6. Durango-Parral	251.09	4:00
7. Parral-Chihuahua	186.47	2:45
8. Chihuahua-Ciudad Juárez	222.51	3:00

he had gained 7 minutes on the short run. Mieres' OSCA dropped out with engine problems.

On leg four between México City and Léon, the three-way rivalry in small sports suddenly became an intrarace contest between the Porsches of Juhan and Herrmann when Bechem spun out and crashed the surviving Borgward. To add insult to injury, two following cars duplicated the accident, hampering aid for the injured driver.

Chiron was now Porsche's only threat. The class had deteriorated to seven cars, and six of them were Porsches. Herrmann won the leg and moved to second for the race behind Juhan, whose lead had dwindled to 12 minutes. Chiron was third overall, and Segura fourth.

The race tightened up on leg five as Herrmann took leg honors for the second time in one day, narrowing Juhan's overall lead to slightly more than 8 minutes. Juhan's Porsche had slowed down with a seized valve, and Herrmann chopped off 4 more minutes in winning the leg. Otto Beckert Estrada was last in the class, with an accumulated time 4 hours back of the leader.

An exhausted Segura passed the wheel of his 550 to mechanic Herbert Linge as Herrmann won the lap from Durango to Parral and had Juhan in his sights. Juhan and Herrmann were still lying third and fourth overall—

Hans Herrmann posed with citizens in Tuxtla Gutiérrez several days before the start of Carrera V. The Porsche 550 was the same car Karl Kling had failed to finish in, in 1953. Don Downie

A bit delicate for the rigors of Mexico was this special based on an MG TC built and driven by El Pasoan Jim Cassidy. It broke on leg one. Cliff Trissel photo, Jim Cassidy collection

Hans Herrmann and Jaroslav Juhan fly in formation across the Juárez finish line, first and second in class, third and fourth overall. Petersen Publishing

behind the Ferraris by 1.5 hours but ahead of the rest of the big sports and stock cars.

On leg seven, Herrmann nearly did it to Juhan, moving to within 23 seconds of the other Porsche driver. In consistent form, he won the leg in record-breaking time, averaging 121mph. If he continued to drive the last leg at the rate he'd been charging for the last 1,000 miles, a victory for him would be ensured, but Porsche Racing Director Huschke von Hanstein called on the drivers to avoid a useless duel that could send the one-two victory up in smoke, especially since the lead cars' engines were beginning to fade.

150

As the largest crowd in Carrera history watched the finish at Juárez in person and on television, the Ferraris of Maglioli and Hill flashed across the finish line at 140mph, followed by Luigi Chinetti, Franco Cornacchia, and Ak Miller. Then came the silver cars of Herrmann, Segura, and Juhan.

Herrmann had picked up nearly a minute on Juhan on the last leg and won the class by 36 seconds—a narrow margin after 19.5 hours of racing the length of a country! His last lap average was 116mph. Chiron finished the race third, followed by Segura and Linge.

Porsche had lived up to its management's expectations that year in Mexico. Its reputation for reliability was beginning to be heard—it had come of age in endurance racing.

Louis Chiron won the Puebla-Mexico City leg in his 1491cc OSCA, besting Jaroslav Juhan's 1953 Porsche record by 9 minutes and 8mph. Petersen Publishing

Jaroslav Juhan, shown here north of Oaxaca, followed the Porsche 550 of Hans Hermann by half a minute at the finish of the race. Mobil Oil Corporation

Mobiloil
CIUDAD JUAREZ
meta
CIUDAD JUAREZ CHIH.
PRENSA
RADIO
C. JUAREZ CHIH.

Chapter 11

1954 Carrera Panamericana V: Small Stock Class

The Stocks Split At The Back Of The Pack

Over half of the 149 entries in the fifth Mexican Road Race were in *turismo especial,* the midsize American car class that had originated in the 1953 event, and a new class, *turismo Europeo* or "European touring stock class," a category for under-2000cc sedans of European manufacture. Sixty-eight American stock cars and nineteen European models were entered by a variety of drivers, and each class would have both leg and overall winners. Although the best individual leg times netted only 1,500 pesos ($120), each class had purses of 50,000 pesos ($4,000), 35,000 pesos ($2,800), and 20,000 pesos ($1,600) for the first three positions, down to a more modest $400 for sixth through tenth place in the final standing.

Eligible models for special stock were termed medium displacement and limited by advertised horsepower. This class included the 90–115hp L-head and overhead-valve fours and sixes of Chevrolet, De Soto, Dodge, Henry J, Ford, Hudson Jet, Kaiser, Nash, Plymouth, Pontiac, Studebaker, and Willys Aero, and the 241ci 150hp V-8s of Dodge, 239ci 130hp V-8s of Ford, and 232ci 120hp V-8s of Studebaker.

The most notable driver in the class was 1951 Pan-Am winner Piero Taruffi, who was driving a Ford six. California speed specialist Mickey Thompson entered a V-8 version, and 1953 small stock winner C. D. Evans moved from a Chevy to a Dodge V-8.

A special Argentinean law that allowed its citizens to import autos duty free induced forty-one largely unqualified drivers to enter the class, much to the disgust of more serious racers.

The European stock class was dominated by Alfa Romeo 1900 TIs, which totaled eleven of the nineteen entries. Six Alfas were official factory entries, assigned to Consalvo Sanesi, an Alfa Formula One and test driver; Sergio Mantovani, a Formula One driver for Maserati; Piero Carini, an Italian touring champion; Mario della Favera; Jose Solona; and Bruno Bonini, Felice Bonetto's codriver in the 1950 race. The balance of the Alfas were private entries. The 1884cc twin-cam fours put out 100hp with two twin-choke Weber carburetors.

The only direct adversary to the Alfas was a lone Borgward Isabella entered by factory driver Adolph Brudes. It could manage only 60hp and an 85mph top speed—however, it was not the slowest in the class.

That honor belonged to a squadron of 31hp Volkswagen 1200s. Although they were not considered competitive, the Mexican importer,

By the time the squadron of 1200cc 36hp Volkswagens finished, the sun was low and the crowd at Juárez was sparse. Running with sealed engines and transmissions, all seven of the VWs that started the race finished, averaging over 60mph for the 1,930 miles. Don Downie

Scott Yantis' Studebaker finishes at Oaxaca in 13th place among small stocks. Yantis had moved to fifth in class—31st overall—by the finish in Juárez. Don Downie

managed by Prince Alfonso von Hohenlohe, wanted to demonstrate their reliability. To prove the point, the engines and gearboxes were sealed at the start, and von Hohenlohe said that oil would be neither changed nor added during the race. Prince Al headed the team of mostly Mexican drivers.

Thompson averaged 75mph to beat out the Ford of Dan Morgan and won leg one in the small stocks, well ahead of Taruffi, who finished eleventh. Sanesi's car led the first of the five official Alfas at an average of over 78mph for the 329 miles in the Euroclass. One Alfa was eliminated with mechanical difficulties, and Brudes' vehicle was tenth, ahead of only the Volkswagens.

On the second leg, the American stock cars finished in front of the Alfas, and Argentine Oscar Calaben was fastest, followed by a charging Taruffi, who moved to third for the race. Thompson suffered valve trouble and finished last in the class, falling to eighth for the average.

1954 Small Stock Category Model Factory Specifications

Model	Price	Engine	Ci	Hp	Weight	Top Speed
Alfa Romeo 1900 T	NA	Dohc 4	120.5	115	NA	112mph
Chevrolet 2dr	$1,782	Ohv 6	235.5	115-125	3,185lb	92
Dodge Coronet	$2,198	Ohv V-8	241	150	3,345	95
Ford 2dr	$1,728	Ohv V-8	239	130	3,207	87
Ford 2dr	NA	Ohv 6	223	115	3,086	93
Studebaker 2dr	$2,287	Ohv V-8	232.6	127	NA	NA
Volkswagen 1200	$1,595	Ohv O-4	72.7	36	1,540	68

Entry Rules Summary For 1954
Turismo Especial and *Turismo Europeo*

Limited to 50 entries. Entry fee 3,500 pesos ($280.00). Same rules apply as on unlimited touring cars.

Turismo Especial
Cars under 3500cc, although Dodge and Studebaker V-8s are allowed. Jaguar Mk VII specifically barred.

Turismo Europeo
English and European sedans with engines up to 2000cc; production sedans with four seats if over 1.0 liter and two seats if less than 1.0 liter.

Prizes (Each Category)

Placing	Prize
First	50,000 pesos ($4,000)
Second	35,000 pesos ($2,800)
Third	20,000 pesos ($1,600)
Fourth	13,000 pesos ($1,040)
Fifth	10,000 pesos ($800)
Sixth through tenth	Each 5,000 pesos (400)
Winner of each leg	1,500 pesos ($120)
Top Mexican driver	10,000 pesos ($800)

Maximum Allowable Times (Each Category)

Leg	Miles	Time
1. Tuxtla Gutiérrez-Oaxaca	329.40	6:30
2. Oaxaca-Puebla	252.95	5:45
3. Puebla-México City	75.13	2:05
4. México City-Léon	261.03	4:45
5. Léon-Durango	329.40	5:45
6. Durango-Parral	251.09	4:30
7. Parral-Chihuahua	186.42	3:00
8. Chihuahua-Ciudad Juárez	222.51	3:30

The finish line at Oaxaca was in front of the parque de beisboll, or baseball park. Bayonet-equipped soldiers guarded the course. Don Downie

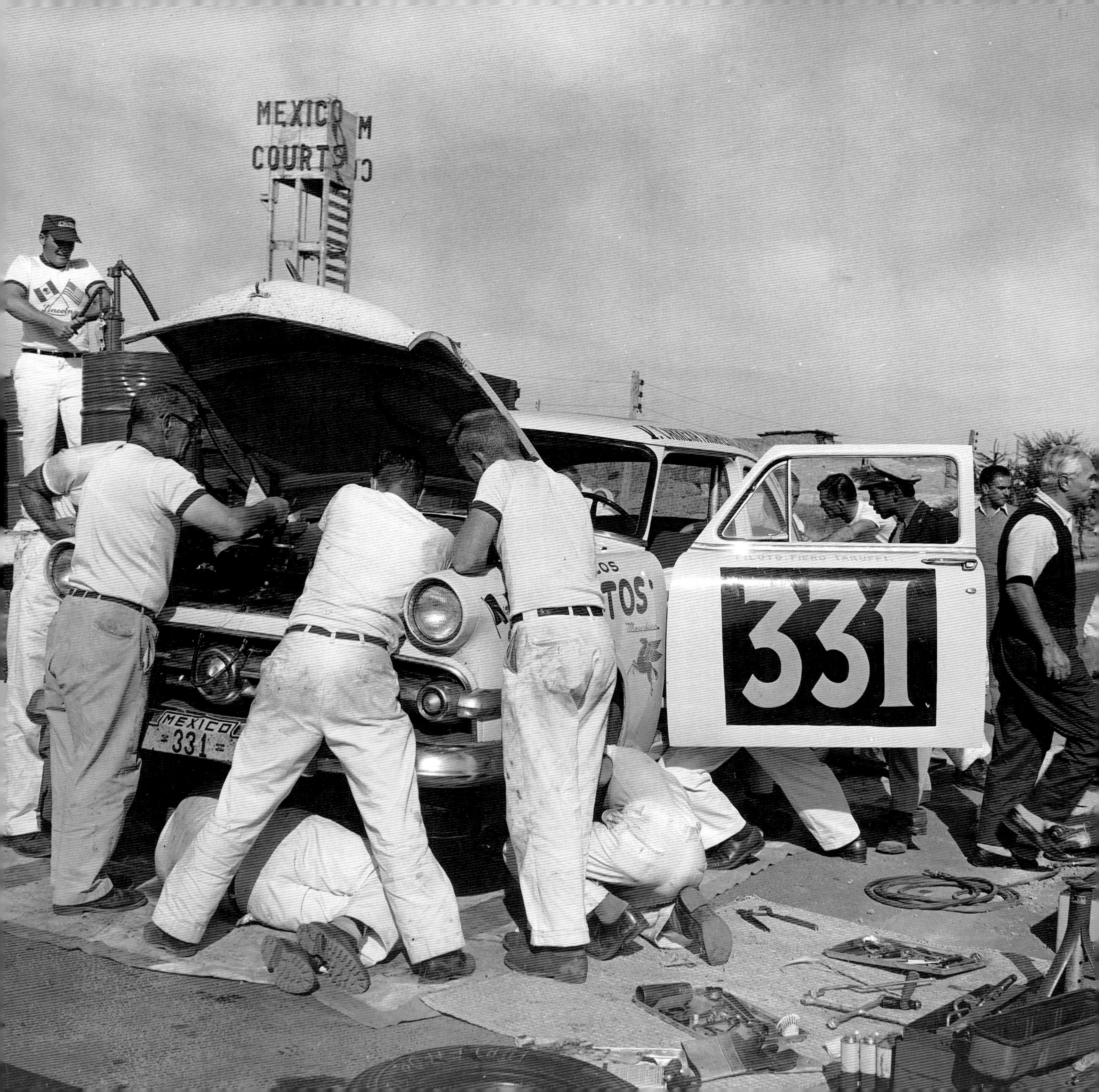
MEXICO
COURTS
331
MEXICO
331

Montovani won in European stocks, leading della Favera, Sanesi, Bonini, and three other Alfa drivers. On the leg into México City, Guatemalan David Cerezo's Alfa plunged off a bridge at San Martin de Temehucan, and another Alfa was eliminated with mechanical trouble. Brudes' Borgward was in ninety-first position overall, already more than 3 hours behind race leader Phil Hill's car after only 657 miles.

The nimble Alfa of Sanesi beat all but one of the big stock cars into the capital and was sitting eleventh overall in the race, still first in its class. The flatter and faster course sections to the north, however, were obviously going to favor the large-displacement cars.

Tommy Drisdale won the next leg, securing his fourth-place position in light stocks. Calaben, who had been leading at

The first five finishers in the European stock car class were Alfa Romeo 1900 Ts. Here, fifth-place Adolpho Valezquez speeds toward Durango. Don Downie

Mickey Thompson, center, supervises work on his Ford after his leg one win in light stocks. Petersen Publishing

*Previous page
Piero Taruffi exits his Ford, right, as Lincoln mechanics swarm over the car during the 1-hour limit for service and repair at Mexico City. The Italian placed eighth in class, 34th overall.* Max Ellis collection

157

Consalvo Sanesi led the group of Alfa Romeo 1900 Ts that swept the first five places in European touring class. Petersen Publishing

Oscar Calaben's Ford Six was an early threat in small stocks, but he finished the race in seventh. Mobil Oil Corporation

México City in his Ford, reached Léon in ninth and lost first place to the Ford of Morgan. Thompson suffered a rollover in his Ford and retired.

By the fifth leg—Léon to Durango—Dodges began dominating the finishing order, with Drisdale, Evans, and Ramiro Aguilar in the first three positions, followed by drivers in two Studebakers and a Chevrolet and then three more Dodges. Although Morgan was holding onto second overall, his grip was loosening as the flat desert roads raised speeds beyond his capability.

Little change in order was seen among the European sedans, as Alfas continued in the top five spots.

Drisdale took over the lead in his Dodge at Durango, winning the leg over Evans, who was nearly 42 minutes behind, sitting in sixth for the race. Morgan maintained second for the

El Abuelito, or The Flying Grandfather, C. D. Evans, competed in all five races, drove four different makes of car, and captured a first and second in class. Petersen Publishing

distance but by a quickly shrinking margin. Ray Elliott replaced Drisdale in third overall.

Also at Durango, Bonini had to withdraw after a flat tire damaged his Alfa's suspension.

Evans set the best time into Chihuahua in his Dodge, ahead of class leader Drisdale. In the European group, Sanesi captured his fourth and last leg victory.

Dodge and Alfa Romeo Win the Day

The leg to Juárez was won by Evans in *turismo especial,* but the overall victory went to Drisdale with an 84.42mph average speed, followed by Elliott and Alvarez Tostado, all in Dodges, and Scott Yantis in a Studebaker.

In the European stock class, the Alfa of Sanesi won, besting the American light stocks by over 45 minutes, averaging 87.33mph and finishing fifteenth overall. Of the eight Alfas that started, five had reached the river.

Brudes' Borgward took sixth place—seventy-third overall—ahead of the seven Volkswagens. The diminutive rear-engine, air-cooled sedans had taken roughly half a day longer in elapsed time to finish the race than the winning Ferrari, but to their credit, the VWs had admirably accomplished their mission. They had driven flat out across nearly the entire length of Mexico without any maintenance or a single mishap, and they had done it at a respectable average speed of 63mph.

Consalvo Sanesi, Alfa Formula 1 and test driver, negotiates the Pan-Am course through a city in his 1900 TI. Mobil Oil Corporation

159

STEVENSON

Chapter 12

1954 Carrera Panamericana V: Large Stock Class

Some Kinda Hero!

Ray Crawford had been haunting the Lincoln camp for a car ever since 1952, but he couldn't seem to make the team. Clay Smith had been tragically killed in a pit accident at DuQuoin, Illinois, on Labor Day just two months before the 1954 Pan-Am was to start. Bill Stroppe was understandably dispirited; he didn't have the will to manage the team with the verve that was present when he and Smith had shared the job. Chuck Stevenson and Chuck Daigh appointed themselves titular team leaders, and Stroppe quietly managed the overall effort. In spite of their loss, they still expected to win.

The Lincoln Boys

The Lincoln team roster read like an all-star line-up: Bill Vukovich (whom the press had somewhat justifiably nicknamed *Ruso Loco* or the Mad Russian, and who had that spring won the Indianapolis 500 for the second consecutive year), Chuck Stevenson, Walt Faulkner, Jack McGrath (who was third at the 1954 Indy), Manuel Ayulo, and Johnny Mantz —three national champions, and drivers who had placed in the top three spots in the Pan-Am the last two years!

In addition, Mexican Fernando Leeuw Murphy and Californian Ray Crawford rounded out the crew of drivers for the Bill Stroppe-prepared Lincolns in the field. Although Crawford was still paying his own way, he was afforded the same privileges as the rest of the team drivers.

Rules called for no variation in weight from stock, so while the 4,250lb Lincolns were lightened by removing unnecessary accessories, the pounds were added back with safety equipment. As in 1953, the engines were blue-printed, dual shock absorbers were used at the front and airlifts at the rear, and the rear ends were raised 4in for better control. New for 1954 were six-ply tubeless tires—inflated with nitrogen to maintain constant pressure despite the changes in temperature—and 12in ribbed brake drums replacing the previous 11in plain drums. While the Lincolns didn't have the then-new power steering option, they were all equipped with power brakes.

Crawford's car was prepared by Stroppe alongside the team cars, and Crawford was paying the team for the use of various facilities—such as the tire stops—although he had his own crew of mechanics.

"The first time I ever saw the cars was on one of the trucks coming into México City," Crawford recalled. "There were probably sixty crew members and five trucks. Ricky Ingesias

On the other side, the Stevenson sign read Vukovich, and that's Bill Vukovich tightening the lug nuts while codriver Vern Houle works the other side of the Lincoln at the special tire stop. The two changed all four tires in 2 minutes, 30 seconds. Max Ellis collection

Bill Vukovich was in second place in unlimited stocks when he flew off a 150ft cliff and somersaulted onto a ledge below the road north of Oaxaca, destroying his Lincoln but escaping injury. What did hurt Vuky, however, was the Lincoln Team custom that if the cars survived the race, they were restored to street condition and awarded to the drivers for their personal transportation. Don Downie

*Next page
When Ray Crawford arrived in Mexico City, Lincoln mechanics took over his car. His standing with the team had improved dramatically—the man watching at right in the dark coat and plaid shirt is Ford Motor Company boss Benson Ford.* Max Ellis collection

The Buick Centuries of Fernando Razo Maciel and Pat Zoccano presented a minor threat to the leaders; by Mexico City, Zoccano had moved to fifth in class, behind the Lincolns and Cadillacs. Don Downie

[Crawford's codriver] and I took it out to check things over, and we went around a corner, and it started to knock! We stopped, and Ricky retarded the spark. I told him Stroppe had set it up that way, but he said we would burn up the engine if we didn't change it!"

Rules had changed for Carrera V: the time allowed for repairs after each leg was reduced to 1 hour after arrival at Oaxaca, Durango, and Chihuahua, but 2 hours were permitted at México City for small repairs, refueling, and tire changing. Lincoln responded by installing compressed air jacks on its team cars and drilling the driver and codriver on tire changes. Each team car was painted a different color for quick crew identification; even the

162

163

Bill Stroppe, right, explains the first-leg tire stop to drivers and codrivers in Tuxtla Gutiérrez. Peering over Stroppe's shoulder and still eating breakfast is Walt Faulkner; behind him is Fernando Leeuw Murphy; to the left are Johnny Mantz and Chuck Daigh. In the foreground with his back to the camera is Ray Crawford; Mickey Thompson is at the far left; directly in front of Thompson are Bill Vukovich, in the dark shirt, and Jack McGrath. Road & Track

color of the tools and wheels matched that of the car they belonged with.

In the typical lemming fashion that seems to pervade racing, many drivers had been switching to Lincoln ever since its first victory in 1952, hoping that they could buy some kind of a win. They apparently didn't realize that Clay Smith and Stroppe—not the cars—created the legend with hundreds of modifications, mostly within the rules, and thousands of hours preparing and working on details.

The scheme had reversed since the first race in 1950, when Cadillac entries outnumbered Lincoln, but with the advent of the latter's new overhead-valve V-8 and its subsequent victories, Lincoln dominated the stock car field in Mexico. The 1954 Cadillac held the Hottest Car title in *Motor Trend* magazine's testing with an advertised 230hp. Even though its delivered weight was 100lb higher than that of the comparable Lincoln, both makes had identical quarter-mile times of 18.4 seconds; the Cadillac's published top speed of 113mph bettered the Capri's by only 2mph. Despite the Cadillac's basically good performance, only two examples were entered in Carrera V, driven by racing veterans Edward Stringer and Keith Andrews.

Buick's new 322ci V-8 might provide some competition as well, especially the Century, which had the 195hp Roadmaster engine in the lighter Special chassis.

Chrysler had finally adapted a four-barrel carburetor to its Hemi engine and advertised

235hp. Packard had somehow managed 212hp from its straight eight, but each of these contenders had an unsophisticated suspension and a 2-ton chassis.

Most drivers said their principal tactic would be to survive safely into México City and then settle any arguments in the deserts to the north, where speed could make up for a lot of time lost in the mountains.

A Time of Surprises

Lincoln had the first seven starting positions locked up, so Ray Crawford asked for the very last stock car number: 149.

"I figured if I started behind everybody and passed someone, I might get some good pictures with my movie camera," he explained. "Also, I didn't want to have to hassle with the Lincoln boys if I was going to do well."

There are a couple of versions of what happened next. The official version says that at Tuxtla, there was a large concrete tank from which all the competitors drew their fuel. Most of the year, the tank contained low-grade fuel. When race time came, officials filled it with a better grade. But in 1954, it apparently didn't get completely emptied before they put in the

The Lincoln Team chuckwagon gets ready for the day's business of feeding factory drivers and mechanics in Mexico. About 80 people made up the race crews that utilized the rolling restaurant; an additional 40 public relations people and visiting executives had to fend for themselves. Max Ellis collection

165

Jack McGrath and codriver Manuel Ayulo pose confidently with their Lincoln before the start. The two had placed third in the 1953 Pan-Am and shared a third at Indianapolis in 1951, and McGrath was again third in the 1954 Indy 500. In Carrera V, their Lincoln went over a cliff in the opening leg, although neither man was hurt. Max Ellis collection

good stuff. The result was a mixture of good and bad—mediocre—fuel.

The other version, from writer-photographer Dean Batchelor, says that the lines for fuel were so long that Crawford and Walt Faulkner decided just to fill up at a local service station—although Lincoln team member Max Ellis disagrees, joking that Faulkner would have been too cheap to buy his own fuel.

In any case, good-quality fuel was essential because of the advanced timing Bill Stroppe used on the Lincolns. The team was carrying bottles of fuel additive, which they could use to boost octane, but they had been warned of a fuel check, so they discussed taking a chance. It is said that Crawford, Bill Vukovich, and Faulkner used the additive; the others didn't.

The Carrera Panamericana V stock car division led off with the Lincolns of Chuck Stevenson, Angel Acar, Johnny Mantz, and Faulkner, followed by Fernando Murphy, Jack McGrath, Vukovich, and the rest of the drivers for the twenty-nine-car field, including Crawford in the cleanup position.

Walt Faulkner had finished second and third in Mexico in previous years and was determined to win in 1954. Petersen Publishing

Ray Crawford crosses the finish line at Mexico City with a 6-minute lead over second-place Walt Faulkner. Petersen Publishing

167

The Lincoln entourage leaves Mexico City well before the racers, bound for Durango, the next night's stop. Max Ellis collection

Awaiting the arrival of the Lincoln team in Mexico City, mechanics prepare for the two leading cars of Ray Crawford and Walt Faulkner. Striding through the pits in a dark jacket is Chuck Daigh, a Lincoln codriver whose mount was among the victims on leg one. Max Ellis collection

At the team's only scheduled tire stop of the race—necessary because of the combination of the length of the leg, the road's abrasive surface, and the weight of the cars—the innovative air jacks paid off. Faulkner and his codriver changed all four tires in 3 minutes, 25 seconds. Shortly thereafter, Vukovich and Vern Houle arrived and broke the record by making a 2-minute, 30-second change.

But that was the high point for Team Lincoln; what else went on between Tuxtla Gutiérrez and Oaxaca was the usual scenario of frustration and danger. The first to go were the Lincolns of Mantz, Murphy, and defending champion Stevenson—all victims of burned pistons from the bad fuel. Then McGrath drove over a cliff and buried his car in the jungle.

Faulkner's vehicle, number 103—the third starter—was the first stock car to Oaxaca, trailed by the number 108 of Vukovich and the number 127 Cadillac of Keith Andrews and the number 110 of Ed Stringer. Then, incredibly, came number 149—the Lincoln of Crawford, who had passed twenty-four of the fastest stock cars in the world and had won the leg with a blistering 82.5mph average speed.

It may have had something to do with emotion, according to Crawford: "We'd practice and practice going into certain curves at certain speeds until we were sure we had it right. There was this little one-lane bridge on leg one at the end of a curve—it just had two planks that you had to hit just right. We wrote that one down at 80—*max*! During the race, we crossed it at 110!"

The wild ride gave Crawford a 1-minute lead over Vukovich and put him 2 minutes, 30 seconds over Andrews and almost 4 minutes in front of Faulkner. Of the seven-car Lincoln team that had begun the day, only two entries—plus Crawford's—were left, and they still had four days and 1,570 miles of racing to go.

During the 1 hour allowed for servicing after each leg, five men were assigned to each

1954 Large Stock Category Model Factory Specifications

Model	Price	Engine	Ci	Hp	Weight	Top Speed
Buick Century 2dr	$2,534	Ohv V-8	322	195	3,795lb	103mph
Cadillac 62 2dr	$3,838	Ohv V-8	331	230	4,347	113
Lincoln Capri 2dr	$3,869	Ohv V-8	317.5	205	4,250	110

Lincoln team car, each with a specific station and specific duties. The driver kept time, and the codriver checked off the list of things to do, crossing off each task as it was completed. Duties included checking—and replacing, if necessary—all four brakes and shock absorbers and the rear end, transmission, steering mechanism, axles, and engine. When these tasks were finished, the car was washed and wiped clean.

Pressure from the Competition

On the 253-mile second leg from Oaxaca to Puebla, the pressure was on Ray Crawford, who was being pursued by Bill Vukovich, who, in turn, had the Cadillac of Keith Andrews on his tail.

"We started out with Vukovich a minute behind us," Crawford remembered. "I assumed he was catching us pretty fast; my codriver was timing the interval between us, and he'd say, 'He's right on our tail!' But you know, he never passed me. I crossed the finish line, but Vuky never showed up!"

Vukovich had crested a hill near Petlacingo at 100mph and found a blind right-hand turn ahead. Unable to make the curve, he braked hard, skidded over a 150ft embankment, and somersaulted several times before coming to rest on a ledge below the road. He and codriver Vern Houle carefully climbed out the space where the rear window used to be and scrambled up to the highway. Vuky hitched a wild ride with Giovanni Bracco, whose Ferrari was already out of the race, but Houle elected to wait for a more leisurely journey aboard the Lincoln team van. Crawford won the leg, retaining the race lead, and was followed by Andrews and Walt Faulkner.

Crawford Makes the Team

When the Lincolns arrived in México City after leg three, instead of the armada that had started, only a pair was left. The hard-charging Walt Faulkner finished in record time ahead of Ray Crawford and Keith Andrews but was still second in his class.

"When I crossed the finish line," Crawford related, "A big Lincoln brass hopped in my car and directed me to the impound area where my five Mexican mechanics were waiting. Lincoln mechanics just pushed them aside and took

---

Entry Rules Summary For 1954 Unlimited Stock Cars

Limited to 100 entries. Entry fee 7,000 pesos ($560.00). 1951-1954 stock sedans of more than 3500cc displacement of which more than 600 have been produced in twelve months. Weight of each entry must be identical to an average of the same model as delivered from the factory. Modifications limited to brake lining, make of shock absorber, ignition coil, spark plugs, crankshaft balancing, overboring to 0.020in, and removal of mufflers. Any optionally listed axle ratio, but "export kits" are prohibited. Roll bars and extra fuel tanks are permitted. Pump fuel is mandatory, but only one hour mechanical attention is permitted between each day's run. Approved racing helmets and seat belts are required.

Prizes

Placing	Prize
First	200,000 pesos ($16,000)
Second	100,000 pesos ($8,000)
Third	40,000 pesos ($3,200)
Fourth	20,000 pesos ($1,600)
Fifth	15,000 pesos ($1,200)
Sixth through tenth	Each 7,000 pesos ($560)
Winner of each leg	5,000 pesos ($400)
Top Mexican driver	20,000 pesos ($1,600)

Maximum allowable times:

Leg	Miles	Time
1. Tuxtla Gutiérrez-Oaxaca	329.40	6:00
2. Oaxaca-Puebla	252.95	5:15
3. Puebla-México City	75.13	2:00
4. México City-Léon	261.03	4:15
5. Léon-Durango	329.40	5:15
6. Durango-Parral	251.09	4:00
7. Parral-Chihuahua	186.47	3:00
8. Chihuahua-Ciudad Juárez	222.51	3:30

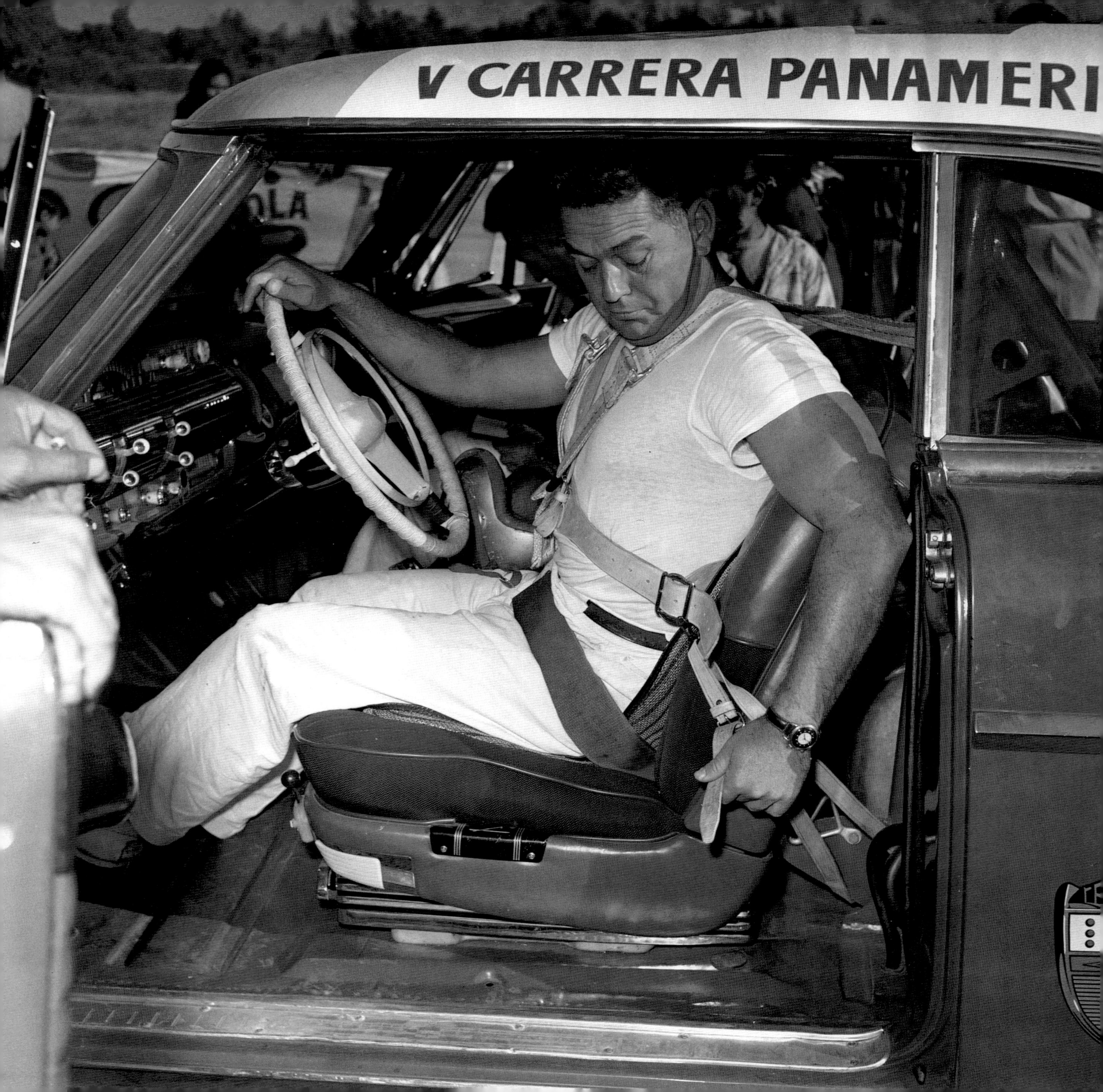
V CARRERA PANAMERI

Walt Faulkner and codriver Frank Hainley practice their tire-changing technique at the Lincoln "pop stand" pit. Petersen Publishing

*Previous page
Ray Crawford demonstrates the complex belting arrangement in the Lincoln team cars—which is essentially an inertia reel to allow necessary movements while keeping belts tight.* Petersen Publishing

The Ford-Lincoln armada arrives in Mexico City: a parts truck, foreground, the chuckwagon, and three transporters filled with race cars. Petersen Publishing

Coloradan Keith Andrews and Ed Stringer drove the only two Cadillacs entered in 1954. They placed third and fourth behind the Lincoln drivers. Petersen Publishing

171

Last-minute preparations are made to Ray Crawford's Lincoln in Tuxtla Gutiérrez before the start of the race.
Petersen Publishing

over. I guess they figured that since I was leading the race, I could join the team, and they could give me a little help!"

Because Crawford was at the head of the race, his Lincoln was the first stock car to leave México City, with the sole surviving team Lincoln, Faulkner's, 1 minute behind. "About 50 miles out, we ran into solid fog," Crawford said. "We had our map from Stroppe, and it showed maybe a 20-mile straight ahead, so we just drove flat out at 130mph! You couldn't see more than about 50ft. Just before we went into the fog, there was a Ferrari closing on Faulkner; it must have been going 40mph faster than he was. We went into the fog and never saw him again. When we came out of it, there was Faulkner, on our tail—hell, he was as crazy as I was! We had to assume there was nothing on the road, and there was no reason to assume that, because all the time there were cattle and horses and Mexican farmers jumping out of the bushes!"

Faulkner beat Crawford to Léon and shaved 2 minutes off his lead. He now trailed the supermarket owner by just 4 minutes, 5 seconds for the race. Pat Zoccano slipped his Buick into third on the leg, behind the second Lincoln.

Even though he was leading the race, Crawford was still acting the tourist—shooting movie film with the camera mounted on his Lincoln's dash. On leg five, he and Faulkner were bumper to bumper, sliding through corners together and generally dicing it up. Crawford kept the camera running, even though all that could be seen were the trunk and rear window of the other Lincoln and the two forms inside.

Faulkner won the leg from Durango to Léon and picked up another 30 seconds on Crawford, who finished second. Andrews stood third in the race, 9 minutes out of the lead.

Faulkner roared into Parral at the end of the sixth leg with a 96mph win and another 1-minute gain on Crawford, and Andrews pulled to within 6 minutes of Faulkner with a second-place finish. Ed Stringer was in fifth, and both Cadillacs were slowly slicing time from the Lincolns' lead. Zoccano, the only

Buick threat, was eliminated with transmission trouble.

Crawford could allow Faulkner his charge, having built up an early lead. He had maintained a smooth and even pace, not pushing his car, but keeping Faulkner in sight and under control.

Andrews won leg seven but was still 4 minutes behind Faulkner in elapsed time for the race. The Lincolns smoked into Chihuahua with Faulkner in the lead and Crawford drafting. It was evident from the horn honking and light flashing that Faulkner had run out of brakes, but that hadn't kept him from making up some more time on Crawford, who now led by only 3 minutes with 223 miles to go in the race.

At the finish line in Ciudad Juárez, the first of the big stocks arrived: Andrews, Faulkner, and Crawford, in that order. It was obvious that one of the three had won.

Andrews had started the last leg 7 minutes, 14 seconds out of first place, less than 3 minutes out of second. The Cadillacs had

Ray Crawford, left, and Enrique Iglesias. Petersen Publishing

173

proved to be faster on the straights than the Lincolns, but Crawford's early lead had prevailed, and he won the race, beating Faulkner by a little over a minute and Andrews by nearly 3 minutes. Crawford pocketed 210,000 pesos ($16,800), and Faulkner 120,000 pesos ($9,600) in leg and finish money.

"Fat, Dumb, and Happy"

After trying for five years, Ray Crawford had finally become successful in Mexico. And it was ironic, because Lincoln had never considered him good enough to be on the team.

But Crawford had the last laugh: he said the Ford Motor Company immediately bought his car from him, painted its team cars red to match his, and sent them all over the country for the next year or so for displays at dealers and car shows.

"Crawford was a good amateur racer," observed Ak Miller. "The Lincoln team was made up of top pros, and there was a world of difference in their comparative abilities, but Crawford had the good luck to see nearly the whole factory team fall apart at the start of the race, and he just motored on—fat, dumb, and happy. When he realized he was in the lead, something happened to him; he was on a 'high' and was able to perform miracles. Hell, he was driving at least 20 percent beyond his abilities once he got in the lead . . . and he knew it!"

Miller continued: "I don't want to take anything away from Ray, and I'm glad that circumstances let him win, but he was probably the luckiest guy in Mexico that year!"

"The next May," Crawford reminisced, "I went over to Indianapolis to watch the 500. I was standing in the pits talking to Sam Hanks —one of the best American drivers around— and this mob of Boy Scouts came wandering by, and they had just seen my Mexican Road Race film the night before. They all began to shout, 'There's Ray Crawford! There's Ray Crawford!' and asked for my autograph. And I said, 'Hey, guys, this here's Sam Hanks!' And this one kid replies, 'Oh?' And Sam says, 'God damn, Crawford—you win one little Mickey Mouse race, and you'd think you're some kinda hero!'"

Hanks had hit the nail on the head: on top of Lincoln's two previous sweeps of the race, Crawford's fortuitous victory had probably meant more credible publicity for the company than had ever been realized by the carefully planned and magnificently executed racing program that the factory had mounted.

From that time on, the 2-ton Capris of the early fifties have always been known as the "Road Race Lincolns," and Crawford as "some kinda hero."

Walt Faulkner and Frank Hainley prepare to leave Tuxtla Gutiérrez at the start of Carrera V. Mobil Oil Corporation

*Previous page
Jack McGrath, right, was third at Indy in 1954, and he and codriver Manuel Ayulo had also shared a third there in 1951.* Petersen Publishing

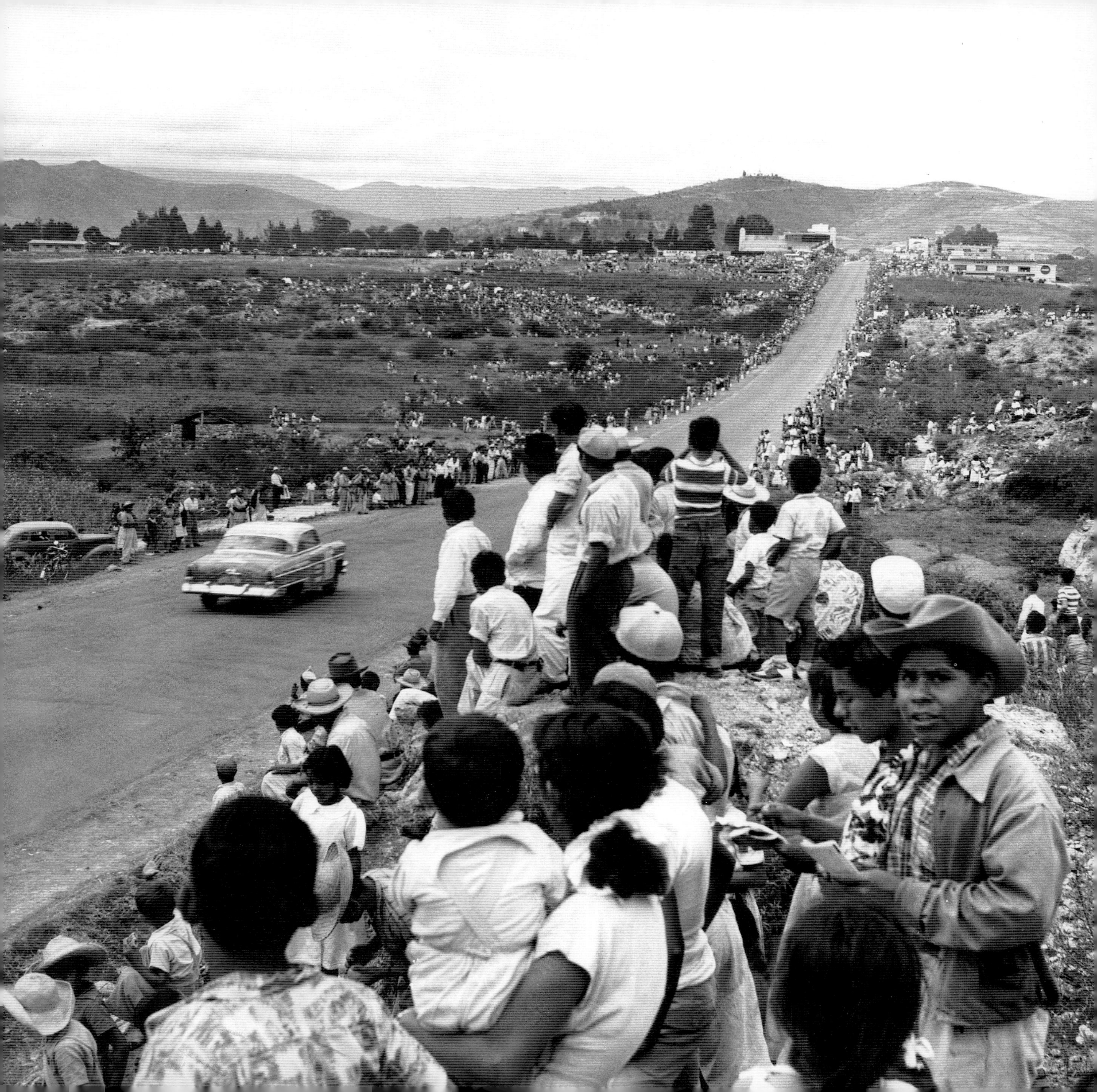

Epilogue

Postmortem

The Mexican Road Race had been conceived and born quickly, then lived a short and intense life before dying at the age of five.

After the 1954 event, pressure to halt the carnage descended on the race committee from both church and state. Not a year had passed without at least two lives being lost: nine had died in 1953, a total of twenty-six in five years, most of them bystanders. Clearly, the Pan-Am was as dangerous for spectators as it was for drivers.

The half decade over which the race was run spanned what was arguably the most exciting development period in motor racing history. The rather uninspired sedans and modest sports cars that competed in the first race were supplanted by a succession of sophisticated and innovative chassis and engines; by 1954, some models featured more than twice the power of their 1950 versions. Since the "City of Roses" Oldsmobile's first win at 78mph, speeds had risen dramatically: the Ferrari's Carrera V average was nearly 30mph faster, and some cars were capable of 180mph on the desert straights.

The biggest shock to Americans and Europeans participating in the race was the Mexican way of doing everything—business, politics, law—and the country's style and attitudes. To Americans, everything seemed upside down. Overt bribery of everyone from hotel clerks to race officials seemed the norm, the law presumed you guilty until you could prove otherwise, gross incompetence appeared to be a prerequisite to an important station, and diarrhea was simply a way of life.

But, as some competitors discovered, if you relaxed, things seemed to go more smoothly. Ak Miller was as laid back as anyone who ever drove in the race, and the Mexican people loved him and his unlikely entries. He said that on a trip to Mexico thirty years after he raced there, he was recognized on the street by one of the race officials and greeted as an old friend.

The South Texans were the least tolerant of Mexico. Their lifelong coexistence along the border provided many of them with an aloofness and superior attitude toward the land and its people. But Mexico had one thing going in its favor: the Carrera Panamericana was its game, played by its rules, on its field, and if you wanted to participate, you had to do it Mexico's way.

Participants had always keyed up to win in Mexico. In an amazingly short time, the Carrera had become a highly sophisticated business, and it undoubtedly gave the world more good, solid endurance engineering experience than any other single race in history. If a car could last through the tortuous Pan-Am, it could probably survive just about anything an average driver would come across in ten years of day-to-day use on the roads of the world.

Lincoln and Ferrari had been the most successful—the American manufacturer with three consecutive one-two finishes, two third places, and two fourths in the stock car division. Ferrari had two outright wins, two seconds, and two thirds. Lincoln's Chuck Stevenson was the only repeat winner, and Piero Taruffi made the most consistent money finishes, with first, second, and fourth placings over the five years. C. D. Evans competed in all five races—driving four different makes of cars—and captured a win and a second in class.

The Mexican decision to cancel Carrera Panamericana after its 1954 running was a wise and timely move. Barely six months later, the terrible tragedy occurred at Le Mans when Levegh's Mercedes 300SLR plunged into the crowd and killed eighty spectators. Then, barely a month after that, during the running of the Tourist Trophy at Ulster, a chain of fiery accidents claimed three drivers; ironically, Driver Lance Macklin of Austin-Healey was involved in both incidents, a fact that made him abandon the sport. The public outcry nearly finished motor racing for a time: Mercedes dramatically withdrew from the sport, and hundreds of events throughout the world were canceled.

The world in 1954 was in the midst of an age when technology and commerce—which had been steadily growing in the nine years since the end of World War II—were gaining momentum. Gigantic strides were being made at a rate faster than the average person could comprehend or absorb. Aircraft were traveling at speeds two to three times faster than had been possible five years previously; the world's first nuclear submarine was launched in January; early computers were taking minutes to do what had formerly been a day's work; and in just three years, the United States would enter the space race with its first satellite.

The contrast between Mexico and the rest of the world was becoming wider than ever. It was inevitable that the experience of the Mexican Road Race at some point had to be relegated to the past. The sophisticated technological world had passed the primitive world, and Mexico got back to normal. That's probably as it should have been. But while it lasted, the Pan-Am was a grand spectacle the likes of which we'll probably never see again.

The heroic memories are still vivid, however. Driver John Fitch summarized it perhaps better than anyone. "The Panamericana," he wrote, "remains one of the magnificent adventures in the history of the automobile."

178

Appendices

Carrera Panamericana Entries 1950-1954

1950

Car	Race #	Driver	Final Standing
1950 Alfa Romeo 6C 2500	90	Felice Bonetto, Italy	8
1950 Alfa Romeo 6C 2500	103	Piero Taruffi, Italy	4
1948 Buick	10	H.R. Lammons, Jacksonville, TX	
1948 Buick	22	Ralph Hop, Norwalk, CA	
1950 Buick	48	E.P. Warren, Inglewood, CA	
1938 Buick	51	Duran Mejia, Mexico	
1950 Buick	61	Carlos Mass	
1942 Buick	75	Jesus Valosi, Mexico	
1940 Buick	80	Andrea Gonzalez, San Francisco, CA	51
1941 Buick	89	Wm. Grover, Colorado Springs, CO	
1950 Buick	96	Joe Thompson, Carlsbad, NM	
1949 Buick	100	Felix Loza, Mexico	
1950 Buick	105	Antonio Casero	42
1950 Buick	107	Wm. Gillespie, Los Angeles, CA	48
1949 Buick	117	Capt. Alfredo Call, El Salvador	
1950 Buick	124	Victor de la Lama, Mexico	44
1950 Buick	130	Arthur Boone, New York, NY	
1949 Cadillac	3	Jose Beltran, Mexico	21
1950 Cadillac	9	Rodolpho Castaneda G., Mexico	26
1947 Cadillac	16	Alberto Rojas, Mexico	
1949 Cadillac	21	Al Rogers, Colorado Springs, CO	3
1948 Cadillac	23	Jose Sanches R., Mexico	
1941 Cadillac	27	Alfonso Oviedo y O., Mexico	46
1950 Cadillac	36	Anthony Musto, Chicago, IL	
1949 Cadillac	47	Joel Thorne, Las Vegas, NV	
1950 Cadillac	53	Rocardo Lopez Mendez, Mexico	
1950 Cadillac	55	George Lynch, Detroit, MI	
1949 Cadillac	59	Robert Clement, Pomona, CA	
1949 Cadillac	63	George Ashley, El Paso, TX	
1950 Cadillac	67	Rafael Norma L., Mexico	
1950 Cadillac	68	Bill Sterling, El Paso, TX	
1949 Cadillac	72	Rafael Mendoza, Mexico	22
1949 Cadillac	81	Lonnie Johnson, Shallowater, TX	
1938 Cadillac	102	Dwight Fox, Mt. Gilead, OH	
1950 Cadillac	111	J.W. Parham, USA	
1950 Cadillac	113	Thomas Deal, El Paso, TX	2
1949 Cadillac	118	Jack McAfee, Manhattan Beach, CA	10
1939 Cadillac	120	Ray Colonbaugh, Des Plaines, IL	30
1943 Cadillac	125	Manuel Lomeli M., Mexico	50
1950 Chevrolet	74	Ramon Lopez	27
1950 Chevrolet	127	P. Miranda	
1950 Chevrolet	131	Emilio Carmargo	41
1947 Chrysler	17	Jacqueline Evans de Lopez, Mexico	47
1950 Chrysler	28	Gutierre Tibon, Mexico	
1950 Chrysler	101	Jose Mateo Topete, Mexico	24
1937 Cord 812	43	Hugh Reilly, Chicago, IL	
1950 Delahaye Type 175	19	Jean Trevoux, France	12
1949 De Soto	58	C.R. O'Brien, Pomona, CA	
1950 Ford	6	Tommy Francis, Los Angeles, CA	35
1939 Ford	18	Fred Steinbroner, Los Angeles, CA	
1950 Ford	41	E.A. Kasold, Huntington Park, CA	14
1949 Ford	50	John Reher, Beauville, IL	
1949 Ford	56	John Fredericks, USA	
1950 Ford	86	Samuel Main, Columbia	29
1950 Ford	92	Rafael Almodovar, Anthony, NM	31
1949 Ford	119	Emillio Portez Medina, Mexico	
1938 Hotchkiss	108	Taylor Lucas/John van Neuman, L.A., CA	
1950 Hudson	1	Luis Davalos, Mexico	
1937 Hudson	4	Ismael Alvarez, Mexico	
1950 Hudson	14	Lou Figaro, Inglewood, CA	
1948 Hudson	20	Chas. Fraley/R. McFee, Columbus, OH	38
1950 Hudson	66	Bob Korf, Beloit, WI	

179

Car	Race #	Driver	Final Standing
1949 Hudson	76	S. Lopez Chavez, Mexico	
1949 Hudson	85	Gustavo Ladeqig	
1950 Hudson	122	Harry Elbel, San Antonio, TX	
1949 Jaguar	110	Jorgen Thayssen	
1947 Talbot-Lago	30	Edward Walker, N. Hollywood, CA	
1950 Lincoln	13	Antonio Exchaiz, Mexico	
1949 Lincoln	25	David Aprezza, Broderick, CA	49
1949 Lincoln	26	Raymond Parks/Red Byron, Atlanta, GA	
1949 Lincoln	31	Ray Crawford, Alhambra, CA	
1949 Lincoln	34	Octavio Esquivel	25
1949 Lincoln	38	John Mantz/Bill Stroppe, Inglewood, CA	9
1949 Lincoln	40	Marie Brookreson, Wilcox, AZ	
1949 Lincoln	42	Jesus Gonzalez, Mexico	13
1949 Lincoln	54	Jimmy Hicks, Houston, TX	
1949 Lincoln	77	Jesus Valezzi, Venezuela	20
1950 Lincoln	88	Harry Sents, Glen Aubry, NY	
1947 Lincoln	106	William Gillespie, USA	34
1949 Lincoln	112	Enrique Hachmeister, Guatemala	
1950 Lincoln	115	Lewis Ruwaldt	
1949 Lincoln	121	Albelardo Acosta, Mexico	19
1949 Lincoln	123	Fonty Flock, Atlanta, GA	
1949 Mercury	11	B.A. Hemesby, San Antonio, TX	
1950 Mercury	15	R.M. de Oca, Mexico	
1950 Mercury	32	Olegario Perez	
1950 Mercury	39	Raul Salgado, Mexico	11
1950 Mercury	57	Alfonso Verdugo	45
1950 Mercury	60	S.S. Barragan, Mexico	
1950 Mercury	64	M. Quintanilla, Mexico	
1950 Mercury	82	L. Almanza, Mexico	15
1950 Mercury	84	C. Almazan, Mexico	
1950 Mercury	93	Gabriel Herrera R., Columbia	
1950 Mercury	104	Arcesio Paz, Mexico	33
1950 Nash	7	Henry Bradley, Peru	
1950 Nash	29	J.A. Solona, Mexico	
1949 Nash	33	S. Santoyo	37
1950 Nash Ambassador	37	Bill France/Curtis Turner, Daytona Beach, FL	
1950 Nash Ambassador	49	Roy Pat Conner, Corsicana, TX	
1950 Nash Ambassador	73	R. Mendoza, Mexico	
1950 Nash Ambassador	114	E.J. Sollohub, Bakersfield, CA	
1949 Nash	116	Lujis Meneses	40
1950 Oldsmobile	5	G. Pirez, Mexico	
1950 Oldsmobile 88	12	Bud Sennett, Los Angeles, CA	12
1949 Oldsmobile	24	Iroeneo Rojas, Mexico	36
1949 Oldsmobile	46	Leal Solares, Mexico	7
1950 Oldsmobile 88	52	Herschel McGriff, Portland, OR	1
1949 Oldsmobile	62	C.G. Mass, Mexico	18
1950 Oldsmobile	71	Owen Gray, Lubbock, TX	16
1950 Oldsmobile	78	A. Cagnasso, Venezuela	
1950 Oldsmobile 88	79	Lewis Hawkins, Spartanburg, SC	6
1950 Oldsmobile	95	Chas. Goldtrap, Port Isabel, TX	
1950 Oldsmobile	97	Ali Rachid, Venezuela	28
1950 Oldsmobile	109	J.V. Hirschfeld, Hollywood, CA	43
1950 Oldsmobile	129	C.D. Evans, El Paso, TX	
1949 Packard	2	Oscar Lopez de Llergo, Mexico	
1949 Packard	8	Jose Estrada Menocal, Mexico	
1949 Packard	35	Javier Razo Maciel, Mexico	

Car	Race #	Driver	Final Standing
1949 Packard	44	Fernando Razo Maciel, Mexico	
1948 Packard	45	John Stewart, Clovis, NM	
1948 Packard	65	Francisco Ibarra Somohano, Portland, OR	
1949 Packard	99	Marano Gomez	
1950 Studebaker	70	Luis Astengo Albizuri	32
1950 Studebaker	87	Andres Wiltz, Mexico	52
1950 Studebaker	94	Fernando Ballardo Amoros, Mexico	
1950 Studebaker	128	H. Inciarte, Venezuela	23

1951

Car	Race #	Driver	Final Standing
1951 Alfa Romeo 6C 2500 SS	19	Carlos Panini, Mexico	
1947 Buick	10	Cecilio Martinez, Mexico	
1938 Buick	26	Fernando Mejia, Mexico	
1951 Buick	64	Luis G. de la P, Mexico	DNS
1949 Buick	73	Angel Gonzalez, Mexico	DNS
1951 Cadillac	8	John Fredricks, USA	24
1951 Cadillac 62	33	Al Rodgers, USA	7
1951 Cadillac	52	Alberto Rojas, Mexico	
1951 Cadillac	57	Jamie Pasquel, Mexico	
1949 Cadillac	89	Jack McAfee, USA	
1951 Cadillac	100	Archie Sarten, USA	DNS
1949 Cadillac	105	Alfonso Oviedo, Mexico	32
1951 Chrysler Saratoga	1	Jose Marin, Mexico	22
1951 Chrysler Saratoga	3	Frank Burani, USA	
1951 Chrysler Saratoga	5	Sebastian Gonzalez, Mexico	
1951 Chrsyler Saratoga	6	Dick Matthews, USA	DNS
1951 Chrysler Saratoga	7	Tony Bettenhausen, USA	16
1951 Chrysler Saratoga	14	Daniel Cayon, Mexico	
1951 Chrysler Saratoga	16	Bill Sterling, USA	3
1951 Chrysler Saratoga	22	Clyde Johnson, USA	11
1951 Chrysler Saratoga	31	Jacqueline Evans de Lopez, Mexico	
1951 Chrysler Saratoga	32	John Fitch, USA	
1951 Chrysler Saratoga	39	Phil Walters, USA	
1951 Chrysler New Yorker	43	Arturo Breton, Mexico	
1951 Chrysler Saratoga	53	Leroy Warnier, USA	
1951 Chrysler Saratoga	72	Reginald McFee, USA	28
1951 Chrysler	84	David Dominguez, Mexico	19
1950 Delahaye Type 175	4	Louis Chiron, France	
1951 Ferrari 212 Inter (0161 EL)	9	Alberto Ascari, Italy	2
1951 Ferrari 212 Inter (0163 EL)	34	Piero Tariffi, Italy	1
1951 Ford	17	Jose Bretto, Mexico	
1951 Ford	42	Jesus Esparza, Mexico	
1951 Hudson Hornet	12	Red Byron, USA	NS
1951 Hudson Hornet	13	Harold Hansen, USA	
1951 Hudson Hornet	24	Luis Leal Solares, Mexico	17
1951 Hudson Hornet	25	Rex Easton, USA	
1951 Hudson Hornet	35	Loren Roberts, USA	NS
1951 Hudson Hornet	37	Salvador Lopez, Mexico	26
1951 Hudson Hornet	44	Marshall Teague, USA	6
1951 Hudson Hornet	51	Enrique Fluchaire, Mexico	
1951 Hudson Hornet	56	Enrique Paredes, Mexico	
1951 Hudson Hornet	75	Clarense Babineau, Canada	NS
1951 Hudson	82	Abelardo Diaz, Venezuela	

Car	Race #	Driver	Final Standing
1951 Hudson Hornet	93	Jorge Limon Escalante, Mexico	35
1951 Hudson	94	Ali Rachid, Venezuela	
1951 Hudson	104	Wayne Hansen, USA	
1951 Jaguar Mark VII	47	Fernando Razo Maciel, Mexico	
1951 Jaguar Mark VII		Bobby Unser, USA	
1951 Lancia Aurelia B 20 GT	91	Felice Bonetto, Italy	
1951 Lancia Aurelia B 20 GT	101	Giovanni Bracco, Italy	
1951 Lincoln	11	Walt Faulkner, USA	
1951 Lincoln Cosmopolitan	54	Ray Crawford, USA	
1951 Lincoln	88	Javier Razo Maciel, Mexico	
1948 Mercury 89M Special	15	Troy Ruttman, Pomona, CA	4
1951 Mercury	38	A.M. Scully, USA	NS
1951 Mercury	59	Arnaldo Alvarado, Peru	21
1951 Mercury	63	Francisco Anza, Mexico	
1951 Mercury	66	Hugo Inciarte, Venezuela	NS
1950 Mercury	98	Emilio Chafardet, Venezuela	
1950 Mercury	99	Salvador Barragan, USA	
1951 Nash-Healey (pace car)		Chuck Stevenson, Milwaukee, WI	
1951 Nash Ambassador	28	C.D. Evans, USA	23
1951 Nash Ambassador	49	Bob Korf, USA	10
1951 Nash Ambassador	68	Robert Christie, USA	29
1951 Nash Ambassador	74	H. Charles Bradley, Peru	
1951 Nash Ambassador	102	Manuel Luz Meneses, Mexico	
1950 Oldsmobile 88	2	Bud Sennett, USA	
1951 Oldsmobile	21	Salvador de Zulueta, Mexico	33
1951 Oldsmobile 88	23	H.L. Fleming, Jr., USA	
1951 Oldsmobile	27	Alberto del Campo, Mexico	30
1951 Oldsmobile 88	29	Jose Antonio Solona, Mexico	9
1951 Oldsmobile	30	Ricardo Ramirez, Mexico	
1951 Oldsmobile	36	Ahelardo Matamoros, Mexico	
1951 Oldsmobile	40	J.C. Trimble, USA	20
1951 Oldsmobile	45	Felix Cerda Loza, Mexico	
1951 Oldsmobile	50	Manual Rocha, Mexico	
1951 Oldsmobile	58	Arcesio Paz, Columbia	
1950 Oldsmobile	60	Olegario Perez Pliego, Mexico	18
1951 Oldsmobile	61	Cesar Lucero, Venezuela	
1951 Oldsmobile	65	Ramon Lopez, Venezuela	
1951 Oldsmobile	67	Oscar Verda, Venezuela	27
1951 Oldsmobile	78	Victor Fernandez, Mexico	NS
1951 Oldsmobile 88	79	Herschel McGriff, Portland, OR	
1951 Oldsmobile 88	81	Jose Garza Castro, Mexico	
1951 Oldsmobile	83	Magin Pastor, Venezuela	
1951 Oldsmobile	85	Oscar Cepeda, Mexico	31
1951 Oldsmobile	92	Leon McMillan, USA	15
1951 Oldsmobile	96	Owen Gray, Lubbock, TX	13
1951 Oldsmobile	97	Luis Salvi, Peru	
1951 Packard	18	Douglas Ehlinger, Mexico	14
1951 Packard	20	Delestino Flores, Mexico	
1951 Packard	41	Jose Estrada Menocal, Mexico	
1951 Packard	46	Francisco Ibarra, Mexico	
1951 Packard 400 Patrician	48	Jean Trevoux, France	5
1951 Packard	55	Chano Ureta, Mexico	
1951 Packard	62	Ramundo Corona, Mexico	12
1951 Packard	87	Tommy Francis, USA	
1951 Studebaker	70	Juan Resendez, Venezuela	
1951 Studebaker	71	Attilio Cagnasso, Venezuela	25
1951 Studebaker	77	Alfredo Gago, Venezuela	

1952 — Categoria Sport

Car	Race #	Driver	Final Standing
1952 Cadillac	1	Fernando Duran, Mexico	
del Campo Special	27	Alberto del Campo, Mexico	
1951 Ferrari 212 Inter Vignale (0239EU)	5	E. R. Echevarria, Mexico	
1952 Ferrari 250S (0156ET) Vig	8	Giovanni Bracco, Italy	
1951 Ferrari 212 Vig Inter (0131 E)	9	Phil Hill, USA	6
1951 Ferrari 212 Inter Vig (0163 EL)	12	Pablo Aguilar, Mexico	
1951 Ferrari 212 Inter Vig (0161 EL)	13	Paco Ibarra, Mexico	7
1952 Ferrari 340 Mexico (0226 AT)	14	Alberto Ascari, Italy	
1952 Ferrari 340 Mexico (0222 AT)	16	Luigi Villoresi, Italy	
1952 Ferrari 340 America (0142 AL)	17	Jack McAfee, USA	5
1952 Ferrari 340 Mexico (0224 AT)	20	Luigi Chinetti, USA	3
1952 Gordini T 15 S (16 S)	15	Robert Manzon, France	
1952 Gordini T 15 S (18 GCS)	19	Jean Behra, France	
1952 Jaguar XK120	7	Santos Letona Diaz, Mexico	
1952 Jaguar XK120	18	Douglas Ehlinger, Mexico	10
1952 Lancia Aurelia B 20 GT (1505)	21	Felice Bonetto, Italy	
1952 Lancia Aurelia B 20 GT (1511)	23	Giulio Casabianca, Italy	
1952 Lancia Aurelia B 20 GT (1506)	26	Umberto Maglioli, Italy	4
1951 Lancia Aurelia B 20 GT	27	Enrique Ortiz Peredo, Mexico	9
1952 Mercedes-Benz 300SL (0005)	3	Hermann Lang, Germany	2
1952 Mercedes-Benz 300SL (0008)	4	Karl Kling, Germany	1
1952 Mercedes-Benz 300SL (0009)	6	John Fitch, USA	
1952 Oldsmobile	34	Chano Ureta, Mexico	
1952 Porsche 356S	10	Graf von Bercheim, Germany	
1952 Porsche 356S (P400 49)	11	Paul Alfons von Metternich, Germany	8
Supremio Especial	100	Gustavo Estrada, Mexico	

1952 — Categoria Standard

Car	Race #	Driver	Final Standing
1952 Cadillac	104	Al Rodgers, Colorado Springs, CO	16
1952 Cadillac	116	Alberto Rojas, Mexico	
1952 Cadillac	125	Guillermo Giron, Guatemala	
1952 Cadillac	136	Bill Sterling, USA	
1952 Cadillac 62	137	Muir Dean Kirby, USA	8
1952 Cadillac	156	Manuel Guevara, Venezuela	
1952 Chrysler Saratoga	103	Bobby Unser, USA	
1952 Chrysler	105	S. Gonzalez Olivares, Mexico	
1953 Chrysler	107	Owen Gray, USA	17
1952 Chrysler	111	Tommy Drisdale, USA	

Car	Race #	Driver	Final Standing
1952 Chrysler	123	Pat Kirkwood, USA	
1952 Chrysler	128	Arturo Alvarez, Mexico	
1953 Chrysler New Yorker	131	C.D. Evans, USA	6
1953 Chrysler New Yorker	132	Allen Heath, USA	10
1952 Chrysler	140	Royal Russell, USA	
1952 Chrysler Saratoga	153	Andrew Moran, USA	
1952 Chrysler New Yorker	155	Reginald McFee, USA	5
1952 Chrysler	174	Jacqueline Evans de Lopez, Mexico	
1952 De Soto	142	Angel Acar, Mexico	
1952 Dodge Coronet	175	Enrique Pedero, Mexico	
1952 Ford	110	Rogelio Anza, Mexico	
1952 Ford	148	H.L. Flemming, USA	
1952 Henry J	165	Juan de Aguinaco, Mexico	
1952 Hudson	101	Salvador Lopez, Mexico	
1952 Hudson	117	Enrique Fluchaire, Mexico	
1952 Hudson	121	Luis Leal Solares, Mexico	
1952 Hudson	135	Attilio Cagnasso, Venezuela	18
1952 Hudson Hornet	144	Salvador de Zulueta, Mexico	
1952 Hudson Hornet	145	Peter Hahn, USA	
1952 Hudson Hornet	146	Abelardo Diaz Gutierrez, Venezuela	20
1952 Hudson Hornet	154	Marshall Teague, USA	7
1952 Hudson	158	Woodrow Rollins, USA	
1952 Hudson	164	Leopoldo Garmendia, Venezuela	
1952 Lincoln	119	W.A. Poston, USA	
1952 Lincoln	120	Duane Carter, USA	
1953 Lincoln Capri	122	John Mantz, USA	2
1953 Lincoln Capri	129	Chuck Stevenson, USA	1
1953 Lincoln Capri	130	Walt Faulkner, USA	3
1952 Lincoln Capri	141	Ray Crawford, USA	
1953 Lincoln Capri	149	Bob Korf, USA	4
1952 Lincoln	159	Archie Sarten, USA	
1952 Mercury	118	Fernando Leeuw Murphy, Mexico	
1952 Nash Ambassador	143	Bob Christie, USA	
1952 Oldsmobile	102	Olegario Perez, Mexico	
1952 Oldsmobile	108	Akton Miller, USA	
1952 Oldsmobile	114	Felix Loza, Mexico	14
1952 Oldsmobile	126	Jose Antonio Solona, Mexico	
1952 Oldsmobile	127	Hector Rivapalacio, Mexico	
1952 Oldsmobile	133	Cesar Yunes, Mexico	
1952 Oldsmobile	138	Herschel McGriff, USA	
1952 Oldsmobile	150	Jim Rathmann, USA	19
1952 Oldsmobile	151	Abelardo Matamoros, Mexico	
1952 Oldsmobile	152	Guy Vincent, USA	
1952 Oldsmobile 88	157	Piero Taruffi, Italy	11
1952 Oldsmobile	163	Juan Dos Santos, Venezuela	12
1952 Packard 400 Patrician	106	Jean Trevoux, France	9
1952 Packard 400	107	Tommy Francis, USA	
1952 Packard	112	Ramundo Corona, Mexico	
1952 Packard	113	Otto Becker Estrada, Mexico	13
1952 Packard	115	Fernando Razo Maciel, Mexico	15
1952 Packard	134	Celestino Flores, Mexico	
1952 Packard	139	Jorge Limon Escalante, Mexico	
1952 Studebaker	147	Emilio Chafardet, Venezuela	

1953 — Sport Internacional

Car	Race #	Driver	Final Standing
1953 Chrysler Special	1	Fernando Razo Maciel, Mexico	
1953 Chrysler Special	3	Owen Gray, USA	
1953 Chrysler Special	16	John Fitch, USA	
1953 Chrysler Special	20	Reginald McFee, USA	
1952 Ferrari 340 Mexico (222 AT)	4	Phil Hill, USA	
1953 Ferrari 250MM (0239 EU)	5	Efrain Ruiz-Echevarria, Mexico	7
1953 Ferrari 375MM (0358AM)	12	Umberto Maglioli, Italy	
1953 Ferrari 375MM (0318 AM)	15	Antonio Stagnoli, Italy	
1953 Ferrari 375MM (0320 AM)	23	Mario Ricci/Maglioli, Italy	6
1953 Ferrari 375MM (0322 AM)	26	Guido Mancini, Italy	4
1953 Ferrari 375MM (0286 AM)	45	Luigi Chinetti, USA	
1953 Ford Special	19	Jorge Moctezuma, Mexico	
1953 Glasspar-Mercury	13	Fernando Duran Mejia, Mexico	
1953 Gordini T 24 S (36 S)	7	Jean Behra, France	
1953 Gordini T 16 S (38 S)	8	Jean Lucas, France	
1953 Jaguar XK120C	14	Guillermo Giron, Guatemala	9
1953 Kurtis-Cadillac	17	Jack Ensley, USA	
1953 Kurtis-Chrysler	21	Tony Bettenhausen, USA	
1953 Lancia D24 (003)	22	Piero Taruffi, Italy	2
1953 Lancia 3.3 Liter	24	Pinheiro Pirez, Brazil	
1953 Lancia D24 (002)	34	Felice Bonetto, Italy	
1953 Lancia D24 (004)	36	Juan Manuel Fangio, Argentina	1
1953 Lancia D23	38	Eugenio Castellotti, Italy	3
1953 Lancia D23	50	Giovani Bracco, Italy	
1953 Miller Special "Caballo de Hierro"	11	Ak Miller, USA	8
1953 Packard Special	9	Jean Trevoux, France	
1953 Post	47	Tommy Francis, USA	
1953 Talbot T.26 GS (110 055)	6	Louis Rosier, France	5
1953 Thorne Sport	2	Joel Thorne, USA	

1953 — Sport Hasa (1,500cc)

Car	Race #	Driver	Final Standing
1953 Borgward 1500	155	Hans Hugo Hartmann, Germany	
1953 Borgward 1500	156	Adolph Brudes, Germany	
1953 OSCA	157	Jacques Peron, France	
1953 Porsche 356	151	Salvador Lopez-Chavez, Mexico	
1953 Porsche 550 (02)	152	Jose Herrarte, Guatemala	1
1953 Porsche 356	153	Guillermo Suhr, Guatemala	
1953 Porsche 550 (01)	154	Jaroslav Juhan, Guatemala	
1953 Porsche 356S	158	Fernando Segura, Argentina	2
1953 Porsche 550 (04)	159	Karl Kling, Germany	
1953 Porsche 550 (03)	160	Hans Herrmann, Germany	
1953 Porsche 356	162	Manfredo Lippman, Guatemala	
1953 Porsche 356	199	Joaquin del Castillo, Uraguay	
1953 Porsche 356	200	Jacqueline Evans de Lopez, Mexico	

Car	Race #	Driver	Final Standing
1953 Siata Sport 8V (BS 513)	165	Ernie McAfee, USA	

1953 Turismo Internacional

Car	Race #	Driver	Final Standing
1953 Buick	88	Ernest Hall, USA	19
1953 Buick	93	Pat Zoccalo, Mexico	12
1953 Cadillac 62	58	Viadimiro Chaterquin, Mexico	
1953 Cadillac 62	72	Bill Sterling, USA	11
1953 Cadillac 62	80	Keith Andrews, USA	
1953 Cadillac 62	92	Edward Stringer, USA	
1953 Chrysler New Yorker	56	Bob Korf, USA	
1953 Chrysler New Yorker	57	Frank Mundy, USA	
1953 Chrysler New Yorker	66	Tommy Drisdale, USA	5
1953 Chrysler New Yorker	67	Royal Russell, USA	6
1953 Chrysler New Yorker	70	Al Rodgers, USA	18
1953 Chrysler New Yorker	78	Murrel Belanger, USA	
1953 Chrysler New Yorker	84	Verlin Brown, USA	
1953 Chrysler New Yorker	90	A.F. Ennis, USA	
1953 Chrysler New Yorker	101	Arturo Alvarez Tostado, Mexico	14
1953 De Soto Diplomat	55	Roberto Balmar, Mexico	13
1953 Jaguar Mk VII	62	Guy Vincent, USA	
1953 Lincoln Capri	51	John Mantz, USA	4
1953 Lincoln Capri	52	Chuck Stevenson, USA	1
1953 Lincoln Capri	53	Walt Faulkner, USA	2
1953 Lincoln Capri	54	Fernando Carriles Pagaza, Mexico	
1953 Lincoln Capri	60	Oscar Galvez, Argentina	7
1953 Lincoln Capri	61	Felix Cerda Loza, Mexico	
1953 Lincoln Capri	63	Luis Leal Solares, Mexico	
1953 Lincoln Capri	64	Ernesto Petrini, Argentina	9
1953 Lincoln Capri	65	Bill Vukovich, USA	
1953 Lincoln Capri	68	Manuel Acosta Munoz, Mexico	
1953 Lincoln Capri	69	Rodger Ward, USA	
1953 Lincoln Capri	79	Jorge Descote, Argentina	8
1953 Lincoln Capri	81	Pablo Birger, Argentina	
1953 Lincoln Capri	82	Gilberto Riega, Argentina	22
1953 Lincoln Capri	84	Rudolph Ryans, USA	
1953 Lincoln Capri	85	Tito Falick, Argentina	
1953 Lincoln Capri	95	Jack McGrath, USA	3
1953 Lincoln Capri	99	Duane Carter, USA	
1953 Lincoln	100	Manuel Arrouge, Argentina	
1953 Lincoln Capri	106	Antiago Pieretti, Argentina	
1953 Lincoln Capri	118	Fernando Leeuw Murphy, Mexico	15
1953 Lincoln Capri	121	Abelardo Maiamoros, Mexico	
1953 Lincoln Capri	149	Ray Crawford, USA	
1953 Mercury	75	Alfredo Macias, Argentina	
1953 Mercury	91	Julio Repetto, Argentina	
1953 Mercury	94	Eugenio Guerrero, Argentina	
1953 Mercury	96	Arquimedes Alfredo, Argentina	
1953 Mercury	97	Mario Andreini, Argentina	
1953 Mercury	147	Clemente Aspe, Argentina	23
1953 Mercury	148	Hugo Inciarte, Argentina	
1953 Oldsmobile 88	102	Alberto del Campo, Mexico	
1953 Oldsmobile 88	113	Ricardo Rivapalacio, Mexico	16
1953 Oldsmobile 88	114	Hector Rivapalacio, Mexico	21
1953 Packard Mayfair	59	Douglas Ehlinger, Mexico	10
1953 Packard Mayfair	74	Ramundo Corona, Mexico	

1953

Car	Race #	Driver	Final Standing
1953 Aero Willys	234	Oscar Mier y Teran, Mexico	
1953 Aero Willys	270	Mario Ribaldi, Argentina	
1953 Chevrolet	217	C.D. Evans, USA	1
1953 Chevrolet	219	Juan Piersanti, Argentina	
1953 Chevrolet	220	Ramiro Aguilar, Mexico	
1953 Chevrolet	230	Ernesto Nanni, Argentina	
1953 Chevrolet	238	Humberto Maneglia, Argentina	
1953 Chevrolet	240	Vincente Tirabasso, Argentina	
1953 Chevrolet	241	Manuel Cobas, Argentina	
1953 Chevrolet	245	Tadeo Taddia, Argentina	10
1953 Chevrolet	256	Baltazar Alaimo, Argentina	12
1953 Chevrolet	259	Scott Yantis, USA	4
1953 Chevrolet	260	Eduardo D'Alessandro, Argentina	
1953 Chevrolet	263	Enrique Canisano, Argentina	
1953 Chevrolet	264	Alfredo Birger, Argentina	
1953 Chevrolet	271	Jorge Cepeda Mier, Mexico	
1953 Chevrolet	273	Carlos Firpo, Argentina	
1953 Chevrolet	285	Eduardo Etchebarne, USA	
1953 Chevrolet	287	Ruben Joly, USA	
1953 Chevrolet	288	Pedro Garcia, USA	
1953 Chevrolet	291	Hector Giogis, USA	
1953 Chevrolet	292	Francisco Ibarra, Mexico	
1953 Ford	201	Octavio Anza, Mexico	
1953 Ford	202	Guillermo Albafull, Mexico	
1953 Ford	206	Othon Aspe Murphy, Mexico	
1953 Ford	207	Norm Patterson, USA	2
1953 Ford	209	Oscar Calaben, Argentina	
1953 Ford	211	Dario Ramonda, Argentina	
1953 Ford	212	Domingo Marimon, Argentina	
1953 Ford	213	Alfonso Franco, Mexico	
1953 Ford	216	Antonio Adrian, Argentina	
1953 Ford	218	Remo Gamalero, Argentina	
1953 Ford	221	Manuel Hidalgo, Argentina	
1953 Ford	223	Jose Rubiol Roca, Argentina	
1953 Ford	224	Robert Christie, USA	
1953 Ford	226	Mickey Thompson, USA	
1953 Ford	227	Sebastian Gonzales, Mexico	
1953 Ford	228	Luis Martonani, Argentina	
1953 Ford	229	Alberto Crespo, Argentina	
1953 Ford	231	Manuel Merino, Argentina	
1953 Ford	232	Alfredo Cogorno, Argentina	
1953 Ford	233	Andres Ferreno, Argentina	
1953 Ford	236	Reoberto Salmon, Mexico	
1953 Ford	239	Daniel Musso, Argentina	
1953 Ford	242	Nestor Lafage, Argentina	
1953 Ford	244	Guillermo Airaldi, Argentina	
1953 Ford Victoria	246	Adolfo Sogolo, Argentina	
1953 Ford	247	Juan Enrique Girotti, Argentina	
1953 Ford	248	Carlos Pfeffer, Argentina	
1953 Ford	249	Pedro Bealmonte, Argentina	
1953 Ford	251	Arnaldo de Tomas, Argentina	
1953 Ford	252	Fernando Tirabasso, Argentina	
1953 Ford	253	Hugo Servetto, Argentina	
1953 Ford	254	Angel Lovalvo, Argentina	
1953 Ford	255	Guillermo Marenghini, Argentina	
1953 Ford	257	Omar Nestor Bide, Argentina	
1953 Ford	258	Domingo Lombardini, Argentina	
1953 Ford	261	Agustin Aguaviva, Argentina	
1953 Ford	265	Ramon Bauzada, Argentina	
1953 Ford	266	Mario de Poli, Argentina	

Turismo Especial

Car	Race #	Driver	Final Standing
1953 Ford	267	Juan Castellano, Argentina	
1953 Ford	268	Miquel Vinardei, Argentina	
1953 Ford	269	Mario Ribaldi, Argentina	
1953 Ford	272	Jorge Daponte, Argentina	
1953 Ford	274	Marcelo Vercher, Argentina	
1953 Ford	275	Balbino Roldan, Argentina	
1953 Ford	276	Miguel Molinero, Argentina	
1953 Ford	277	Oscar Martorani, Argentina	
1953 Ford	278	Robert Barkimer, USA	
1953 Ford	279	Carlos Battilana, USA	
1953 Ford	280	Alberto Fulvi, USA	
1953 Ford	281	Jose Brea, USA	
1953 Ford	282	Luis Manzeo, USA	
1953 Ford	283	Ravael Larocca, USA	13
1953 Ford	284	Enrique Etchebarne, USA	
1953 Ford	286	Francisco Casuscello, USA	
1953 Ford	289	Eugenio Veicier, USA	
1953 Ford	290	Juan Leon, USA	
1953 Ford	295	Benito Estadillo, Mexico	
1953 Ford	300	Rogelio Anza, Mexico	
1953 Hudson Jet	204	Francisco Ramirez, Mexico	8
1953 Hudson Jet	225	Enrique Paredes, Mexico	9
1953 Hudson Jet	235	Malcom Eckart, USA	5
1953 Hudson Jet	237	Alfredo Suarez, Mexico	
1953 Kaiser	250	Manuel Meneses, Mexico	
1953 Kaiser	293	Alfonso de la Pena, Mexico	
1953 Kaiser	294	Heliodoro de la Pena, Mexico	
1953 Mercury	296	Buenaventura Perez, Mexico	
1953 Nash Statesman	215	Rafael Gonzalez, Mexico	19
1953 Plymouth	205	Jose Marin, Mexico	
1953 Plymouth	208	Frank Davis, USA	
1953 Plymouth	222	Hector Ortiz, Mexico	
1953 Studebaker	203	Olegario Perez Pliego, Mexico	
1953 Studebaker	210	Carlos Diaz, Mexico	14
1953 Studebaker	214	Carlos Alvarado, Mexico	

1954 Sports

Car	Race #	Driver	Final Standing
1954 Austin Healey 100S	7	Lance Macklin, Britain	
1954 Austin Healey 100S	8	Carroll Shelby, USA	
Cabero Special	32	Alberto del Campo, Mexico	
1954 Chevrolet Corvette	12	Bill von Esser, USA	
1954 Ferrari 375 Plus (0362 AM)	1	Jack McAfee, USA	
1954 Ferrari 750 Monza	2	Alfonso de Portago, Spain	
1954 Ferrari 500 Mondial (0464 MD)	3	Porfirio Rubirosa, Dominican Republic	
1954 Ferrari	4	Roberto Bonomi, Argentina	
1954 Ferrari 750 Monza	14	Giovanni Bracco, Italy	
1954 Ferrari 375 Plus (0392 AM)	19	Umberto Maglioli, Italy	1
1953 Ferrari 375MM (0286 AM)	20	Phil Hill, USA	2
1954 Ferrari 250 Monza (0442 M)	22	Franco Cornacchia, Italy	3
1954 Ferrari 375MM (0376 AM)	24	Luigi Chinetti, USA	4
1954 Jaguar XK120C	13	Francisco Ibarra, Mexico	
1954 Jaguar XK120	16	Oscar Fano Bush, Mexico	
1954 Kurtis-Cadillac 500S	6	Jack Ensley, USA	
1954 Kurtis-Oldsmobile 500S	17	Duane Carter, USA	
1954 Miller Special	11	Ak Miller, USA	5
1954 Packard Special	9	Jean Trevoux, France	6
1954 Pegaso Z102BS (0142)	10	Joacquin Palacios, Spain	

1954 Sport Hasa (1,500cc)

Car	Race #	Driver	Final Standing
1954 Borgward RS 55	60	Karl Bechem, Germany	
1954 Borgward RS 55	61	Franz Hammenick, Switzerland	
MG Special	99	Jim Cassidy, USA	
1954 OSCA MT4-1500	52	Roberto Mieres, Argentina	
1954 OSCA MT4-1500 (1151)	54	Louis Chiron, France	3
1954 OSCA MT4-1500 (1152)	62	Manfredo Lippmann, Germany	
1954 Porsche 550 (01)	51	Salvador Lopez-Chavez, Mexico	5
1954 Porsche 356	53	E.J. Hirz, Germany	7
1954 Porsche 550 (04)	55	Hans Herrmann, Germany	1
1954 Porsche 550 (05)	56	Jaroslav Juhan, Guatemala	2
1954 Porsche 550 (06)	58	Fernando Segura, Argentina	4
1954 Porsche 356	59	Otto Beckert Estrada, Mexico	6
1954 Porsche 356	100	Jacqueline Evans de Lopez, Mexico	

1954 Turismo

Car	Race #	Driver	Final Standing
1954 Buick	107	Manuel Acosta Munoz, Mexico	13
1954 Buick Century	111	Luis Leal Solares, Mexico	5
1954 Buick	112	Fernando Razo Maciel, Mexico	
1954 Buick Century	113	Ricardo Ramirez, Mexico	6
1954 Buick Century	114	Riva Palacio	
1954 Buick Century	115	"Yuyo" Mariscal	
1954 Buick	116	Cesar Campo	
1954 Buick	122	Pat Zoccano, Mexico	
1954 Cadillac	110	Edward Stringer, USA	4
1954 Cadillac	127	Keith Andrews, USA	3
1954 Lincoln Capri	100	Chuck Stevenson, USA	
1954 Lincoln	101	Angel Acar, Mexico	
1954 Lincoln Capri	102	John Mantz, USA	
1954 Lincoln Capri	103	Walt Faulkner, USA	2
1954 Lincoln Capri	104	Fernando Leeuw Murphy, Mexico	
1954 Lincoln	105	Manuel Ayulo, USA	
1954 Lincoln	106	Felix Cerda Loza, Mexico	
1954 Lincoln Capri	108	Bill Vukovich, USA	
1954 Lincoln Capri	109	Jack McGrath, USA	
1954 Lincoln	117	Tony de Rosa, Argentina	11
1954 Lincoln	123	Rafael Garzon	
1954 Lincoln	124	Fernando Ramirez, Mexico	10
1954 Lincoln Capri	149	Ray Crawford, USA	1
1954 Oldsmobile	130	Guillermo Suhr, Guatemala	12
1954 Packard	119	Douglas Ehlinger, Mexico	7
1954 Packard	133	Raimundo Corona, Mexico	9

Car	Race #	Driver	Final Standing
1954 Turismo Europeo			
1954 Alfa Romeo 1900 T	251	Consalvo Sanesi, Italy	1
1954 Alfa Romeo 1900 T	252	Adolpho Valazquez, Mexico	5
1954 Alfa Romeo 1900 T	255	Piero Carini, Italy	4
1954 Alfa Romeo 1900 T	256	Sergio Montovani, Italy	2
1954 Alfa Romeo 1900 T	257	Jose Solona, Mexico	
1954 Alfa Romeo 1900 T	260	Airaldi	
1954 Alfa Romeo 1900 T	265	Cerezo	
1954 Alfa Romeo 1900 T	267	Mario della Favera, Italy	3
1954 Alfa Romeo 1900 T	268	Bruno Bonini, Italy	
1954 Borgward Isabella	253	Adolph Brudes, Germany	6
1954 Volkswagen 1200	261	Alfonso von Hohenlohe, Mexico	7
1954 Volkswagen 1200	262	Jan Wyers, Germany	9
1954 Volkswagen 1200	263	Manuel Hinke, Mexico	8
1954 Volkswagen 1200	269	Juan de Aguuinaco, Mexico	13
1954 Volkswagen 1200	270	Alfonso de la Pena, Mexico	10
1954 Volkswagen 1200	271	Axel Wars, Mexico	11
1954 Volkswagen 1200	272	Ara Arakelian, Mexico	12
1954 Turismo Especial			
1954 Chevrolet	216	Jorge Descotte, France	19
1954 Chevrolet	221	Rafael Larocca, Argentina	27
1954 Chevrolet	229	Marcos Cianni, Argentina	22
1954 Chevrolet	240	Salvador Torisse, Argentina	31
1954 Chevrolet	241	Pablo Gulle, Argentina	33
1954 Chevrolet	243	Osvaldo Mantega, Argentina	16
1954 Chevrolet	245	Raul Jaras, Chile	24
1954 Chevrolet	247	Hernan Videla, Chile	30
1954 Chevrolet	301	Jorge Sorai, Argentina	28
1954 Chevrolet	303	Angel di Rosa, Argentina	32
1954 Chevrolet	320	Vincente Tiraba, Argentina	18
1954 Chevrolet	326	Raimundo Caparos, Argentina	15
1954 Chevrolet	340	Tadeo Taddia, Argentina	20
1954 Chevrolet	342	Baltazar Alaino, Argentina	21
1954 Dodge	205	Roberto Belmar	
1954 Dodge V-8	208	Moises Solana, Mexico	6
1954 Dodge V-8	211	Alvarez Tostado, Mexico	4
1954 Dodge V-8	217	C.D. Evans, USA	2
1954 Dodge	218	Francisco Rodriguez, Mexico	12
1954 Dodge	222	H. Palacios	
1954 Dodge V-8	226	Tommy Drisdale, USA	1
1954 Dodge V-8	231	Ray Elliott, USA	3
1954 Dodge	235	Frank Davis, USA	

Car	Race #	Driver	Final Standing
1954 Dodge	237	Ramiro Aguilar	9
1954 Dodge		Ramon Aguilar	
1954 Dodge	328	R. Caparros	
1954 Ford	201	Octavio Anza, Mexico	10
1954 Ford	204	Mickey Thompson, USA	
1954 Ford	206	P. Ovies Sanchez	
1954 Ford	207	Olegario Perez	
1954 Ford V-8	209	Oscar Calaben, Argentina	7
1954 Ford	210	T. Gordon	
1954 Ford	212	Dan Morgan	
1954 Ford	227	Enrique Paredes, Mexico	23
1954 Ford	228	Pepe Ruso	
1954 Ford	230	Pilnio Larocca	
1954 Ford	232	Alberto Peduzzi, Argentina	14
1954 Ford	233	Andres Ferreno, Argentina	34
1954 Ford	242	Antonio Pingeon, Argentina	44
1954 Ford	246	Bartolo Abello, Argentina	46
1954 Ford	249	Eugenio Guerraro	
1954 Ford	259	P. Achuzza	
1954 Ford	284	E. D'Alessandro	
1954 Ford	303	Angel de la Rosa	
1954 Ford	305	Alberto Legulo, Argentina	39
1954 Ford	310	Ernesto Beronto, Argentina	29
1954 Ford	311	Bartolome Ortiz	
1954 Ford	312	Oscar Cremer, Chile	42
1954 Ford	313	Americo Guizzini, Argentina	45
1954 Ford	314	Daniel Musso, Argentina	35
1954 Ford	316	Pedro Petinari, Argentina	43
1954 Ford	318	Antonio Gomez	
1954 Ford	319	Santos Martin	
1954 Ford	321	Melvin Stickney	36
1954 Ford	323	Joaquin Salas, Chile	38
1954 Ford V-8	325	Luis Parnisari, Argentina	37
1954 Ford	328	Carlos Battilana	
1954 Ford	330	Robert Lillienthal	26
1954 Ford 6	331	Piero Taruffi, Italy	8
1954 Ford	332	Carlos Pfeffer, Argentina	40
1954 Ford	334	Cesar Vidales, Argentina	41
1954 Hudson	219	Malcom Eckart, USA	11
1954 Studebaker	205	Roberto Belmar	25
1954 Studebaker	213	Abelardo Matamoros, Mexico	17
1954 Studebaker	215	C.D. Garcilazo	
1954 Studebaker	220	Manuel Menendez, Mexico	13
1954 Studebaker	238	Scott Yantis, USA	5

Carrera Panamericana Results 1950-1954

1950 Carrera Panamericana Final Positions
Ciudad Juárez to El Ocotal, 2,135 miles
132 entries, 52 finishers

Place	Driver/Codriver	Car	Time/Average Speed
1	McGriff/Elliott (USA)	1950 Oldsmobile 88	27:34:25/78.421mph
2	Deal/Cresap (USA)	1950 Cadillac 62	27:35:41/77.362
3	Rodgers/Rodgers (USA)	1949 Cadillac 62	27:55:39/76.440
4	Taruffi/Ceroli (Italy)	1950 Alfa Romeo 6C 2500	28:01:04
5	Sennett/Baich (USA)	1950 Oldsmobile 88	28:02:21
6	Hawkins/Burgess (USA)	1950 Oldsmobile 88	28:19:15
7	Leal/Concha (Mex)	1949 Oldsmobile 88	28:23:54
8	Bonetto/Bonini (Italy)	1950 Alfa Romeo 6C 2500	28:25:36
9	Mantz/Stroppe (USA)	1949 Lincoln Cosmopolitan	28:27:10
10	McAfee/Robinson (USA)	1949 Cadillac 62	28:28:03

1950 Leg Winners

Leg	Start/Finish Points	Winner	Speed
1	Ciudad Juárez—Chihuahua	Sterling (Cadillac)	100.425mph
2	Chihuahua—Parral	Lynch (Cadillac)	95.885
3	Parral—Durango	Sterling (Cadillac)	85.993
4	Durango—Léon	Johnson (Cadillac)	90.133
5	Léon—México City	Deal (Cadillac)	93.169
6	México City—Puebla	Maciel (Packard)	79.777
7	Puebla—Oaxaca	Bonetto (Alfa Romeo)	68.129
8	Oaxaca—Tuxtla Gutiérrez	Mantz (Lincoln)	73.032
9	Tuxtla Gutiérrez—El Ocotal	Taruffi (Alfa Romeo)	57.153

1951 Carrera Panamericana II Final Positions
Tuxtla Gutiérrez to Ciudad Juárez, 1,933 miles
91 entries, 35 finishers

Place	Driver/Codriver	Car	Time/Average Speed
1	Taruffi/Chinetti (Italy)	1951 Ferrari 212 E	21:57:52/88.09mph
2	Ascari/Villoresi (Italy)	1951 Ferrari 212 E	22:05:56/87.55
3	Sterling/Sandiege (USA)	1951 Chrysler Saratoga	22:13:46/87.04
4	Ruttman/Smith (USA)	1948 Mercury club coupe	22:18:03/86.98
5	Trevoux/Lesurque (France)	1951 Packard 400 Patrician	22:22:17
6	Teague/Snow (USA)	1951 Hudson Hornet	22:41:40
7	Rodgers/Rodgers (USA)	1951 Cadillac 62	22:52:43
8	Crawford/Valdez (USA)	1951 Lincoln Cosmopolitan	23:04:06
9	Solona/Iniesta (Mex)	Oldsmobile 88	23:12:29
10	Korf/Reiner (USA)	Nash Ambassador	23:12:49

1951 Leg Winners

Leg	Start/Finish Points	Winner	Speed
1	Tuxtla Gutiérrez—Oaxaca	Trevoux (Packard)	78.54mph
2	Oaxaca—Puebla	Ascari (Ferrari)	76.03
3	Puebla—México City	Taruffi (Ferrari)	85.82
4	México City—Léon	Ascari (Ferrari)	98.01
5	Léon—Durango	Ascari (Ferrari)	97.99
6	Durango—Parral	Ascari (Ferrari)	95.88
7	Parral—Chihuahua	Bettenhausen (Chrysler)	112.57
8	Chihuahua—Ciudad Juárez	Bettenhausen (Chrysler)	113.35

1952 Carrera Panamericana III Final Positions, Sports Class
Tuxtla Gutiérrez to Ciudad Juárez, 1,934.4 miles
27 entries, 10 finishers
Winning average: 102.527mph

Place	Driver/Codriver	Car	Time	Overall Place
1	Kling/Klenk (D)	Mercedes-Benz 300SL	18:15:19	1
2	Lang/Gruff (D)	Mercedes-Benz 300SL	19:26:30	2
3	Chinetti/Lucas (Italy/USA)	1952 Ferrari 340 México	19:32:45	3
4	Maglioli/Bornigia (Italy)	1952 Lancia Aurelia B 20	20:11:20	4
5	McAfee/McAfee (USA)	1952 Ferrari 340 America	20:21:15	5
6	Hill/Stubbs (USA)	1951 Ferrari 212 E	20:33:46	6

Place	Driver/Codriver	Car	Time	Overall Place
7	Ibarra/Solar (Mex)	1951 Ferrari 212 E	23:14:18	24
8	Metternich (Es)	Porsche 356S	23:18:15	25
9	Ortiz/Armaida (Mex)	1951 Lancia Aurelia B 20	23:52:47	28
10	Ehlinger (Mex)	Jaguar XK120	24:37:37	31

1952 Leg Winners, Sports Class

Leg	Start/Finish Points	Winner	Speed
1	Tuxtla Gutiérrez—Oaxaca	Behra (Gordini)	89.1mph
2	Oaxaca—Puebla	Villoresi (Ferrari)	83.8
3	Puebla—México City	Villoresi (Ferrari)	100.7
4	México City—Léon	Villoresi (Ferrari)	112.8
5	Léon—Durango	Kling (Mercedes)	111.7
6	Durango—Parral	Kling (Mercedes)	104.0
7	Parral—Chihuahua	Kling (Mercedes)	126.8
8	Chihuahua—Ciudad Juárez	Kling (Mercedes)	135.8

1952 Final Positions, Stock Class
Tuxtla Gutiérrez to Ciudad Juárez, 1,934.4 miles
64 entries, 29 finishers
Winning average: 90.78mph

Place	Driver/Codriver	Car	Time	Overall Place
1	Stevenson/Smith (USA)	1953 Lincoln Capri	21:15:38	7
2	Mantz/Stroppe (USA)	1953 Lincoln Capri	21:16:09	8
3	Faulkner/Daigh (USA)	1953 Lincoln Capri	21:20:27	9
4	Korf/Carrington (USA)	1952 Lincoln Capri	21:25:09	10
5	McFee (USA)	1952 Chrysler New Yorker	21:43:00	11
6	Evans/Aguilar (USA)	1952 Chrysler New Yorker	21:54:55	12
7	Teague/Snow (USA)	1952 Hudson Hornet	22:08:00	13
8	Kirby (USA)	1952 Cadillac 62	22:17:50	14
9	Trevoux/Dubois (France)	1952 Packard 400	22:35:00	15
10 (tie)	Heath/Czyca (USA)	1953 Chrysler New Yorker	22:43:59	16 (tie)
	Taruffi/Vargas (Italy)	1952 Oldsmobile 88		

1952 Leg Winners, Stock Class

Leg	Start/Finish Points	Winner	Speed
1	Tuxtla Gutiérrez—Oaxaca	Faulkner (Lincoln)	79.1mph
2	Oaxaca—Puebla	Russell (Chrysler)	72.0
3	Puebla—México City	Taruffi (Oldsmobile)	83.5
4	México City—Léon	Korf (Lincoln)	95.1
5	Léon—Durango	Mantz (Lincoln)	98.2
6	Durango—Parral	Carter (Lincoln)	96.5
7	Parral—Chihuahua	Stevenson (Lincoln)	109.9
8	Chihuahua—Ciudad Juárez	Mantz (Lincoln)	115.4

1953 Carrera Panamericana IV Final Positions, Large Sports Class
Tuxtla Gutiérrez to Ciudad Juárez, 1,911.9 miles
31 entries, 9 finishers
Winning average: 105.14mph

Place	Driver/Codriver	Car	Time	Overall Place
1	Fangio/Bronzoni (Arg/Italy)	Lancia D 24	18:11:00	1
2	Taruffi/Maggio (Italy)	Lancia D 24	18:18:51	2
3	Castellotti/Luodni (Italy)	Lancia D 23	18:24:52	3
4	Mancini/Serena (Italy)	Ferrari 375MM	19:40:25	4
5	Rosier (France)	Talbot T.26 GS	20:11:22	5
6	Magliolo (Ricci) (Italy)	Ferrari 375MM	20:15:25	6
7	Ruiz/Villegas (Mex)	Ferrari 250MM	20:48:29	11
8	Miller/Harrison (USA)	Akton Miller Special	22:07:36	12
9	Giron (Guatemala)	Jaguar XK120	23:01:49	14

1953 Leg Winners, Large Sports Class

Leg	Start/Finish Points	Winner	Speed
1	Tuxtla Gutiérrez—Oaxaca	Bonetto (Lancia)	94.89mph
2	Oaxaca—Puebla	Taruffi (Lancia)	87.93
3	Puebla—México City	Taruffi (Lancia)	102.81
4	México City—Léon	Maglioli (Ferrari)	115.79
5	Léon—Durango	Taruffi (Lancia)	116.50
6	Durango—Parral	Maglioli (Ferrari)	111.57
7	Parral—Chihuahua	Maglioli (Ferrari)	127.46
8	Chihuahua—Ciudad Juárez	Maglioli (Ferrari)	138.31

1953 Final Positions, Small Sports Class
Tuxtla Gutiérrez to Ciudad Juárez, 1,911.9 miles
14 entries, 2 finishers
Winning average: 79.827mph

Place	Driver/Codriver	Car	Time	Overall Place
1	Herrarte (G)	Porsche 550	23:47:11	15
2	Segura (Arg)	Porsche 356S	24:18:25	16

1953 Leg Winners, Small Sports Class

Leg	Start/Finish Points	Winner	Speed
1	Tuxtla Gutiérrez—Oaxaca	Herrmann (Porsche)	86.82mph
2	Oaxaca—Puebla	Juhan (Porsche)	73.81
3	Puebla—México City	Juhan (Porsche)	80.18
4	México City—Léon	Juhan (Porsche)	93.32
5	Léon—Durango	Hartmann (Borgward)	96.75
6	Durango—Parral	Hartmann (Borgward)	90.03
7	Parral—Chihuahua	Hartmann (Borgward)	106.36
8	Chihuahua—Cuidad Juárez	Herrarte (Porsche)	101.13

1953 Final Positions, Large Stock Class
Tuxtla Gutiérrez to Ciudad Juárez, 1,911.9 miles
49 entries, 23 finishers
Winning average: 93.15mph

Place	Driver/Codriver	Car	Time	Overall Place
1	Stevenson (USA)	1953 Lincoln Capri	20:31:32	7
2	Faulkner (USA)	1953 Lincoln Capri	20:32:55	8
3	McGrath (USA)	1953 Lincoln Capri	20:33:07	9
4	Mantz (USA)	1953 Lincoln Capri	20:33:30	10
5	Drisdale (USA)	Chrysler New Yorker	21:21:19	12
6	Russell (USA)	Chrysler New Yorker	21:34:26	13
7	Galvez (Mex)	Lincoln Capri	22:18:44	15
8	Descote (Mex)	Lincoln Capri	22:27:01	16
9	Petrini (Argentina)	Lincoln Capri	22:28:36	17
10	Ehlinger (Mex)	Packard Mayfair	22:34:40	18

1953 Leg Winners, Large Stock Class

Leg	Start/Finish Points	Winner	Speed
1	Tuxtla Gutiérrez—Oaxaca	Stevenson (Lincoln)	83.27mph
2	Oaxaca—Puebla	Stevenson (Lincoln)	75.07
3	Puebla—México City	Mantz (Lincoln)	84.49
4	México City—Léon	McGrath (Lincoln)	97.49
5	Léon—Durango	Mantz (Lincoln)	101.61
6	Durango—Parral	McGrath (Lincoln)	93.69
7	Parral—Chihuahua	Mantz (Lincoln)	114.30
8	Chihuahua—Ciudad Juárez	Mantz (Lincoln)	115.40

1953 Final Positions, Small Stock Class
Tuxtla Gutiérrez to Ciudad Juárez, 1,911.9 miles
97 entries, 26 finishers
Winning average: 77.07mph

Place	Driver/Codriver	Car	Time	Overall Place
1	Evans (USA)	1953 Chevrolet 2100	24:48:21	34
2	Patterson (USA)	1953 Ford 6	24:58:55	35
3	Calaben (Argentina)	1953 Ford 6	25:03:49	36
4	Yantis (USA)	1953 Chevrolet 2100	25:09:51	37
5	Eckart (USA)	1953 Hudson Jet	25:17:05	38
6	Maneglia	1953 Ford 6	25:34:27	39
7	Ortiz (Mex)	1953 De Soto Diplomat	25:53:31	40
8	Ramirez (Mex)	1953 Hudson Jet	25:59:48	41
9	Paredes (Mex)	1953 Hudson Jet	26:00:42	42
10	Taddia (Argentina)	1953 Chevrolet 2100	26:03:33	43

1953 Leg Winners, Small Stock Class

Leg	Start/Finish Points	Winner	Speed
1	Tuxtla Gutiérrez—Oaxaca	Davis (Plymouth)	73.45mph
2	Oaxaca—Puebla	Patterson (Ford)	64.62
3	Puebla—México City	Airaldi (Ford)	71.67
4	México City—Léon	Eckart (Hudson)	79.08
5	Léon—Durango	Yantis (Chevrolet)	79.95
6	Durango—Parral	Airaldi (Ford)	82.05
7	Parral—Chihuahua	Airaldi (Ford)	92.58
8	Chihuahua—Ciudad Juárez	Yantis (Chevrolet)	91.20

1954 Carrera Panamericana V Final Positions, Large Sports Class
Tuxtla Gutiérrez to Ciudad Juárez, 1,908 miles
20 starters, 6 finishers
Winning average: 107.955mph

Place	Driver/Codriver	Car	Time	Overall Place
1	Maglioli (Italy)	Ferrari 375 Plus	17:40:26	1
2	Hill/Ginther (USA)	Ferrari 375MM	18:04:56	2
3	Cornacchia (Italy)	Ferrari 250 Monza	19:34:06	5
4	Chinetti/Shakespeare (USA)	Ferrari 375MM	20:10:18	6
5	Miller/Harrison (USA)	Akton Miller Special	20:21:09	7
6	Trevoux (France)	Packard Special	20:48:31	13

1954 Leg Winners, Large Sports Class

Leg	Start/Finish Points	Winner	Speed
1	Tuxtla Gutiérrez—Oaxaca	Hill (Ferrari)	96.19mph
2	Oaxaca—Puebla	Maglioli (Ferrari)	87.32
3	Puebla—México City	Hill (Ferrari)	95.98
4	México City—Léon	Maglioli (Ferrari)	115.78
5	Léon—Durango	Maglioli (Ferrari)	115.55
6	Durango—Parral	Maglioli (Ferrari)	112.40
7	Parral—Chihuahua	Maglioli (Ferrari)	131.39
8	Chihuahua—Ciudad Juárez	Hill (Ferrari)	137.64

1954 Final Positions, Small Sports Class
Tuxtla Gutiérrez to Ciudad Juárez, 1,908 miles
17 starters, 7 finishers
Winning average: 97.22mph

Place	Driver/Codriver	Car	Time	Overall Place
1	Herrmann (D)	Porsche 550	19:32:33	3
2	Juhan (G)	Porsche 550	19:33:09	4
3	Chiron/Delpech (France)	OSCA MT-4-1500	20:34:56	8
4	Segura/Linge (Arg/D)	Porsche 550	20:46:23	12
5	Lopez (Mex)	Porsche 356	22:56:31	28
6	Becker (Mex)	Porsche 356	26:07:56	66
7	Hirz (D)	Porsche 356	26:22:24	69

1954 Leg Winners, Small Sports Class

Leg	Start/Finish Points	Winner	Speed
1	Tuxtla Gutiérrez—Oaxaca	Bechem (Borgward)	88.90mph
2	Oaxaca—Puebla	Bechem (Borgward)	82.52
3	Puebla—México City	Chiron (OSCA)	88.86
4	México City—Léon	Herrmann (Porsche)	104.35
5	Léon—Durango	Herrmann (Porsche)	105.43
6	Durango—Parral	Herrmann (Porsche)	104.59
7	Parral—Chihuahua	Herrmann (Porsche)	121.42
8	Chihuahua—Ciudad Juárez	Herrmann (Porsche)	119.46

1954 Final Positions, Large Stock Class
Tuxtla Gutiérrez to Ciudad Juárez, 1,908 miles
26 starters, 13 finishers
Winning average: 92.3mph

Place	Driver/Codriver	Car	Time	Overall Place
1	Crawford (USA)	1954 Lincoln Capri	20:40:19	9
2	Faulkner (USA)	1954 Lincoln Capri	20:42:07	10
3	Andrews (USA)	1954 Cadillac	20:43:14	11
4	Stringer (USA)	1954 Cadillac	21:15:13	14
5	Leal (Mex)	1954 Buick Century	21:51:17	16
6	Ramierez (Mex)	1954 Buick Century	21:59:34	17
7	Ehlinger (Mex)	1954 Packard	22:23:34	21
8	Mariscal	1954 Buick Century	22:30:39	22
9	Corona (Mex)	1954 Packard	22:51:20	25
10	F. Ramirez (Mex)	1954 Lincoln Capri	22:51:38	26

1954 Leg Winners, Large Stock Class

Leg	Start/Finish Points	Winner	Speed
1	Tuxtla Gutiérrez—Oaxaca	Crawford (Lincoln)	82.42mph
2	Oaxaca—Puebla	Crawford (Lincoln)	74.33
3	Puebla—México City	Faulkner (Lincoln)	82.54
4	México City—Léon	Faulkner (Lincoln)	94.34
5	Léon—Durango	Faulkner (Lincoln)	101.61
6	Durango—Parral	Faulkner (Lincoln)	99.28
7	Parral—Chihuahua	Andrews (Cadillac)	113.71
8	Chihuahua—Ciudad Juárez	Andrews (Cadillac)	117.48

1954 Final Positions, Special Stock Class
Tuxtla Gutiérrez to Ciudad Juárez, 1,908 miles
66 starters, 46 finishers
Winning average: 84.42mph

Place	Driver/Codriver	Car	Time	Overall Place
1	Drisdale (USA)	1954 Dodge V-8	22:35:53	23
2	Evans (USA)	1954 Dodge V-8	22:50:44	24
3	Elliott (USA)	1954 Dodge V-8	22:52:16	27
4	Tostado (USA)	1954 Dodge V-8	23:00:18	29
5	Yantis (USA)	1954 Studebaker V-8	23:02:04	31
6	Solona (Mex)	1954 Dodge V-8	23:08:40	32
7	Calaben (Mex)	1954 Ford	23:08:55	33
8	Taruffi (Italy)	1954 Ford	23:15:21	34
9	Aguilar (Mex)	1954 Dodge V-8	23:18:45	35
10	Anza (Mex)	1954 Ford	23:19:06	36

1954 Leg Winners, Special Stock Class

Leg	Start/Finish Points	Winner	Speed
1	Tuxtla Gutiérrez—Oaxaca	Thompson (Ford)	75.93mph
2	Oaxaca—Puebla	Calaben (Ford)	71.58
3	Puebla—México City	Drisdale (Dodge)	77.68
4	México City—Léon	Morgan (Ford)	87.08
5	Léon—Durango	Drisdale (Dodge)	90.73
6	Durango—Parral	Drisdale (Dodge)	88.58
7	Parral—Chihuahua	Evans (Dodge)	102.04
8	Chihuahua—Ciudad Juárez	Evans (Dodge)	105.7

1954 Final Positions, European Stock Class
Tuxtla Gutiérrez to Ciudad Juárez, 1,908 miles
17 starters, 13 finishers
Winning average: 87.33mph

Place	Driver/Codriver	Car	Time	Overall Place
1	Sanesi/Cagna (Italy)	Alfa Romeo 1900 T	21:50:42	15
2	Mantovani/Chiappa (Italy)	Alfa Romeo 1900 T	22:06:25	18
3	Della Favera/Campignotto (Italy)	Alfa Romeo 1900 T	22:06:50	19
4	Carini/Sambrotta (Italy)	Alfa Romeo 1900 T	22:19:04	20
5	Valazquez (Mex)	Alfa Romeo 1900 T	23:00:57	30
6	Brudes (D)	Borgward Isabella	27:02:36	73
7	Von Hohenlohe (Mex)	Volkswagen 1200	30:14:12	77
8	Hinke (Mex)	Volkswagen 1200	30:15:54	78
9	Wyers (Germany)	Volkswagen 1200	30:17:56	79
10	De la Pena (Mex)	Volkswagen 1200	31:01:43	80

1954 Leg Winners, European Stock Class

Leg	Start/Finish Points	Winner	Speed
1	Tuxtla Gutiérrez—Oaxaca	Sanesi (Alfa Romeo)	80.31mph
2	Oaxaca—Puebla	Mantovani (Alfa Romeo)	75.69
3	Puebla—México City	Mantovani (Alfa Romeo)	83.29
4	México City—Léon	Sanesi (Alfa Romeo)	89.47
5	Léon—Durango	Sanesi (Alfa Romeo)	91.04
6	Durango—Parral	Carini (Alfa Romeo)	90.81
7	Parral—Chihuahua	Sanesi (Alfa Romeo)	98.19
8	Chihuahua—Ciudad Juárez	Della Favera (Alfa Romeo)	100.39

Bibliography

Bentley, John, and Coles Phinizy. "New King of the Mountains." *Sports Illustrated*, December 6, 1954.

Business Week, December 5, 1954.

Cimarosti, Adriano. *Carrera Panamericana "Mexico."* Milan, Italy: Automobilia, 1987.

Crane, L. C. "Carrera Porsches." *Vintage Racer*, Summer 1982.

Eaton, Godfrey. *Ferrari: The Road and Racing Cars*. Publications International, 1982.

El Automovil Mexicano, June 1950.

El Paso Herald-Post, 1950–54.

El Paso Times, 1950–54.

Evangelisti, Athos. "An Italian in America." *Ferrari World*, January–February 1992.

Flying, December 1954.

Girdler, Allan. *American Road Race Specials 1934–70*. Motorbooks International, 1990.

—. *Stock Car Racers*. Motorbooks International, 1988.

Goodman, Roland. *Mexican Road Race*. Floyd Clymer Co., 1950.

Harnell, Boyd. "Last Real Road Race." *Cars & Parts*, August 1980.

Hendry, Maurice D. "The Car Named for Jackson's Wife's Uncle—Hudson." *Automobile Quarterly* Vol. IX-4.

Hot Rod Magazine, February 1955.

Howley, Tim. "The Launch of the Rocket 88." *Automobile Quarterly* Vol. XV-4.

—. "A Look at the Postwar Lincolns." *Automobile Quarterly* Vol. XVII-2.

Jones, Chris. *Road Race*. New York: David McKay Co., 1977.

Langworth, Richard M. "Carrera Panamericana Mexico." *The Milestone Car*, Winter 1975.

Levine, Leo. *Ford: The Dust and the Glory*. MacMillan Co., 1968.

Life, December 7, 1953.

Ludvigsen, Karl. *The Mercedes-Benz Racing Cars*. Bond/Parkhurst Books, 1971.

Madigan, Tom. *Boss: The Bill Stroppe Story*. Darwin Publications, 1984.

Moss, Stirling. *In the Track of Speed*. G. Putnam's Sons, 1957.

Motor Trend, May 1950, July 1950, December 1951, February 1952, March 1952, January 1953, February 1953, October 1953, November 1953, February 1954, January 1955, and January 1989.

Newsweek, December 3, 1951, and December 6, 1954.

Owen, David. "Lancia." *Automobile Quarterly* Vol. XII-4.

Popular Science, November 1952, January 1953, and January 1954.

Presto, Kay. "He Keeps On Runnin'." *Grand National Illustrated*, November 1982.

Richards, Michael. "Carrera Panamericana, the Races: 1950–1954." *The Milestone Car*, Winter 1975.

Road & Track, June 1950, January 1952, February 1953, February 1954, February 1955, and March 1982.

Rudy, Tom. "The Great Mexican Road Race." *Auto Sport Review*, April 1952.

Russo, Bob. "Carrera Panamericana." *Speed Age*, March 1955.

Scalzo, Joe, and Bobby Unser. *The Bobby Unser Story*. Doubleday & Co., 1979.

"Shapes of Things to Come." *300 Star Letter*, Winter 1982.

—. "The Outsider." *Car and Driver*, April 1974.

The Motor, March 12, 1952, and January 14, 1953.

Time, December 3, 1951; December 1, 1952; December 30, 1953; and December 6, 1954.

Wilkinson, Sylvia. *Dirt Tracks to Glory*. Algonquin Books, 1983.

Index

Alfa Romeo 1900T, 153, *157, 158, 159*
   6C 2500, 19, 23, *45*
American Automobile Association (AAA), 15, 40
Andrews, Keith, 168, *171*, 173
Ascari, Alberto, 42, 46-49, 57, 59, 73-74
Ashley, George, *14, 32*
Asociacion Mexicana Automovilistica (AMA), 13
Asociacion Nacional Automovilistica (ANA), 13
Austin-Healey 100S, 124-125, *127, 136*
Ayulo, Manuel, 102, 161, *166*

Bechem, Karl, 130, 144-149
Behra, Jean, 57, 60, 77, 82
Bettenhausen, Tony, 44, 47-50, *82, 88*
Bonetto, Felice, 19, 23, *34*, 39, 47, 58-59, 73, 81-82
Bonini, Bruno, 153
Borgward Isabella, 153
   1500, 93, 96, *98*
   RS 55, 144, *147*
Bracco, Giovanni, *41*, 42, 47-48, 57, 60-62, 73, 82, 122, 126, *129*, 169
Brudes, Adolph, 93, 153
Buick, *118, 162*, 164
Byron, Red, 44

Caballo de Hiero, 77-82, 89, 125-143
Cadillac, 17, 23, 41, 67, 103, 164
Calaben, Oscar, 119-121, 154
Castellotti, *1*, 73, *75*, 81-89
Carini, Piero, 153
Carter, Duane, 68-70, 125, 128

Chinetti, Luigi, 42, 51, 57, *60*, 62, 74, 82, 122, 129-141, 143
Chevrolet, 103
   Corvette, *121*, 125, *135*
Chiron, Louis, 43, 47, 141, 147, 151
Christie, Bob, 117
Chrysler FirePower V-8, 43-44, 164
   New Yorker, 103
   Saratoga, 41, 67
Conner, Roy Pat, 35
Cord 812, 19
Cornacchia, Franco, 57, 122, 129-141, *138-139*
Cornejo, Antonio, 13
Crawford, Ray, 44, 50, 68-69, 102-104, *106*, 161, *164*, 165, 169, *170, 173*, 174
Cunningham, Briggs, 43, 144

Daigh, Chuck, 66, *114*, 161, *164*
Davis, Frank, 113, 119, 130
Daimler-Benz AG, 52, 53
Deal, Thomas A., 19, 26-27, 33-36, 69
Delahaye Type 175, 19, 43
della Favera, Mario, 153
De Soto, *100*
Dodge V-8, 158
Drisdale, Tommy, 69-70, *107*, 111, 113, 157

Eckart, Malcom, 118-119, 121
Ehlinger, Douglas, 47, 57, 105
Elliott, Ray, 15, *22*, 36
Ellis, Max, 166
Ensley, Jack, 79, 81, 125
Entries, 179-185

Entry rules
   1950, 24
   1951, 42
   1953 Sports cars, 76
   1953 Small Sport cars, 96
   1953 Stock cars, 104
   1954 Sports cars, 126
   1954 Small sports cars, 148
   1954 Unlimited stock cars, 169
   1954 Special and European stock cars, 155
Estes, Bob, 16
Evans, C. D., 69-70, *109*, 113-121, *159*, 178

Fangio, Juan Manuel, 73, 81-91
Faulkner, Walt, 44, 48, 66, *68*, 69-70, 102, 105-113, *115*, 161, *164, 167*, 172
Ferrari 212 Inter, 40-41, *44, 46, 53*, 57
   250MM, 75
   250S, 55, 57
   340 America, 55, 57, *58-59*
   340 Mexico, 55, *57*, 75, *85*
   375MM, 74, 75, *81, 83, 90*, 122, *139, 141*
   375 Plus, 122, 125, *133*
   500 Mondial, 122, 125
   750 Monza, 122, 125, *129, 132, 138*
Fitch, John, 44, 47, 55, 59-63, 79, 81, 105, 178
Fletcher Aviation, *94*, 144
Flock, Bob, 19
Flock, Fonty, 19
Ford, *158*
France, Bill, 19, 26, 34-35, *37*
Francis, Tommy, 33, 50, 69

Ginther, Richie, 75, 82, 122-143
Glasspar, 79
Gordini
    T 15S, 57
    T 16S, 77, *86*
    T 24S, 77
Guiberson, Allen, 57, 75, 122

Hansen, Swede, 44, 47, 50
Harrison, Doug, 77, 81
Hartmann, Hans, 93-98
Herrarte, Jose, 93, 144-151
Herrmann, Hans, 93-94, 132, 141, 144-151
Hill, Phil, 57, 60-61, 75, *79*, 81-82, 122, 129-143
Holman, John, 68
Houle, Vern, 66, *160*
Hudson, 23
    Hornet, 41, 44, 67
    Jet, 103

Iglesias, Enrique, *173*

Jaguar
    XK120, 55, 57
    XK120C, *89*, 125
    Mk VII, 41
Juhan, Jaroslav, 93-99, 141, 144-151

Kaiser, 103
Keikhaefer, Carl, 44, 70, 79, 105
Kirkwood, Pat, 69
Klenk, Hans, 55, 59, 63
Kling, Karl, 54-55, 59-63, 93-94, *95*
Korf, Bob, 47, 69-70, 105, *114*
Kurtis-Cadillac, 79, *133*
Kurtis-Oldsmobile, *143*

Lancia, *77*
    Aurelia GT, 41
    B20 GT, *41*, 42, 55, 58
    D20, 73
    D23, 73, *75*, *82*, *85*
    D24, *72*, 73, 75, *84-85*, *90*
Lang, Herman, 54-55, 60-63
Lincoln Capri, 67, 103
Lincoln-Mercury, 64, 70, *102*
Lincoln team, 67-70, 102, *103*, *105-106*, *108-109*, *112*, 113, *117*, *119-120*, *160*, 161, 164, *165*

Lucas, Jean, 77, 82
Lynch, George, 21-22

Macklin, Lance, 125, 128, 178
Maglioli, Umberto, 58, 60, 62, *63*, 73-74, 81-91, 122, *123*, 129-143
Mancini, Guido, 74
Mantovani, Sergio, 153
Mantz, John, 16, 21, *23*, 26-36, 66, *69*-70, 102, 105-113, 161, *164*
Manzon, Robert, 57, 59
McAfee, Ernie, 57, *58*, 93
McAfee, Jack, 26, 28, 57, *58*, 60-61, 122, 126
McFee, Reginald, 69-70, 79, 81, 105, 107
McGrath, Jack, 102, 107, 111-113, 161, *164*, 166
McGriff, Herschel, 11, 13-15, *20*, 21, *22*, 26-27, 34-36, 44-47, 69
Menocal, Jose Estrada, 47
Mercedes-Benz 300SL, *53*, 54-63
Mercury, *66*, 103
Miller, Ak, 52, *65*, 70, *78*, 81, 129, *130-132*, *136*, 141-142, 174, 177
Mundy, Frank, 105, 107
Murphy, Fernando Leeuw, *66*, 161, *164*
Musto, Anthony, 21-22

NASCAR, 19
Nash Ambassador, 23
Nash-Healey pace car, 39
Neubauer, Alfred, *55*, 56, 60-61

Oldsmobile 88, 17, 23, 41, *44*, 67, 103, *118*
OSCA MT4, 93, 95, 144, 147, *151*

Packard, 17, 23, 41, 67, 164
Pan-American Highway, 12-13, *40*
Panini, Carlos, 47
Patterson, Norm, *110*, 113, 118-121
Pegaso Z102BS, 124-125, 129-130
Plymouth, 103
Porsche
    356, 55, 57, 93, 95, *96*, *145*, 147
    550, *92*, 93, *94*, 95, *97-99*, 144-151
Portago, Alfonso de, 75, 122, *125*, 128

Rathmann, Jim, 69, 105, 111, 113
Ricci, Mario, 74, 83
Robinson, Ford, 26, 126

Rogers, Al, 19, 34, 36, 44, *51*, 69, 105, *113*
Rogers, Ralph, 19, 34, 36, 44, 69, 105, *113*
Rosier, Louis, 75, 83
Royal, C. R., 33, 111
Rubirosa, Porfirio, 122, *124*, 126, 128
Russell, Royal, 50, 69, 111
Ruttman, Troy, 44-45, 47-50, 64

Sanesi, Consalvo, 153, 158
Segura, Fernando, 144-151
Sennett, Bud, 22
Shelby, Carroll, 125, 128-129, *136*
Siata Sport 8V, 93, 95, *99*
Smith, Clay, *43*, 44-45, 47-50, 64, 69-70, 113, 164
Spear, Bill, 57
Stagnoli, Antonio, 74, 81
Sterling, Bill, 19, 21, 26-27, 31, 43, 49-50, 69, 108, 111
Stevenson, Chuck, 39, 47, 66, *68*, 69-70, 102-113, *116*, *120*, 161
Stringer, Ed, *110*, 168, *171*
Stroppe, Bill, 19, 30-31, 64-66, 69-70, 102, 113, 126, 161, *164*
Studebaker, 103, 158

Talbot-Lago T26 GS, 75, *86-87*
Taruffi, Piero, 19, 21, 34-35, 39, 46-51, 69, 73, 81-89, *116*, 153, *157*
Teague, Marshall, 44, 49-50, 69
Thompson, Mickey, 113, 117, 153, *157*
Thorne, Joel, 19, *26*, 79
Trevoux, Jean, 19, 22, 47, 49-50, 69, *74*, 79, 82, 125
Turner, Curtis, 19, 26, 34-35, *37*

Unser, Bobby, 44, 47, 69
Unser, Jerry, 44, 69

Villoresi, Luigi, 42, 57, 59-62
Volkswagen, *152*, 153-154, 159
von Hohenlohe, Alfonso, 154
Vukovich, Bill, 102, *117*, *160*, 161, *164*

Walters, Phil, 43
Ward, Rodger, *114*

Yantis, Scott, 113, 121, 159

Zoccano, Pat, 162